Pretty Evil

NEW YORK

NEW YORK

TRUE STORIES OF MOBSTER MOLLS, VIOLENT VIXENS, AND MURDEROUS MATRIARCHS

ELIZABETH KERRI MAHON

Globe
Pequot
GUILFORD, CONNECTICUT

Globe
Pequot

An imprint of Globe Pequot, the trade division of
The Rowman & Littlefield Publishing Group, Inc.
4501 Forbes Blvd., Ste. 200
Lanham, MD 20706
www.rowman.com

Distributed by NATIONAL BOOK NETWORK

British Library Cataloguing in Publication Information available

Library of Congress Cataloging-in-Publication Data

Names: Mahon, Elizabeth Kerri, author.
Title: Pretty evil New York : true stories of mobster molls, violent
  vixens, and murderous matriarchs / Elizabeth Kerri Mahon.
Description: Guilford, Connecticut : Globe Pequot, [2021] | Includes
  bibliographical references. | Summary: "In Pretty Evil New York, author
  Elizabeth Kerri Mahon takes you on a journey through a rogue's gallery
  of some of New York's most notable female criminals"—Provided by
  publisher.
Identifiers: LCCN 2021018772 (print) | LCCN 2021018773 (ebook) | ISBN
  9781493055005 (trade paperback) | ISBN 9781493055012 (epub)
Subjects: LCSH: Female offenders—New York (State)—Biography. | Crime—New
  York (State)—History. | New York (State)—History—1865-
Classification: LCC HV6046 .M2925 2021 (print) | LCC HV6046 (ebook) | DDC
  364.3/7409227471—dc23
LC record available at https://lccn.loc.gov/2021018772
LC ebook record available at https://lccn.loc.gov/2021018773

♾™ The paper used in this publication meets the minimum requirements of American National Standard for Information Sciences—Permanence of Paper for Printed Library Materials, ANSI/NISO Z39.48-1992

Cover image credit: Prisoner identification photograph of Ruth Snyder at Sing Sing Prison. Lewis Lawes Papers, Lloyd Sealy Library, John Jay College of Criminal Justice/CUNY url: https://dc.lib.jjay.cuny.edu/index.php/Detail/Object/Show/object_id/119

CONTENTS

INTRODUCTION VII

HENRIETTA ROBINSON (1827–1905) 1
THE VEILED MURDERESS

EMMA CUNNINGHAM (1818–1887) 24
THE BOND STREET TRAGEDY

FREDERICKA "MARM" MANDELBAUM (1818–1894) 43
QUEEN OF FENCES

SOPHIE LYONS (1848–1924) 61
QUEEN OF CRIME

ROXALANA DRUSE (1847–1887) 79
THE LAST WOMAN TO BE HANGED IN NEW YORK

LIZZIE HALLIDAY (1859–1918) 97
THE WORST WOMAN ON EARTH

MARY ALICE LIVINGSTON (1861–1948) 117
CLAM CHOWDER MURDER

MARY FARMER (1880–1908) 138
WATERTOWN TRUNK MURDER

CELIA COONEY (1904–1992) 157
THE BOBBED HAIRED BANDIT

CONTENTS

RUTH SNYDER (1895-1928) 175
THE DOUBLE INDEMNITY MURDER

STEPHANIE ST. CLAIR (1897-1969) 200
THE NUMBERS QUEEN OF HARLEM

NOTES 219

SELECTED BIBLIOGRAPHY 247

ABOUT THE AUTHOR 255

INTRODUCTION

Historically, women have been thought of as less criminally inclined than men. But this image is hard to mesh with reality, for history is crowded with women who broke the law. When women do commit a criminal act, the story is even more fascinating. It makes front-page news, and a curious public clamor to know the dirty details of the wicked woman who dared commit such an act. Women may have committed less-violent crimes throughout history, but they were certainly a match for men when it came to theft, burglary, forgery, and prostitution. It might be argued that the only difference between men and women is the belief that women were too emotional to commit violent crimes.

The Empire State has certainly produced its fair share of notorious women. After all, if you can make it there, you can make it anywhere as the song goes. From the nineteenth century to near the present day, *Pretty Evil New York* looks at criminal women of all types, from all walks of life. These eleven women secured their places in New York's history by committing some of the most sensational crimes of their day. A few of the women in these pages perpetrated their misdeeds because they were truly rotten, but several were driven into a life of crime. Questions still go unanswered in a couple of cases.

Many of these women were immigrants, lured by tales of streets of gold in the New World and seeking new starts, only to find themselves facing the same grinding poverty they had left behind. Only the toughest and most resourceful women could survive and thrive. It was certainly a man's world, which is not to glorify the lifestyles and choices made by these women but to illustrate what people will do to survive. All of these women have a story to tell. Some of them had a traumatic event that led to them seeing a life in the underworld. The one thing that ties these women together is the fact that they were all either born or ended up in New York State. *Pretty Evil New York* recounts the thrilling tales of the Empire State's most clever and misunderstood criminals.

Each chapter of *Pretty Evil New York* chronicles the life of a woman who committed a crime. Fascinating portraits of these criminal women as individuals emerge from their stories; their cases come to life—as does the state in which they lived. They include Marm Mandelbaum who ran a school for thieves; Lizzie Halliday, one of the earliest known female serial killers; Emma Cunningham, who was sensationally acquitted of murder; and, perhaps most famous of all, Ruth Snyder; the photo of her execution at Sing Sing in 1927 shocked the nation. These shocking but true stories turn common assumptions about crime and women upside down.

HENRIETTA ROBINSON (1827-1905)

THE VEILED MURDERESS

In the spring of 1851, a woman named Henrietta Robinson, along with her maid, came to live at 627 River Street in the largely Irish neighborhood in the north end of Troy. Her small white cottage, set well back from the road, was near Oliver Boutwell's mill. The back of the cottage faced the river, far enough from prying eyes. For about a year, she hardly ventured from her comfortable cottage, although she was cordial to her neighbors. She appeared to be in her late twenties, was "of medium height, with coal-black hair, dark blue eyes, a complexion fairer than art could imitate, and teeth whiter than the snows of her native north."[1] She claimed that her husband was "on the rails," meaning that he worked for the railroads. But people noticed that a mysterious carriage would show up late at night, leaving at the crack of dawn.

It wasn't until the winter of 1853, after she'd lost her maid, that Mrs. Robinson began to venture forth into Troy. Directly across the street stood a low wooden building occupied by Timothy Lanagan, a thirty-seven-year-old Irish immigrant; his wife; and their four small children. The building was divided into two, one half serving as the family dwelling, the other as a small grocery and liquor store, a popular hangout for his fellow countrymen. Ever since Mr. Lanagan had opened his business in the fall of 1852, Mrs. Robinson had been one of his most devoted customers, coming in nearly every day to purchase her groceries, along with a steady supply of beer and brandy. She paid her bills on time and was friendly enough with the Lanagans to borrow

1

Engraved by J. C. Buttre

Henrietta Robinson

Fenimore Art Museum

small sums of money from them when she ran low on funds. Despite her eccentricities, the Lanagans regarded her as a friend.

She also became friendly with a young dressmaker named Mary Jane Dillon, the daughter of her gardener, who was only seventeen. Mrs. Robinson hired her to do some mending, but she also tried to turn her into a sort of companion. She gave her a great deal of sewing work and encouraged her to linger at her home for tea and long talks. Mrs. Robinson complained a great deal about her next-door neighbors, the Boutwells, especially Oliver Boutwell, who owned the nearby mill. She alleged that he, his family, and several of his friends had slandered her.

Mrs. Robinson also confided details of her romantic past. Was she the daughter of a French count or was it an Irish lord? Her father threw her out for marrying beneath her, or was it her cruel stepmother? Mary Jane didn't question the inconsistencies because she enjoyed the stories and the attention of this sophisticated woman who spoke French. When Mary Jane glimpsed a middle-aged man at the cottage, Mrs. Robinson said that it was her husband, Mr. Robinson. On another occasion, she told her that the man was Dr. Potter, a clergyman from Albany. "The days I passed at her house were very pleasant part of the time," she recalled. But sometimes Mrs. Robinson's language became coarse. "It consisted of such language as ladies do not often use." In other words, Mrs. Robinson could swear like a sailor when she chose.[2]

Her neighbor, Oliver Boutwell, noticed that Mrs. Robinson sometimes acted in a bizarre manner that spring. "I used to see her in the streets, prior to March '53, when I thought she was the worse for wear for liquor." Mrs. Robinson continued to slowly unravel. On a rainy day in late April, she walked alone from her home to the Rensselaer County Courthouse. It was unusual and highly dangerous for a respectable woman to be out walking late at night. A woman could be arrested on suspicion of prostitution simply for walking alone.

When she failed to find the chief of police, she poured out her problems to Edwin Brownell, Overseer of the Poor, who was working late. She complained that there had been a group of ruffians around her house, that they had broken in, and she was afraid that they were going to attempt it again. She wanted the chief of police to send someone to protect her house. Brownell tried to get her to go home, but she wouldn't leave unless he escorted her. Suddenly she mentioned that she had not been well attended of late.

Brownell asked who had neglected her. She replied, John C. Mather. John Cotton Mather was well known to Brownell. He was not only part owner of a brand-new bank in Troy, but he was also a New York State canal commissioner and a direct descendant of Increase Mather and Cotton Mather, a judge at the Salem Witch trials. Mrs. Robinson told Brownell that she had not seen him for some time. She'd heard that he was going to be married, but she was his lawful wife. He would have to avow it when he came back, or she was going to take his life! Brownell noticed that Mrs. Robinson was clearly agitated and probably intoxicated as well.[3]

But in the spring of 1853, Mather was in trouble. He was charged with ten counts of mismanagement of the seven-million-dollar bill to make improvements to the canal. He was the first person ever impeached in New York. It was so unprecedented that no one knew how to hold an impeachment trial.[4] So he probably dropped Mrs. Robinson like a hot potato to focus on his trial.

Then there was the trouble the night of the dance.

It happened in early March of 1853. It wasn't a big affair, since the Lanagans didn't have much room, just a single musician played for the dancers. A young man named David Smith approached Mrs. Robinson and asked her to dance. No one overheard the conversation, but Mrs. Robinson claimed he'd insulted her. Pulling out the pistol she kept concealed in her bodice, she aimed it at the young man and threatened to "blow his brains out," if he ever insulted her again. Seeing the disturbance, Mr. Lanagan hurried over, told her that he would not tolerate "such a noise, and that she must leave." Mrs. Lanagan took her firmly by the arm and escorted her across the street to her own home.[5] Later that night, Mrs. Robinson returned and asked to speak to David Smith. Smith went out, but no one knows what happened between the two of them. However, Smith was known to be a bully and a troublemaker.[6]

A few days later Mrs. Robinson showed up at the Lanagans' front door and began to berate Mrs. Lanagan, telling her that she was a "mean woman" who had invited "rowdies to her house to insult me." She threatened to get the family evicted and their grocers' license revoked. Roused from his bed by the uproar, Mr. Lanagan ordered Mrs. Robinson to leave the store immediately. "Do you mean to throw out so good a customer?" cried Mrs. Robinson. Mr. Lanagan told her that he "did not want her custom" and repeated the demand. Mrs. Robinson refused. If he wanted her to leave, "he would have to get a constable to do it." In the end, Mrs. Lanagan convinced her to return home.[7]

For several weeks Mrs. Robinson boycotted the store, shopping at Peter Cox's establishment instead. Cox sold hard liquor as well as beer. "I expect she has got the worse for liquor sometimes," Cox said. "She generally purchased the very best liquor I had and sometimes got a little intoxicated. She usually bought a half pint of brandy or a quart of beer at a time."[8] Gradually, however, she resumed her visits to the store, and by the middle of May, the relationship had returned to its former friendly status. Or so it seemed at the time.

Around this time, Mrs. Robinson's relationship with Mary Anne Dillon ended. Sometime toward the end of April, Mrs. Robinson showed up at the Dillons' home, early in the morning, wearing nothing but her nightgown. She requested the loan of a dress so that she could "go down the street and purchase a revolver and take out a warrant for Dave Smith." Mary Jane supplied the dress, but she sent her sister to pick it up later that day. When Mrs. Robinson called again, Mary Jane turned her away. When she returned three days later, Mary Jane recalled later for the court, "She came in and said she had a warrant for me, that I had slandered her. I asked her what I had said about her. She made no reply, but came up and kissed me, and asked me to forgive her."[9] Mrs. Robinson had employed Mary Jane's father as a gardener, but now after the break with the family, she hired an elderly neighbor named Mr. Haley. He subsequently moved in with her, probably to provide a measure of security.

So, we have a kept woman, whose protector is otherwise occupied fighting for his political future; who is drinking too much; and who is suffering from anxiety and paranoid delusions that her neighbors are out to get her. Truthfully, the neighbors had probably been gossiping about Mrs. Robinson since she moved to Troy, but now she had become aware of it and it bothered her, especially since her relationship was on the rocks. It was a recipe for disaster.

Shortly after daybreak on Wednesday, May 25th, Mrs. Robinson appeared at the Lanagans' store, where she purchased a quart of "strong beer" and a pound of soda crackers. A few hours later, she sent her gardener, Mr. Haley, to ask for a loan of two dollars. "I did not let Haley have it. I had the money in the house but did not want to let Mrs. Robinson have it." While Mrs. Lanagan spoke to Mr. Haley, Mrs. Robinson appeared, wondering what was taking so long. Mrs. Lanagan then told the same lie to Mrs. Robinson, that she didn't have the money but would try to borrow it. Mrs. Robinson said that she was sorry but that she would be happy to loan Mrs. Lanagan a hundred dollars tomorrow. If Mrs. Robinson had the wherewithal to loan Mrs. Lanagan a hundred dollars, why did she need to borrow two dollars, unless she was testing the woman, to see if she would still oblige her in this way. Now, she had hard proof that they would not.

She returned at eleven o'clock, extremely agitated. She had just received a dreadful telegram, she exclaimed. Her husband, "a very prominent citizen" who was traveling out west, had been hurt in a railway accident. Some of Mr. Lanagan's buddies were hanging around the store, and one of them joked that he didn't see what Mrs. Robinson was so upset about. "I have a wife out West," he said, "and if she was dead, I wouldn't fret about it." The remark brought forth a burst of laughter from the others. Clearly the men knew Mrs. Robinson didn't have a husband. Turning on the men, Mrs. Robinson went off on them. Strangely Mrs. Lanagan, who was only a few feet away, didn't hear what was said. When Mrs. Robinson came into the kitchen, Mrs. Lanagan told her to go home, this was no place for her to be. Mrs. Robinson left, no doubt stewing about the slights and rebuff of that morning.

She wasn't gone long. Less than two hours later, Mr. Lanagan, his wife, and his wife's sister-in-law—twenty-five-year-old Catherine Lubee—were finishing their midday meal at the kitchen table in the back when Mrs.

Robinson reappeared. Inviting herself to join them, Mrs. Robinson pointed to an uneaten hard-boiled egg and asked, "Whose is that?"

"Yours if you want it," Mr. Lanagan said. He rose from his chair and disappeared into the store.

Mrs. Robinson made herself comfortable at the table, while Mrs. Lanagan peeled a potato and set it before her. As she did, she noticed a piece of white paper, folded into a small packet, clutched in one of Mrs. Robinson's hands. Later she would realize that the little packet contained arsenic. At the time Mrs. Lanagan thought nothing of it.

After polishing off her simple meal, Mrs. Robinson asked for a glass of beer and invited the other two women to join her. Mrs. Lanagan declined, and Catherine Lubee said she didn't like beer. Clearly, they were hoping that Mrs. Robinson would simply go away but were too polite to tell her. Mrs. Robinson insisted that she wouldn't leave until the two women joined her. As Mrs. Lanagan rose to fetch the beer, Mrs. Robinson asked if she had any sugar. Mrs. Lanagan was surprised. Why did Mrs. Robinson need sugar? She had already bought nine pounds during the past week. "No, no," Mrs. Robinson replied. She didn't want to buy any. She only wanted to mix a little in her beer to make it good.

Mrs. Lanagan returned a few moments later with a saucer with powdered sugar. After she brought in the sugar, she went to fetch a quart measure of beer. When she returned, she noticed that Mrs. Robinson was walking the floor with the saucer in her hand. Having decided to join Mrs. Robinson in a drink after all, she poured the beer into two glasses. Mrs. Robinson complained that the glasses were not full. Indulgent of such a good customer, Mrs. Lanagan went back into the store for more beer. When she returned, Mrs. Robinson was stirring sugar into the tumblers.

After filling the glasses to the brim, Mrs. Lanagan reseated herself and took hold of her glass. As she lifted the glass to her lips, however, she noticed a powdery film on the top of the beer. Thinking, as she later testified, that "it was some dust from the sugar," she picked up a teaspoon to skim it off. Immediately, Mrs. Robinson grabbed the spoon from her hand, exclaiming, "Don't do that! That's the best part!" Then all of a sudden Mrs. Robinson decided that she didn't want to drink any beer after all.

7

Just as Mrs. Lanagan was about to take a sip, her husband called out to her. Placing her untouched beer back on the table, she went into the grocery, where he asked her to mind the store while he ran an errand downtown. On his way out he passed through the kitchen, spotted the untouched beer, and paused to drink it. As soon as he drained the glass, he departed. Mrs. Robinson left a few minutes later.

Left alone at the table, Catherine Lubee, who had initially turned down the offer of a drink, decided not to let the beer go to waste. She thought it tasted a little peculiar, but she finished it off. Within minutes, she began to feel sick. Not long afterward, Mrs. Robinson returned yet again. She found Mrs. Lanagan tending to Catherine, who lay groaning on a bed in the back room. Hovering nearby, Mrs. Robinson asked how she felt. "Very poorly," moaned Catherine. She accused Mrs. Robinson of putting "something in the beer that sickened her." Mrs. Robinson denied any wrongdoing. She "had put nothing in it," she told the stricken young woman, "but what would do you good."

Mr. Lanagan, his normally ruddy face drained of color, showed up a short time later. Staggering across the room, he collapsed on a sofa, convulsed with nausea.

"Run for the doctor," he managed to gasp. "I am done for."

Turning on Mrs. Robinson, who stood watching with detached interest, Mrs. Lanagan shrieked, "What have you done? You have killed the father of my children!"

"I have done no such thing," Mrs. Robinson said. She then stepped toward the sofa, to speak to the agonized grocer, who raised his hands and cried, "Go, woman! Go!"

Dr. Henry Adams, the Lanagans' family physician, arrived moments later. By then Mr. Lanagan was racked with excruciating abdominal pain and vomiting uncontrollably. Dr. Adams, recognizing his patient had been poisoned, did what he could to relieve his suffering and to bolster his spirits. But Mr. Lanagan was under no illusions about his condition. "The villain has destroyed me," he told the doctor, "and I shall not recover."

While Mrs. Lanigan tended to her stricken husband, Mr. Haley returned with a note from Mrs. Robinson, asking if she could visit her at the cottage as soon as possible. Reeling with disbelief that Mrs. Robinson could be so callous, she told Mr. Haley that she could not possibly go. A few hours later, with his family and friends kneeling by his bedside in prayer, he died in the arms of his sobbing wife.[10]

Despite her pain, Catherine Lubee managed to make her way back to James Lanagan's where she'd been staying. At nine o'clock that evening, the Rensselaer County coroner, Dr. Reed Bontecou, met with a hurriedly called coroner's jury. There the men took a bedside deposition from Catherine Lubee. According to Catherine, Mrs. Robinson was particularly concerned that all the sugar in the glass be consumed to the point of holding the spoon containing the dregs and forcing it into her mouth.[11] She clung to life until five o'clock the next morning. Her final hours, like those of Timothy Lanagan, were full of unremitting torment.

By the time death finally came for Catherine Lubee, Mrs. Robinson was in custody. She had been arrested the previous evening while out shopping for new furniture at Perkins Cabinet Store. On her way to jail, she laughed and joked with the police officers, apologizing for not being properly dressed. She wore a short, loose wrap called a "Jenny Lind," above her skirt; it was a garment that women normally wore at home, for lounging without a corset. For some reason she assumed that Officer Burns was taking her to the recorder's office, not the jail. When she realized that her destination was the jail, she asked Officer Burns, if she could go in by herself. "She seemed quite surprised when she went into the jail," he later testified.

Inside the jail, Burns discovered that Mrs. Robinson carried two pistols in her bodice. When she resisted handing them over, Sheriff Price and one of his men had to help Burns wrestle them away from her. Burns also found a small piece of paper in her pocket, but since it had no writing on it, he decided it wasn't important and threw it away.[12] The coroner, Reed Bontecou, then searched Mrs. Robinson, because there were no female guards or deputies. She offered no resistance but stood and held up her arms to facilitate the process. Bontecou noticed that her eyes had a wild quality and that she didn't respond to any of the questions that he asked. He asked for the keys to her house for a search.

Bontecou arrived at Mrs. Robinson's house with three officers. While searching the house, the police found a packet marked "poison" hidden under a carpet in her back parlor. A second packet contained Spanish fly, which was still considered an aphrodisiac in the nineteenth century. It was also not the type of item that one usually found in the bedroom of a respectable woman. In her bedroom they found a man's watch, a box of jewelry, and a locket.[13]

Within twenty-four hours, they had traced the poison to a local druggist named William Ostrom, who confirmed that a few weeks earlier Mrs. Robinson had purchased four ounces of arsenic from him, ostensibly to deal with an infestation of rats from Oliver Boutwell's flour mill. Mrs. Robinson had paid for the poison in cash, so the sale was not recorded in his book. He sold her four ounces divided into two packets, clearly marked "poison." He also told the police that shortly before Mrs. Robinson was arrested, she had arrived at his shop, clearly apprehensive. She said that she was in trouble and had been charged with poisoning a couple of people. When Ostrum asked why they would suspect her, she replied that it was out of revenge, because she would not loan them a hundred dollars. She implied that there was some sort of mix-up with the glasses, Mr. Lanagan was taken sick, and now they thought she had poisoned the beer.[14]

The *Troy Daily Whig* alleged that stolen goods were found at the cottage—boots, shoes, jewelry, and silverware—estimated at one thousand dollars. It was later learned that Mrs. Robinson owned all the items, but the damage was done. From the beginning of the case, newspapers went out of their way to blacken her character. Henrietta Robinson was clearly an alias. The press alleged that she was either living off criminals or was a kept woman. What kind of respectable woman needed to use an alias? The *Troy Daily Times* asserted that "Attempts of late had been made to drive her from the neighborhood."

A coroner's jury was held on May 26. The coroner, Dr. Bontecou, later testified that during the autopsy, they discovered that Timothy Lanagan had forty grains of arsenic in his stomach, enough to kill ten men. The coroner also tested the beer at the Lanagans' by drinking it. "It produced no very unpleasant effect. It did not kill me. I think there was no poison in it."[15]

Ann Lanagan also drew drafts of beer for the men on the coroner's jury to taste. Clearly the beer barrel wasn't tainted. The sugar box, when analyzed, was also poison-free. After deliberation, they found that Timothy Lanagan and Catherine Lubee were poisoned by Mrs. Robinson and their deaths were premeditated.

By the second day of her incarceration, Mrs. Robinson's mania had reached the tipping point. She seemed possessed by paranoid delusions that a mob of two or three hundred people had broken into the jail and tried to kill her and that a couple in an adjoining cell had heated a cauldron of water and threatened to boil her alive. One of her jailers, Dr. William Hegeman, took to visiting her two or three times a day. On the first day, she told him that Oliver Boutwell's men were out to destroy her; she could hear them sharpening their knives in the cell next to hers. She refused to believe his denials, demanding her pistols back so that she could defend herself.[16]

A lawyer named Richard Jennyss came to visit Mrs. Robinson. He claimed that he was there on a personal matter not a professional one. "I went to see Mrs. Robinson as a friend of Mr. Mather. I had heard his name made use of in connection with hers prior to her arrest. I had also heard that she had letters of his, and to avoid the scandal that might arise from an exposure of these letters, I went to see her to see if I could get them." He found Mrs. Robinson to be "excited and strange," unable to converse in a normal manner. When he asked her to sign an order for the letters, she refused to sign her name. Instead, William Hegeman signed her name for her, but the order was protested, and Jennyss never got the letters back.[17]

While his visit may not have accomplished his purpose, it did alert her jailors that Mrs. Robinson was the special friend of a powerful man. She was soon moved to the top floor of the jail, for her comfort. Dr. Bontecou continued to visit to ask what she wanted done with her possessions, but he believed that she wasn't rational. She continued to talk about whatever was on her mind. Eventually most of her furnishings and clothing ended up in her cell, which was sizable compared to the one downstairs. Her bed, wardrobe, washstand, divan, five chairs, mirrors, carpets, several trunks, and a rocking chair soon made her cell a home away from home.

Because so many people dropped by the jail, a system was set up so that one had to be either connected to the case or given permission by Mrs. Robinson. Only her lawyers, the sheriff, and his deputies were allowed. At this point, Mrs. Robinson began to wear a heavy veil. Even her lawyers weren't allowed to see her without it. Rumors flew during her time in jail that she was one of the Woods sisters, a prominent Canadian family. The father, Robert Wood, was a successful merchant and trader. Out of his five daughters, four of them married into the British aristocracy. And four of the five also attended Troy Female Seminary. Based on snippets of information that Mrs. Robinson let slip, they deduced that she must be Emma Wood.

In July, Emma Willard, the founder and owner of the Troy Female Seminary, and her son, Dr. John Willard, posted a letter to the editor of the *Troy Whig* stating emphatically that Henrietta Robinson was not one of the Wood sisters of Quebec, nor was she a graduate of Troy Female Seminary. If she were, she would surely have dropped by while she was in town. Willard also claimed that he had gone to the jail with William Wood to visit Mrs. Robinson. She was so covered up that they could see only the top of her face and one of her hands. But just from her hand and wrist, he was most definitely, positively, 100 percent sure that she was not Emma.[18] But the note raised more questions than it answered. Willard claimed that it was Mrs. Robinson who had said that she was one of the Wood sisters, which was false. Even her lawyers had no idea who she really was. Of course, it makes sense that the Willards would deny that Mrs. Robinson had been a student. The school, the first school in the nation to offer high school and college-level instruction, had attracted students from Europe and Canada, as well as the American South and Midwest, since it opened in 1819. The last thing it needed was the scandal of one of their former students being tried for murder.

Mrs. Robinson's first biographer, David Wilson, interviewed her in jail. At the time they met, Wilson had written two well-received books, *Twelve Years a Slave,* as told to him by Solomon Northrup, and a biography of Jane McCrea, a young woman who had been killed by a Huron-Wendat warrior associated with the British army of General Burgoyne, during the American

Revolution. Wilson was also a New York assemblyman, so he would have been well acquainted with John C. Mather.

In his book, *Henrietta Robinson,* published in 1855, shortly after Mrs. Robinson was sentenced, he wrote that she came from a well-known family in Quebec. She was educated at Emma Willard's Troy Female Seminary. While she was there, she fell in love with a young man from a middle-class family. Her family did not approve, wanting her to make a grander match. Back home in Quebec she met an aristocratic Englishman, a Cavalry officer. She was not in love with him, but she was pressured into marriage. The couple were unhappy, although her husband tried to please her by taking her abroad. They had two children, but she resolved to leave him.

When she arrived at the family home in Canada, her parents were livid at the idea of her leaving her husband. They tossed her out. Instead of reaching out to friends, or attempting to reconcile with her parents, she turned bitter, letting her grievances fester. She decided to return to Troy, to seek work as a teacher or governess. On the voyage to Troy, she met John Cotton Mather. He had just been elected to a three-year term as canal commissioner in 1850. He was also married but separated from his wife. Although Wilson doesn't name Mather in his book, readers at the time could guess the identity of her protector. Mrs. Robinson told Wilson that she took the name Robinson after Mary Robinson, actress, playwright, and mistress of George III of England.[19] She claimed that she was a descendent of Robinson and the king.

Because of Mather's high profile and her previous life in Troy, it was necessary for Henrietta to be a recluse. If she ever ventured out, she was heavily veiled. While Mather kept her in the lifestyle to which she was accustomed to, it was socially isolating. Being Mather's mistress meant she missed out on a social life, theater, parties, friends. Her only companions, apart from Mather, were her maid and a gardener. Allegedly she began to make plans to return to England and her husband, if he would have her, but Mather wouldn't let her go. He pursued her to Boston, convincing her to return.[20]

Her lawyers had no choice but to go for an insanity defense, but Henrietta resisted the idea. She had recovered her wits after her first few months in jail. Besides, she was innocent; she was sure that a jury would acquit her. Several people would later testify at her trial that for the first two weeks she was in jail, she was practically incoherent. After months of heavy drinking, she was probably suffering from delirium tremens. In the following months of her incarceration, she would often fly into uncontrollable rages, demolishing the furnishings in her cell. These outbursts alternated with bouts of deep depression.[21] One day in April, the grand jury came to the jail to see the inmates. Henrietta placed a dummy dressed in her clothes and a dark veil, in a rocking chair in the cell. When one of the jurors removed her veil, they were shocked to find the dummy sitting there. A general search found Mrs. Robinson hiding under the bed.[22]

In July, a few weeks after John Willard and William Wood tried to see her, Henrietta attempted suicide by swallowing sulfuric acid. Only the quick action of her jailers, who immediately summoned two physicians to her cell, administered the appropriate antidote and saved her. But she was very sick for weeks afterward. But where did she get the poison?[23] The *Troy Daily Whig* speculated that she had it on her when she was arrested. But Mrs. Robinson had been searched by Dr. Bontecou the night she was arrested.[24] And why wait until now? Either she tried to kill herself, or someone tried to poison her. She was clearly an inconvenient woman to Mather, his friends, and the city of Troy. Or the third explanation is that Henrietta was able to bribe a jailer to buy her the sulfuric acid, or something like laudanum, to help her sleep, and he got the medicines mixed up.

Many people thought Henrietta might be faking insanity to get out of going to prison. But no one could figure out what her motives were for killing Timothy Lanagan and Catherine Lubee. It wasn't until October 1853 that a grand jury arraigned her on two charges of murder in the first degree. She pleaded not guilty. In court she wore a heavy, dark blue veil to conceal her face. While the judge wanted the trial set for November, Martin Townsend, one of Henrietta's lawyers, asked for more time to prepare. The judge granted the stay.[25]

In the spring District Attorney Anson Bingham hired an attorney from out of the county, Henry Hogeboom, to assist in the prosecution. While reviewing the indictment, he found some irregularities. He also asked for a stay so that a new bill of charges could be drafted. The judge once again agreed to postpone the trial.[26] After a long delay, her trial finally began in

May 1854. It had been almost a year to the day since the murders of Timothy Lanagan and Catherine Lubee.

The trial was supposed to start at eleven o'clock in the morning, but there were only eleven potential jurors left in the pool. Sheriff Price had to go out and literally pull people off the street to serve. Another problem: the men had to be property owners to serve on a jury, which made the pool of potential jurors even smaller. District Attorney Anson Bingham and his team—Henry Hogeboom and George Van Santvoord—decided that Henrietta would only be tried for Timothy Lanagan's murder. By having separate trials for each victim, it gave the prosecution a chance to learn from the first trial. If she were found not guilty of murdering Lanagan, they still had another opportunity for justice. If she was convicted, there was no need for a second trial. Either way, the prosecution won.

Hordes of curiosity seekers showed up, eager to glimpse the notorious madwoman and hoping for a display of her notoriously bizarre behavior. They were not disappointed. She arrived at the courthouse "magnificently attired in an elegant black dress, a white shirred bonnet ornamented with artificial flowers, white kid gloves, and a rich black mantilla lined with white satin."[27] The most striking feature was the heavy blue veil that shrouded her face. For the length of the trial this veil would never fully be removed. Henrietta's legal team consisted of Job Pierson, her senior defense counsel, and his two partners William A. Beach and Levi Smith. Clearly Mather or someone was making sure that she had a more-than-adequate defense.

Judge Harris made it clear that he would tolerate no nonsense in his courtroom. Whispering and conversation would not be allowed. Thirty-three potential jurors were called. Of the twenty-one men excused, they fell into two categories: those who said they had already formed an opinion of her guilt, or those who were not aware of the case. The jury members were to be sequestered throughout the trial. Henry Hogeboom gave the opening statement, explaining the case to the jurors. During the first days of the trial, the prosecution needed to establish not only that a crime had been committed, but that Henrietta had the motive, the means, and the opportunity to commit said crime.

Dr. Henry Adams, who had treated the Lanagans for years, was the first witness called. He testified that he believed the cause of death was poison. The defense was able to get Mr. Lanagan's deathbed statement thrown out. Hogeboom asked the witness to identify Henrietta Robinson. The judge requested that she lift her veil, which she did only part way. Only Dr. Adams and the judge could see her face. William Beach, during his cross-examination, tried to suggest that Lanagan died from cholera. Dr. Adams testified that although many of the symptoms were similar to arsenic poisoning, it wasn't cholera.[28] Dr. Skilton, who was present at the autopsy, gave the jury a picture of how painful death by poisoning could be. He also told the court that he had seen white powder that looked like arsenic in Lanagan's stomach. The defense pointed out that if the arsenic had been in the beer, it would have dissolved into the liquid.

Mrs. Lanagan, Timothy's widow, testified next. She was emotional as she described to the jury what happened that day: Henrietta's five visits and how she had almost consumed the beer that killed her husband, implying that she had been the intended victim. Two interesting things occurred during her testimony. First, she took parts of Catherine Lubee's statement and ascribed those incidents to herself. For example, she told the court that she had tried to remove the powdery film on the beer, but Henrietta stopped her. However, that happened to Catherine, not to her. And second, she testified to seeing Henrietta with a piece of white paper in her hand.

The weakest part of the prosecution's case was motive. What possible reason could Henrietta have had to harm the Lanagans? Mrs. Lanagan told the court about the events at the dance in March, and how abusive Henrietta had been at the store the next day. And she testified that she had refused to loan Henrietta two dollars on the day of the murders. Job Pierson took over during the cross-examination of Mrs. Lanagan. He realized that she needed a more delicate touch in questioning than William Beach could provide. Beach's specialty was attacking a witness, confusing them, making them stumble over their words.

Pierson got Mrs. Lanagan to admit that Henrietta had taken her business elsewhere for several weeks after the dust-up at the dance. She could also remember incredible details on some points but not others. He even got her to admit that she lied to Henrietta about the two dollars. Her testimony at the inquest had implied that there was no enmity between her family and Henrietta, but now a year after her husband's death, she'd had some time to think about events. Another revelation was that Henrietta and Catherine Lubee had been friends; the two women had met several times during Catherine's ten-day visit. Catherine would visit her at her cottage. Mrs. Lanagan also admitted that she, too, had visited Henrietta at her home in the weeks before the murders, and that her children had also called on her.[29]

Surprisingly, the prosecution didn't call any other witnesses to testify about the incident at the dance, nor did they call any of the people who were in the room with Mr. Lanagan just before he died. William Ostrum testified about selling the arsenic to Henrietta, allegedly to kill rats. She also had visited him the night of her arrest. He had thought that she was drunk, but he told the court that it also could have been a sign of madness.

On day three of the trial, Judge Harris decided that something needed to be done about Henrietta's heavy veil. "We had the singular spectacle of a prisoner on trial, charged with a high capital crime without the jury or the court ever having seen the prisoner." He went on to say that he felt a "repugnance at trying a prisoner whose face had never been seen." The exasperated judge ordered her to unveil herself, to which she haughtily replied, "I am here, your Honor, to undergo a most painful and important trial, I do not wish to be gazed at."[30] The newspapers of the day quickly dubbed her the "Veiled Murderess."

Officer Charles Burns, who had arrested Henrietta, testified that she had laughed and joked on the way to the jail. This seemed to indicate a woman who was either totally callous to the nature of the charges, or who knew she was innocent. He also took her pistols from her. Regarding the search of her house, he told the jury that he found a packet of arsenic under the rug, which was nailed to the floor. William Beach established that Henrietta had been out shopping when she was arrested. Not the usual behavior for someone who had allegedly just murdered two people.[31]

Coroner Bontecou was called as a witness for the prosecution. The district attorney wanted Catherine Lubbee's statement before the jury, but when Bontecou took her statement, he still thought she might recover, which meant that it couldn't be considered a deathbed statement, because she didn't know she was dying. Judge Harris refused to allow her statement into evidence. During his testimony Bontecou admitted that while he had tasted the beer by drinking it, he hadn't tested the sugar by tasting it. He also testified to Henrietta's behavior the night of her arrest, her anxiety, and her rambling and meaningless conversation.

The prosecution on redirect tried to prove that Bontecou had become infatuated with Henrietta, given how often he had visited her in jail. Bontecou replied that it had been only to talk about the disposition of her property. His visits were necessary because he was responsible for her possessions. Once that was taken care of, he never visited her again. He recalled only one instance when she acknowledged the existence of the Lanagans, when Mrs. Lanagan asked for her pot and other personal items returned. When Beach broached the issue of insanity with Dr. Bontecou, Judge Harris stopped him. If the defense was going to be based on insanity, then the jury needed to see the face of the accused. They needed to be able to see her expressions to determine sanity. Finally, Henrietta lifted her veil briefly, exposing her face to the judge and jury. She then shielded the bottom half of her face with a fan.[32]

The prosecution had called only nine witnesses, four of whom were doctors. Three of the doctors had either treated the victims or had been involved with the autopsy. The fourth doctor was the coroner, Dr. Bontecou. The prosecution failed to call her gardener, Mr. Haley, who had lived with Henrietta, or William Brickley who had carried Lanagan to bed on the day that he died. On the third day, they rested, sure that they had proven their case. They had proved that Lanagan had been poisoned and that Henrietta had access to arsenic, as well as access to poison the beer via the sugar. But they still hadn't established a motive.

The defense's problem was that if Henrietta hadn't poisoned Mr. Lanagan or Catherine Lubee, the only other potential suspect was Mrs. Lanagan. Attacking the grieving widow might backfire with the jury. But then what was her motive? There was no proof of an inappropriate relationship between her husband and Catherine Lubee, although there had been gossip.

Job Pierson made the defense's opening statement to the jury. He reminded them that he had at one time been a district attorney. But he had never tried to introduce a deathbed statement that wasn't one. He informed the jury that he and his fellow counsel were defending Henrietta for free. He had never met her before taking her case. He learned of her arrest from a jailor, who believed that she was insane. He believed that was indeed the case after meeting her.

"Indeed gentlemen, the conduct here in court shows you that she is not in her right mind. I do not say, or believe that she is insane, but her mind has lost its balance in a degree." In other words, she was temporarily insane at the time of the murders. He pointed out that if she'd had a lawyer at the grand jury, she never would have been charged. Pierson also pointed out the lack of evidence that Henrietta had poisoned the beer and the fact that there was no motive.[33] The defense didn't consider putting Henrietta on the stand, because legally she was not allowed to testify in her own defense. It wasn't until an amendment to the state constitution in 1867 that a person could testify in his or her own defense.

The first witness for the defense was William Hegeman, one of the sheriff's deputies. He testified that he believed Henrietta to be irrational. He told the court about her breaking up and burning her furniture, her obsession with her appearance, and her fears that she was being attacked in the jail. The prosecution tried to hammer home a theme that Henrietta had men under her spell, that she bewitched them somehow. When asked, Hegeman informed the court that he was twenty-six years old, that he had seen Henrietta in her nightclothes, and that although he was a doctor, he was not an authority on insanity.[34]

Mary Ann Dillon testified that Henrietta's stories about her past changed often. She also explained that occasionally she had been frightened of her: "She took hold of me the same as she said she did hold of the man; but she laughed and seemed so pleasant about it that I thought little of it afterwards; when she saw I was frightened she laughed; I was not frightened by her much afterwards." She also told the court about the middle-aged man that she had seen with Henrietta. Mary Ann also testified that she had never seen Henrietta under the influence of alcohol.[35]

Edwin Brownell testified that he had met with Henrietta in early May 1853 when she was looking for the sheriff. He told of her fear regarding her neighbors. He also spoke the name John C. Mather in court, the first positive link between the two. He told the court that after he escorted her home, she pointed to some shirts that she claimed belonged to Mather. John Upton of Albany was called to testify for the prosecution regarding the nature of the relationship between Henrietta and John C. Mather. The defense objected. Judge Harris refused to let Upton testify further.[36]

Martin Townsend gave the first closing argument. He pointed out that since Henrietta had a habit of pulling a gun out whenever she was angry, why would she suddenly resort to poison? He also asked why no one considered Mrs. Lanagan to be a suspect. She too had a motive and the means, while Henrietta had no motive. Also, Henrietta hadn't tried to flee Troy after Lanagan and Lubee took ill; she'd gone shopping for furniture. In defense of his client, Townsend attacked John C. Mather for caring more about power and his position, and casting Henrietta adrift. "He may make money his idol, he may dive into business and secure forgetfulness of the gnawings of a lacerated heart." After five hours, Townsend sat down. Henrietta leaned over and whispered loudly, "That was all very well said, but it could have all been said in fifteen minutes."[37]

During George Van Santvoord's closing argument, he pointed out that while they suspected the defense would bring up the question of Henrietta's sanity, they were surprised that they would put forward another suspect. He asked the jury to consider what proof, if any there was, to suspect Mrs. Lanagan. He suggested that Henrietta was not insane, but an alcoholic. And a crime committed under the influence was still a crime. Job Pierson spoke on the last day of the trial. He pointed out the same issues: motive and sanity. He referred to Henry Hogeboom losing an election as a Supreme Court judge. "The gentleman to follow me on the other side, is distinguished as a lawyer, and for his ability and ingenuity of argument. He will attempt to convict the prisoner. He feels his reputation is at stake."

Judge Harris may have sealed Henrietta's fate when he told the jury, "But I have not understood the counsel for the defense as contending that the evidence justifies such a conclusion." As Harris heard it, the defense accepted Henrietta's guilt, that she had poisoned the beer. It was clear from Judge Harris that he also believed her to be guilty when he pointed out that the credibility of "Mrs. Lanagan has never been questioned." He continued, "You cannot hesitate, however painful it may be, to come to the conclusion that it was the accused, and no one else, who administered the arsenic." Harris then explained the legal issues regarding insanity as well as the use of alcohol. He explained, "It is my duty to say to you, gentlemen, that if she was intoxicated, even to such an extent that she was unconscious of what she was doing, still the law holds her responsible for the act."

The jury deliberated for two and a half hours before reaching a verdict. A throng of people had gathered at the courthouse to hear it. There were so many people, that some had to remain outside in the street. A full one-third of the spectators were women, despite the late hour. Sheriff Price, observing the crowd, elected to convey Henrietta into the building through the back door. As usual she was heavily veiled. The court remained silent when the foreman stepped forward to pronounce Henrietta guilty. Pierson asked that the jury be polled. When each member's name was called, he responded "guilty." Henrietta stood up and began shouting, "Shame on you Judge! Shame on you! There is corruption here! There is corruption in the court!" Pierson tried to quiet her, but then gave up, asking the judge to postpone sentencing. Henrietta continued to shout about corruption, demanding another judge.[38]

On the Sunday before sentencing, Henrietta was in a manic mood. Dressed all in white, she ranted for hours, calling for vengeance against the prosecution. At other times she could be heard saying, "He shall never pass sentence against me! No, never, never, never!" Minutes later, she would be joking. At one point she fainted from exhaustion. Sheriff Price put her on suicide watch.

Once again, the courtroom was packed to the rafters with spectators. Half the audience was women, many of whom had brought their children with them. Parents held their children up so that they could catch a glimpse of the "Veiled Murderess." Beach asked the judge to continue to suspend sentencing, because he claimed that one of the jurors had been heard to say prior to the trial that he was certain Henrietta was guilty. The same man had said during jury selection that he had formed no opinion regarding her guilt. The judge ruled for the defense.

While she waited in jail to be sentenced, the question was raised again as to the real identity of Henrietta. Emma Willard issued another statement refuting that she had ever been a student at the academy. William Wood also issued a statement in the *Troy Whig* denying that she was any of his sisters. He also brought a libel suit against the *Troy Daily Times* for saying so.[39] The *Montreal Transcript* published an article stating that Henrietta was the daughter of a lumber dealer who had married an officer. After his death, she married a Dr. Robinson, whom she later abandoned. But the *Transcript* was wrong. The woman in the article was married to a Dr. Robertson, and she'd died in an asylum nine years before.[40]

Henrietta waited months for her sentencing, sitting comfortably in her jail cell surrounded by all her things. During this time, she converted to Catholicism. She became resigned to her fate. It was not until May 1855, two years after the murders of Timothy Lanagan and Catherine Lubee, that the courts in Albany heard arguments for a second trial. Unfortunately for Henrietta, the court refused to hear the case any further. On June 19, 1855, again the courthouse was packed with spectators waiting to see what sentence she would receive. At three o'clock Judge Harris took his seat upon the bench. And at three fifteen, Henrietta, led by Sheriff Price, came into court finely dressed and heavily veiled. She walked in with a firm and buoyant step, greeting her counsel with a smile. The district attorney asked that Henrietta receive the death penalty. Judge Harris asked her to remove her veil, which she did willingly for once. He asked her if she had anything to say as to why she shouldn't be given the death penalty. "Yes, a great deal to say, but I do not wish to be interrupted; I have been the victim of a conspiracy of you politicians at Albany." Job Pierson tried to get her to be quiet as the judge proceeded. "You have been convicted of the murder of Timothy Lanagan." "Yes, and upon false evidence! Shame! Judge, Shame!"

"If you would hear me," Judge Harris said. "I would advise you to cease battling with your fate but submit to it like a true woman, but as you will not hear me, it only remains for me to pass upon you the sentence of the law."

He announced that her date of execution would be August 3. While the judge was saying, "You will be hanged by the neck until dead," Henrietta very coolly drew her hand across her throat and said, "A very pretty throat for a halter; isn't it Judge?" And when he had finished, she told him, "He had better pray for his own soul."

When Sheriff Price tried to remove her from the courtroom, she ordered him to wait. She wasn't finished yet. In a commanding voice and with a proud glance, she said, "May the Judge of Judges thus deal with you."[41]

When she returned to her cell, she burned most of her possessions, knowing she would not be allowed the same luxury as she had in the Troy jail. A few days after her sentencing, accompanied by Sheriff Price and his wife, she took the train headed for Sing Sing. On the train ride her mood swung from recognition of her plight to crying. Sometimes she thought she was going home to Quebec.[42] Sheriff Price very politely told her she was on her way to Sing Sing. Other times she would be perfectly rational, complaining about the fact that she wouldn't be allowed to wear her own clothes; she would have to wear prison clothing. She asked the sheriff to intercede with the prison authorities for her. When she arrived at prison, a party of young men and women did not greet her with much enthusiasm. Henrietta turned to the sheriff and exclaimed, "What queer people these are, they have no manners!" She begged to be taken home.

On July 27, 1855, a week before the day of her scheduled execution, Governor Clark commuted her sentence to life imprisonment in Sing Sing.[43] After twenty years she was transferred to the Matteawan State Hospital for the Criminally Insane, where she passed the last fifteen years of her life making lace to pass the time. Toward the end, when it was clear that she was dying, she was urged to reveal to the world her real identity. She answered that she had "kept the secret for half a century" and intended to "die with it." No one came forward to claim her body, and she was buried in the hospital cemetery, veiled in mystery to the end.[44]

EMMA CUNNINGHAM
(1818–1887)

THE BOND STREET TRAGEDY

The townhouse at 31 Bond Street was, to all appearances, a model of sober middle-class propriety. But on the morning of January 31, 1857, dentist Harvey Burdell was found brutally murdered in his office strangled and stabbed fifteen times. The walls and doors were smeared with blood. A search of the building revealed a bloody towel and shirt, as well as what was thought to be the murder weapon. The prime suspect was Emma Cunningham, a thirty-eight-year-old widow with five children who had been serving as the landlady of the boarding house that Burdell ran out of his home. The murder trial dominated the attention of the local and national press and public in much the same way O. J. Simpson's trial did in the late twentieth century. Behind the closed doors of 31 Bond Street lurked a hotbed of greed, lust, intrigue, and depravity.

Emma Cunningham didn't seem a likely candidate for a murderer. The daughter of a rope-maker, she was born Emma Hempstead in Brooklyn, on August 15, 1818. The oldest of three daughters, Emma had always had big dreams. She could see the lights of Manhattan from the waterfront, and she longed to be a part of it. And she had no qualms about using her beauty and sexuality to begin her social climb.

At nineteen, she shocked her devout Methodist parents by marrying George Cunningham, the son of a local brewer, who was not only twenty-two years her senior but also Presbyterian. When Emma married George, she moved up in the world, but her relationship with her family was severed.

For a brief time, things were good in the Cunningham household. They were even able to move to a rented townhouse on Irving Place in Manhattan, giving Emma the chance to become a part of upper middle-class society.

But Cunningham soon suffered a series of financial reversals that slid the family back down the economic ladder. Like many others, he left for California to seek his fortune, but he was back after a year. He died in 1853, leaving Emma ten thousand dollars (the equivalent today of about three hundred thousand dollars), which wasn't nearly enough after paying off his debts to support herself and her children.[1] With no help from her family, Emma's only hope was to marry again. At the age of thirty-three, she was still an attractive woman, with a comely figure and a vivacious personality. Realizing that she would not be able to find a husband or the life she desired living in Brooklyn, Emma used a portion of her husband's bequest to move back into Manhattan.

While Emma met many single men, finding one willing to take on five children was another story. Sometime around late 1854, Emma met and began a whirlwind courtship with Harvey Burdell. A native of Herkimer County, in upstate New York, Burdell had come to the city in 1834 to join his brother John's dental practice. The two were soon highly successful, catering to members of New York's high society.[2] Described as "a fine-looking man, well proportioned, and of singularly youthful appearance,"[3] Burdell also owned property in New Jersey and Herkimer County, New York.[4] Burdell thought Emma "pleasant, ladylike in her appearance & conduct," but he also thought she was a wealthy widow, someone who not only looked good on his arm, but who had the potential to invest in one of his properties.[5]

By the summer of 1855, their relationship was serious enough that he invited Emma to join him for the month of August in Saratoga, a fashionable and wealthy resort in upstate New York. Emma brought along her fourteen-year-old daughter Helen, to see about enrolling her in a proper school. At the end of the summer, Burdell insisted that Emma and her children move into 31 Bond Street, first as boarders. After months of instability, it looked like Emma and her family finally had it in Harvey Burdell. Eventually Emma took over as the landlady of the boarding house. On the surface, the situation seemed ideal for both, Harvey had a convenient bed partner, and Emma had hopes that the proximity would convince him to pop the question. Emma certainly behaved as if they were married, ordering the food, hiring the maids, and dining at his table.

But by the fall of 1856, the relationship between the couple had become hostile. Here were two people who were at cross purposes—a woman desperate to marry and a man just as desperate to avoid it. Emma was jealous of Burdell's beautiful young cousin, Dimis Hubbard, who was a frequent house guest. She suspected they were having an affair. The couple had frequent arguments, with neighbors reporting later that shouts and crashes came from 31 Bond Street almost nightly. One night, Burdell accused Emma of stealing a promissory note from his office safe.[6] He summoned the police to have her arrested. When Emma struck Burdell across the face in the presence of the two officers, they declined to make an arrest. Burdell retaliated by telling the policemen that Emma could often be seen, with a male companion, in the local "houses of assignation."[7] Outraged, Emma brought lawsuits against him for breach of promise, as well as slander. Burdell was arrested and released after paying the six-thousand-dollar bail.[8]

In her suit Emma claimed that Burdell had seduced her. The pair had been visiting a property in Elizabethtown, New Jersey that Burdell was thinking of buying. They missed the last train back to New York, and that's when Emma claimed Burdell made his move. She eventually withdrew her suits against Burdell after he gave her a signed statement vowing to "extend to herself and family my friendship through life," and that he would never again "do or act in any manner to the disadvantage of Mrs. Emma A. Cunningham." He also promised to continue leasing her 31 Bond Street for eight hundred dollars a year.[9]

Although he kept his professional office at the residence, Burdell was seen taking his meals alone at several of the hotels on Broadway. Neighbors gossiped that all was not well between Burdell and his landlady. By January, Burdell had had enough of the situation. He not only wanted Emma out of his house, but he had begun telling friends that he feared for his life. He wrote to his cousin Dimis claiming that Emma was about to take steps to injure him.[10] A few days before his death, Burdell showed the house to his friend Caroline Stansbury, persuading her to take over the lease in May. Eavesdropping under the stairwell, Emma heard everything. Burdell's plan would leave her and her family homeless.

Caroline was due back on January 31st to sign the lease, but that morning, when Burdell's house boy, John Burchell, entered his office, he discovered something out of a horror movie. Blood was everywhere, and lying crumpled on the floor was the battered, liberally gashed body of Harvey Burdell.[11] Burchell immediately informed Hannah Conlon, the cook, that the doctor was lying dead on the floor. Crying, Conlon ran upstairs to alert the rest of the family. George Snodgrass, one of the boarders, informed Emma of Burdell's death. When Emma heard the news of Burdell's death, she dramatically swooned before recovering. She was the very picture of grief, weeping and tearing at her hair.[12]

Burchell ran to summon Dr. J.W. Francis from across the street, and then to the 15th Ward police station. At first it was thought that Burdell had burst a blood vessel and died before he could summon help but after a closer examination of the body, it was soon changed to murder.[13]

The *New York Herald* eagerly gave readers every gory detail of the scene: "The condition of the room wherein the bloody scene was enacted bore evident traces of a long and desperate struggle having been made by the deceased ere he yielded to the knife of the assassin."[14] Burdell had not only been stabbed fifteen times, his carotid artery severed, but he'd also been strangled.

When the police arrived at the house, they discovered a trail of blood that led all the way to the attic. Burdell's body was moved to his bedroom while the house and clinic were searched. In one of the unoccupied bedrooms on the top floor, the fireplace contained a piece of recently burned fabric. They determined that the murderer had to have been someone inside the house. There were no signs of a break-in, and Burdell's pocket watch and purse were still on his person.

News of the murder traveled quickly, and throughout the day a curious crowd surrounded 31 Bond Street, discussing the subject of the murder. Several policemen were required to keep spectators from storming into the house to look at the crime scene. A favorite ruse for trying to get in was to claim, "I'm a reporter." Eventually, the police discerned who the actual reporters were and barred the doors to imposters.[15]

The city coroner, Edward Downes Connery, an avuncular Irishman with a flair for the dramatic, convened the inquest the afternoon of Burdell's murder. A former journalist, he knew how to play to the audience that crowded into the tiny parlor to watch the proceedings. Twelve men from the neighborhood were quickly rounded up to serve as jurors. The double parlor had been converted into a makeshift interrogation room for the purpose of the inquest, while the body was moved into the victim's bedroom. The dentist chair was brought down from the crime scene on the second floor to serve as the witness stand. Extra chairs had to be brought in; every seat was filled, and spectators stood along the walls and leaned against the mantel. A table on one side of the room was for the stenographers, members of the press who were recording the interviews word for word. The *New York Times* donated this service to city proceedings, and in exchange, the newspaper was permitted to print the reports verbatim, making them "The Paper of Record."

Connery paused the inquest so that a further search of the house could be conducted. In a storeroom a bloody sheet was found, also a man's shirt, smeared on one arm, with the name Charles J. Ketchum printed on it. There was also a night shirt and a towel that appeared to be smeared with blood. There were several spots of blood inside and outside of the storeroom.[16]

Burdell's autopsy was performed inside the house by a battery of doctors, including Connery's son-in-law. This was a privilege of the wealthy (a morgue autopsy was common for the poor). Microscopes were brought into the house to analyze the blood evidence, including that on the shirt and the knife that was found. After careful examination, the towel, shirt, and knife were determined to have been stained with cow's blood, not human blood, so those were eliminated as evidence. Connery, proud of his impressive credentials, considered himself a medico-legal detective who had little use for the city's police force. He had no intention of sharing the fame or glory for solving the Burdell murder case. Emma was fortunate in retaining the services of Henry L. Clinton, a prominent criminal attorney. Connery barred

Clinton from seeing his new client, forcing Clinton to go to court to file a habeas corpus petition to gain access.[17]

Burdell had died an extremely violent, messy, and no doubt noisy death. But curiously none of the inhabitants of 31 Bond Street had heard anything during the night. Not Emma and her children; not the boarders Daniel Ullman, John Eckel, and George Snodgrass; and not any of the servants, who had all been in residence the night of the murder. They all later testified at the inquest that they had slept peacefully through the brutal murder of Harvey Burdell. And no one at 31 Bond Street had seen Burdell from the time he'd left the house on January 30 to go to dinner until John Burchell found him the next morning. While no one within the house had heard anything, neighbors testified that they heard someone shout "Murder!" around ten-thirty and several neighbors said they smelled smoke and burning wool coming from the general direction of 31 Bond Street.[18]

From the beginning Emma was the main suspect in the case. The police and Connery refused to consider any other alternative to their theory, despite receiving multiple tips about potential suspects. The streets around Burdell's house were notoriously dangerous, only a few steps away from the beer halls and saloons of the Bowery. There had long been a call to strengthen the New York police force. The number of officers available for patrol was woefully inadequate. Solving the murder quickly was a political expediency to quell the fears of the populace. And Emma had the means, a hell of a motive, not to mention the opportunity. The medical examiner determined that the murderer was left-handed; so was Emma.[19] Burdell's business partner, Alvah Blaisdell, testified that the day before the murder Burdell had asked him to spend the night at 31 Bond Street because he feared violence from Emma, John Eckel, George Snodgrass, and Emma's oldest daughter, Augusta.[20] One of the maids testified that Emma once stated that Burdell was "not fit to live" and that it was time he "was out of this world." Furthermore, Emma had called Burdell "a bad man."

The jury was shocked when the cook Hannah Conlon testified that Emma's relationship with Burdell was not only illicit but that she had become pregnant by him. Burdell had rejected her pleas that they marry, forcing her to have an abortion.[21] The real bombshell was Emma's revelation on the witness stand that she and Burdell had married in late October 1856, at the Greenwich Street parsonage of Reverend Uriah Marvine of the Dutch Reformed Church.[22] To prove her story, Emma provided the marriage certificate, and Augusta testified that she had witnessed the ceremony. Emma claimed that Burdell asked her to keep the marriage a secret until June. When Reverend Marvine took the stand, he could only definitively identify Augusta Cunningham as a witness. When taken to view Burdell's corpse, he couldn't positively identify him as the man he had married on October 28, nor could he positively identify Emma Cunningham as the bride.[23]

However, one of his servants, a young woman named Sarah McManilen, testified that she was positive the two women who came to Reverend Marvine's home that night were Emma and Augusta, and she believed that the groom was Harvey Burdell.[24] Contradictory evidence was then presented about where Burdell was on October 28, 1856, the day he supposedly married Emma. Some witnesses placed him in New York, while others insisted that he was in Saratoga. Several witnesses, including Burdell's cousin Catherine Dennison, testified to Burdell's frequent and vehement denunciations of marriage and how he vowed that he would never be drawn into wedlock.[25] Emma had also revived her breach of promise suit against Burdell three weeks after the supposed wedding took place.[26] Why would she do that if she and Burdell were legally wed?

During the inquest, aspersions were cast against Emma. A witness named John Hildreth testified that he had known Emma in Brooklyn when she was a teenager, that she had been a Vinegar Hill girl of dubious morals. He further stated that she was George Cunningham's mistress at first, that George was actually married to another woman. Hildreth suggested that they disinter Cunningham's body, accusing Emma of murdering her late husband.[27]

Suspicion soon extended to two newcomers to 31 Bond Street, eighteen-year-old George Vail Snodgrass, the son of a clergyman, and thirty-five-year-old John Eckel, a dealer in hides and fats, who was a former butcher and lover of canaries. When his room was searched, private papers belonging to Dr. Burdell were found, including an agreement signed by Emma that she would vacate the premises on May 1.[28] A servant girl, Mary Donoho, testified that Eckel's and Emma's rooms were not only right next to each other, but that Eckel was often seen spending time with Emma alone in her room. Could Eckel have replaced the good doctor in Emma Cunningham's bed? Another witness testified that Emma and Eckel had come into his barbershop to buy a toupee (Eckel had a receding hairline).

A man named John Farrell testified that on the night of January 30, he was tying his shoe on the front steps of 31 Bond Street when he heard sounds like choking, which were followed by a fall. A man, whom he identified as John Eckel, opened the front door and ordered him away. Blood was found on the door exactly where Farrell claimed Eckel had touched it.[29]

Mrs. Alvetis, the wife of the proprietor of a store on Broadway, testified that three days before Burdell was murdered, she sold a dagger known as a four-cornered blade to George Snodgrass, who vehemently denied it. This was enough for police to keep Emma under house arrest while Snodgrass and Eckel were held at the 15th Ward Police Station while the inquest continued. Connery led the jurors on a search of the house, where they found female undergarments in Snodgrass's room, along with a love poem presumably to Emma's daughter Helen. He also had Eckel, Snodgrass, and Emma examined for any bruises or blood, but the examination didn't take place until three days after the murder, when any blood would have been cleaned away.

The reports of the inquest in the daily papers kept New York entertained with the twisted tale of Harvey Burdell and Emma Cunningham. On February 2, the *New York Herald* wrote: "The Bond Street tragedy continues to be the all-absorbing topic of conversation. The shocking death of Dr. Burdell was spoken of in every circle."[30] The reporters of the various dailies vied with the coroner in raking up evidence, regardless of the source, and embellishing it with their own viewpoint. The average reader knew as much about the case as the jurors did. Virtually every family in New York was buying a daily paper. The story was a windfall for the press. Thanks to the telegraph, the story was not only carried nationwide but also internationally. The story had everything: sex, lies, and manipulation. Then, as now, readers loved to read about the foibles of the upper classes. Emma was convicted in the court of public opinion before her trial even started.

While the general tone of the stories tried to be objective, the editorials were free to moralize on the character of the victim and his alleged murderer. More than one thousand column inches were written about the Burdell case. There was fierce competition between the major daily papers (the *Sun,* the *Herald,* the *Tribune,* and the *New York Times)* and two newcomers *Harper's Weekly* and *Frank Leslie's Illustrated Newspaper.* The papers relentlessly covered the events, adding to the mountain of material printed about the case.

The murder of Burdell was a boon to Frank Leslie because it gave him the chance to define news in his illustrated newspaper by taking readers to crime scenes. He sent artists over to 31 Bond Street, who connived their way into the crime scene. He even hired actors to re-create the murder scene for the illustrators. The resulting illustrations sent circulation through the roof. Thirty thousand extra copies were printed of the February 14 issue. Coverage of the crime saved the publication from failure.

More details about the good doctor were revealed in the newspapers. Although Burdell was successful and highly regarded in his profession, he also had a darker side. He was constantly being accused by his creditors of reneging on debts. In 1835 Burdell caused a scandal when, on his wedding day, he demanded twenty thousand dollars from the wealthy father of the bride-to-be to go through with the marriage. Furious, the bride's father refused, threw Burdell out of his house, and canceled the wedding. Another engagement to a wealthy heiress was broken after he punched her father in the eye. He was well-known in the Bowery, where he often went to gamble and partake of the brothels. As an act of thriftiness, he would service the dental needs of the prostitutes working in his neighborhood and take his fee in trade.[31]

Interest in the case was so intense that people were lining up as early as eight o'clock in front of Grace Church on the morning of Burdell's funeral. Thousands of spectators jammed the muddy corner of Broadway and Tenth Street by the church's gate. The *New York Times* reported, "Among these were individuals of all degrees of society. The rowdy, of course, were there; everybody who was idle was there; but there were others who never attend any demonstration of a kindred nature unless something very extraordinary or exceedingly peculiar characterizes the incident."[32] The crowds pressed forward, anxious to gain access to the limited pew space.

Until the morning of the funeral, Emma had been barred from the room were Burdell lay in a satin-lined rosewood coffin. She was not allowed to attend the funeral of her alleged husband, but she begged Connery for the chance to pay her respects. Clad in deepest mourning, the *Herald* reported, "Having descended the staircase half-way, she burst into a fit of tears, sobbing heavily, she at length entered the dread apartment." She was taken to see his body before the coffin lid was screwed shut. Crying hysterically, she said, "Oh, I wish to God you could speak, and tell who done it."[33] Emma was so distraught that she needed medical assistance. Following the funeral, Burdell was buried in Green-Wood Cemetery in Brooklyn.

Over the fourteen days of the inquest, more than one hundred witnesses testified, including four of Emma's five children, the youngest being William, only nine years old. Both of Emma's daughters Augusta and Helen testified that the three of them retired on Friday night between ten and eleven o'clock, and that all three slept in the same bed, Emma in the middle. The reason being that Helen was leaving the next morning to go attend school in Saratoga.

Although the evidence was extremely circumstantial, after six hours of deliberation, the jury declared that Emma and John Eckels were responsible for Burdell's death.[34] George Snodgrass was charged as an accomplice. Emma's daughters Augusta and Helena were found to "have some knowledge of the facts connected with the said murder, which they have concealed from the jury; that it is the duty of the coroner to hold them for the future action of the grand jury."[35] The grand jury was summoned on February 16, 1857. The proceedings were held in secret, so reporters were forced to turn to other sources for stories.

Emma had already been removed from 31 Bond Street before the inquest was over into her new home at the city prison nicknamed the Tombs to await the verdict. Now it was to be her new home until the trial. Curious strangers paraded through the open corridors daily to gawp shamelessly at Emma, depriving her of privacy and rest for the three months before her trial. Her daughters Augusta and Helen, along with the two boys were allowed to continue to reside at 31 Bond Street. A reporter from the *New York Herald* was able to get an interview with the prisoner. He found her remarkably calm given the circumstances. Emma claimed that her signature was forged on the agreement giving her consent to leave 31 Bond Street.[36]

What must have been going through Emma's mind during those months while she awaited her trial? How had her life come to this after such a promising beginning—marriage to the once wealthy George Cunningham? Now she faced the possibility of death if found guilty. What would become of her children? Marrying Burdell was supposed to return Emma to the prosperous life she'd once lived. But Emma was not down for the count; there was still the possibility that not only would she be found innocent, but that she would inherit Burdell's estate if the marriage was proved valid.

While Emma awaited the start of her trial in the Tombs, the court moved to liquidate the contents of 31 Bond Street. Emma provided a list of items, including furniture, china, and books, that she claimed belonged to her.[37] On March 30 a public auction of the furnishings and dental equipment was held in the house. Eager New Yorkers could now own a souvenir from the crime scene. Crowds lined up to get in. Fights broke out amongst the prospective bidders. The blood-soaked carpet from Burdell's consulting room was a sought-after item. The *New York Herald* noted that for weeks "a crowd stood gaping at the premises of No. 31 Bond Street, anxiously desiring to get a view of the interior of the house in which such a strange and fiend-like tragedy had been enacted." The stream of people who filed through the house were less interested in the items up for auction than in ghoulish curiosity. "The back room on the second floor, the walls and doors of which are still bespattered with the blood of the deceased, was the central point of attraction."[38] By the end of the auction, a few hundred dollars had been raised.

Emma moved swiftly to try and take control of Burdell's assets as his widow. Burdell's will, if he had one, never turned up in the search of 31 Bond Street. But Burdell's relatives also laid claim to the estate estimated to be worth between eighty thousand and one hundred thousand dollars (over two million dollars today). Burdell's relatives hired prominent attorney Samuel J. Tilden to represent them. Emma's lawyer, Henry L. Clinton, asked the surrogate court that she be recognized as Burdell's widow. The star witness was once again the Reverend Uriah Marvine, who had changed his mind and now stated conclusively that the two people he married were Emma Cunningham and Harvey Burdell. Clinton argued that the marriage had been kept secret at Burdell's insistence, implying that he had only agreed to the marriage as a way of settling Emma's legal claims against him. At the end of the proceedings, the surrogate court judge announced that he would reserve his decision until after the criminal trial.[39]

Emma's trial began on May 5, 1857, with the trial of John Eckel scheduled to take place after hers. The trial lasted a few days. She had to sit in the courtroom while the prosecution, led by District Attorney A. Oakey Hall, smeared her as a bad, immoral woman who made no bones about her hatred for the victim and who was eager to get her hands on his money.[40] Hannah Conlon testified regarding Emma's abortion at Burdell's hands. Clinton objected to the testimony of Conlon and Mary Donoho, claiming that their memories were unreliable, but he was overruled by Justice Davies.

Clinton and his co-counsel Gilbert Dean countered that yes, Mrs. Cunningham-Burdell (as she was now calling herself), had had her share of disputes with Burdell, but she also had suffered greatly at his hands. They stressed his shady past, his gambling habits, his willingness to screw over his family for money, and his habit of performing dental work on prostitutes in exchange for sexual favors. They brought up the lack of evidence connecting Emma to the crime. She had an alibi, from both of her daughters, who claimed they had spent the night of the murder with her, and she had slept in between them. Gilbert Dean focused on providing another suspect, claiming that Dimis Hubbard's ex-husband William Vorce had a motive. Burdell convinced Dimis to seek a divorce. Vorce was heard to have sworn vengeance.

When Edward Downes Connery took the stand, Henry Clinton took the opportunity to call into question his ethics. Not only had he hired his son John to assist during the inquest, but also his son-in-law Dr. William Knight was part of the post-mortem team. Clinton played on the Irish stereotype by implying that both Connery and Hannah Conlon were drunks. The jury was taken to 31 Bond Street to survey the crime scene. It was noticed that the house could be entered from both the side and rear doors as well as the front entrance.

When Clinton gave his final summation to the jury, he claimed that Emma was the victim of a witch hunt, doing his best to portray her as victim of prosecutorial misconduct. Clinton argued that Emma's marriage to Burdell proved that she had no motive for murder. There were others who had stronger incentives to want Burdell dead. Clinton even managed to get in a dig at Coroner Connery for denying Emma her civil rights.[41]

On May 9, after deliberating for only half an hour, the jury found Emma not guilty of murder. John Eckel, who had been charged with being her accessory, was also freed.[42] It was a popular verdict. Despite the negative revelations about Emma's morals, the weak evidence against her, coupled with the vile character of the deceased, had earned her some sympathy.[43] Many expressed the opinion that if she didn't murder Harvey Burdell, she should have. The *New York Times,* citing the incompetence of police and authorities to solve the murder, offered a five-thousand-dollar reward to anyone who could solve the murder at what was, in their eyes, a gross miscarriage of justice. After the trial, Emma returned to 31 Bond Street with her children to await the outcome of the surrogate court. A large crowd had gathered outside the house hoping for a glimpse, but Emma and her family very prudently kept out of sight. The crowd became so unruly that the cops were called to disperse them. Two officers kept watch, telling curious onlookers to "move along" unless they had business at the house.

If only Emma had trusted Clinton to win her suit in surrogate court, the way that he'd won her freedom, her life might have turned out differently.

Unfortunately for Emma, she let greed overpower her common sense. During her weeks in prison, she had cooked up a plan to claim that she was pregnant with Burdell's child. She showed up in court, noticeably thicker around her middle, claiming that the infant was due around the end of July or beginning of August. Emma refused to let anyone but her doctor examine her, and Victorian morality made it impossible for Hall to order Emma to submit to a thorough medical examination.

Trusting in doctor/patient confidentiality, she enlisted the help of Dr. David Uhl who had given her medical care since Burdell's death. Informing him that she was pregnant, she asked him to supervise her prenatal care. But a brief examination informed Uhl that she was not pregnant. Using her most persuasive manner, she offered to pay him one thousand dollars if he helped her to procure a baby. Dr. Uhl, no doubt worried about his medical license, informed District Attorney Hall of Emma's scheme.

Still smarting from his failure to put Emma behind bars for murder, he saw the chance to get his revenge. Hall counseled Uhl to play along, and he would be more than happy to take things from there. Uhl went back to Emma, telling her that he knew of a young married woman who had a husband prospecting for gold in California. Alas, she was expecting a child that wasn't her husband's. No doubt she would be happy to have Emma take the infant off her hands. Uhl went to Bellevue Hospital, where he convinced a woman named Elizabeth Ann Anderson to loan her baby for Emma's little performance. Emma, dressed as one of the Sisters of Mercy, carried the baby from Uhl's office back to 31 Bond Street in a basket.

August 3 was the date chosen for Emma to "give birth." To make the birth seem authentic, Emma had taken the precaution of procuring a bucket of lamb's blood and a placenta. Contorting under bloody sheets, "and in due time, after considerable groaning and moaning, the expectant heir was brought forth," reported the *New York Daily Tribune*. "Dr. Uhl left the house and the case to the charge of others, who were on hand at the door." As soon as Emma produced the infant, detectives rushed in and arrested all the participants, including the baby. Alas, for Emma, the district attorney had taken the precaution of marking the baby with silver nitrate under the armpits, which made it easy to prove that the baby was not actually hers.[44]

During this time Henry Clinton had left for a month's vacation in Sharon Springs, returning to New York on August 4. The morning following his return, he discovered that his client, whom he had believed to be pregnant, had been charged with a felony and imprisoned once again in the Tombs. He refused to represent her in connection with these charges, and she had to scramble to find a new lawyer, who applied unsuccessfully for bail several times before it was granted.

This little escapade was too much for the judge in surrogate court. Emma's marriage to Burdell was ruled invalid, barring her from receiving a cent of Burdell's estate. The idea being that if she could fake a pregnancy, she was probably capable of faking a marriage as well.[45] Emma was left with nothing, but at least she didn't have to worry about going to prison, thanks to a technicality. She hadn't attempted to claim Burdell's estate for her "baby," so a judge ruled that she could not be charged with attempted fraud. Strike two for District Attorney Hall.

While the murder is considered unsolved, the fascination with the case and the coverage continued until the 1860s, when the Civil War eclipsed crime reporting. In 1863 a career criminal by the name of George Symonds confessed to the murder while incarcerated in the Mercer County Penitentiary. He was about to be executed for the murder of a Princeton jeweler. He was not the first to confess to the murder of Dr. Burdell, and while most death row confessions are suspect, his was one that seemed plausible. The story was reported in two issues of the *National Police Gazette*. His motive? His estranged wife Eliza Jane was once a patient of Burdell, and she had fallen in love with his nephew, Galen Burdell, who was also a dentist. Symonds apparently got the two confused. He also claimed that he had lost a large sum of money to Harvey Burdell in a card game.[46]

On July 31, 1897, the front-page story of the *New York Times* declared: "Burdell Murder Cleared. William F. Woods of Chicago Says Mrs. Cunningham Confessed the Crime." A man named William Woods provided the information to the newspaper that in 1860 Emma had confessed to his grandmother, whose husband had briefly been Burdell's business partner. The *Times* offered few other details, like what reason Emma would have had to confess three years after Burdell's death, other than that the crime had been solved.

As for the other players in the tragedy, although he failed to convict Emma of either murder or fraud, Hall went on to serve two terms as mayor of New York. Henry L. Clinton tried many important cases after Emma's, including the prosecution of New York's notorious Tweed ring and the contested wills of Cornelius Vanderbilt and department store magnate A. T. Stewart. Hall and Clinton would face off again when Hall was indicted along with William Marcy "Boss" Tweed for bribery in 1872.[47] After three trials Hall was acquitted in 1873, but his career was ruined. Emma's alleged accomplice, John J. Eckels, was charged with tax evasion in 1869, serving time in Sing Sing prison for tax evasion, where he died later that year. Before he died, he denied any involvement in Burdell's murder.[48]

Emma and her children were evicted from 31 Bond Street after the surrogate court's ruling. To pay her legal fees, she was forced to sell an investment property that she had bought with her first husband's insurance money at a thirty percent loss. For the next few years, she was sighted everywhere from California to Ohio and back to New York, where her daughter Augusta married a well-to-do Southern planter.

Emma eventually married a former beau from her Brooklyn childhood, a miner named Whitehead Hyde. "Fickle, false, and full of fraud," Emma had rejected Hyde when they were younger probably because he was only a poor clerk, and she had her sights on bigger fish. The exact date of their marriage is unknown but by 1864, Emma, her two sons William and George, and her daughter Helen were living with Hyde in Loreto, in Lower (Baja) California where she had taken over the running of his mine La Sauce.[49] Soon after the marriage, Hyde signed a power of attorney giving Emma complete control over his property. Emma promptly transferred the deeds to the ranch and the mine to her two sons William and George.[50]

But the marriage was unhappy, and Hyde feared for his life after two of his children died under mysterious circumstances. According to an article published in the *New York Sun* on January 23, 1876, and reprinted in the

San Francisco Chronicle, Emma had not only run off with the superintendent of the mine, but she sold the mine for a considerable sum. Even after the divorce, rumors abounded that Emma had tried to poison Whitehead Hyde multiple times.

Almost twenty years after the murder, Emma once again appeared in the news. The February 11, 1876, edition of the *San Francisco Chronicle* featured a rare interview with Emma, who now went by the name Mary Caroline Williams. Living in San Francisco, she had remarried again in 1870, this time to a silver miner named William E. Williams, who was thirteen years her junior. Whether he was the same man Emma was rumored to have had an affair with no one knows. Emma greeted the reporter "with a profound bow," appearing to the visitor "as a pleasant-looking, stout, matronly lady of apparently 50 or 55 years of age." The *Chronicle* reporter offered readers the following description: "No signs of remorse—if she be guilty of the horrible butchery with which she was charged—are visible in her countenance, nor have the agonies of a terrible, persistent persecution—if she be innocent—left any traces in her face. She simply presents the appearance of a well-preserved, well-dressed, quiet, lady-like middle-aged woman, in whose arms a grandchild would not look out of place."

Emma wanted to set the record straight about the recent article in the *New York Sun,* which she claimed was full of falsehoods. Of course, she herself wasn't above telling a few little white lies herself to make a better story. Bursting into tears, Emma claimed that she had never met Hyde before 1861, a year after she moved to the West Coast, and she divorced in 1868 for drunkenness and squandering her money. She denied that she'd had anything to do with the mysterious deaths of Hyde's children. Emma flat out denied the charge that Hyde ever owned or operated a copper mine. In fact, Emma purchased a half-interest in the mine in Loreto with her own money, which she had made over to her children William and Helen. Emma denied not only murdering Burdell but claimed that she was framed in regard to the bogus baby plot, that it was a scheme by Burdell's relatives to drive her from 31 Bond Street. As for her name change, it was because of the constant persecution she faced by the press.[51]

Soon after her husband's death in 1883, Emma was swindled by a group of investors in a copper mining scheme in Baja. Thrice-widowed and broke, Emma moved back to New York to live with her niece, Phoebe Morrell, in East Harlem, where she died in September 1887.[52] She now lies in New York's Green-Wood Cemetery, only a few hundred yards away from the resting place of Harvey Burdell.

FREDERICKA "MARM" MANDELBAUM (1818-1894)

QUEEN OF FENCES

How did a poor immigrant German-Jewish peddler woman rise to the top of the male-dominated underworld of Gilded Age New York? How was she able to achieve all that she did in an era when women were not only considered second-class citizens but also property? Known as the "Queen of Fences," Fredericka "Marm" Mandelbaum reigned as the most successful and notorious fence in New York City for over thirty years in the late nineteenth century. From humble beginnings, she became a larger-than-life figure in the nineteenth century professional criminal world. The *Boston Globe* called her "the smartest female 'fence' or receiver of stolen goods, who ever lived in this country, or probably in any other."[1] Between 1857 and 1884, most New York thieves knew their best chance to realize their ill-gotten gains was to trust Mandelbaum. At the height of her power, she handled as much as 10 million dollars in stolen goods, roughly the equivalent to between 120 million and 200 million dollars today. A July 1884 *New York Times* article called her "the nucleus and center of the whole organization of crime in New York City."

Marm was born Fredericka Wiesner on February 17, in 1827 in Hanover, Prussia. Very little is known about her life in Germany before she emigrated, but as a young Jewish girl, Fredericka probably had at least an elementary education.[2] In 1848 she married Wolf Mandelbaum, a peddler, one of the few professions that Jews could hold. The couple set about scratching out

43

a living as itinerant peddlers, but it was a hard life, especially for a Jewish couple. They were just barely scraping by when their daughter Bessie was born.

In 1850 the couple decided to emigrate to New York City, like other immigrants who left poverty, political upheaval, economic depression, and religious persecution behind them to seek opportunities in America. Wolfe left first, traveling on the steamship *Baltimore* in July,[3] Fredericka and their daughter Bessie followed in August 1850 via the *Erie.*[4] They traveled in steerage, the cheapest fare possible, paying twenty dollars for the passage. They were forced to endure the long voyage below deck with the other third-class passengers for the six-week journey. More than one hundred immigrants would be packed tightly like sardines in one of three lower decks. A row of tiny, hay lined bunks was stacked against the wall.

Passengers were provided with an "immigrant kit," which consisted of a horse blanket, a tin plate, and a knife and fork. Meals consisted of bread and salted meat. Seasickness was rampant; personal space and hygiene were nonexistent. Fredericka must have questioned the decision to emigrate constantly during the long and perilous journey.[5] At six feet tall, she was cramped in a space that was six feet high, two feet wide, and seven feet long. Despite the inhumane conditions, Fredericka and Bessie managed to make it to the New Word relatively unscathed.

New York Harbor must have been a welcome sight after the long voyage. The bustling port teemed with barges and small ferries vying with steamships and schooners filled with goods for entry. It was the largest port in the

United States, bustling with goods and people being loaded and unloaded onto the crowded wharves. The Mandelbaums were just a few of the two million immigrants who landed in the city in the 1850s. The city's population was around five hundred thousand citizens, which almost doubled to eight hundred thousand by the 1860s.[6] For the immigrants who arrived in the 1850s, life was not easy; they were often taken advantage of by landlords, who charged inflated rents and then evicted them when they could not pay. Employment wasn't easy to find either. Life was hard, but life back in the old country was harder.

The Mandelbaums settled in Kleindeutschland (Little Germany) on the Lower East Side. The area comprised an area from the East River, on the north by 14th Street, on the west by the Bowery and the notorious Five Points neighborhood, and on the south by Division Street. The neighborhood had the largest German-speaking population in the world outside of Berlin. The Germans tended to cluster together more than other immigrants and those from particular German states preferred to live amongst their compatriots. Tompkins Square formed the center. Avenue B, occasionally called the German Broadway, was the main commercial artery. Avenue A was the street for beer gardens, oyster saloons, and groceries, and the Bowery was filled with theaters. By the end of the decade, it would become the most heavily populated neighborhood in the city.[7]

The streets of their new city weren't paved with gold; they were unpaved, muddy, and dirty. Garbage was tossed out into the street; chamber pots were also emptied out into the alleys, producing rivers of human excrement. Factories intermixed with housing in increasingly crowded conditions. The neighborhood was squalid, with people squeezed into tenement apartments measuring just three hundred and twenty-five square feet. The only heat was from a fireplace in the kitchen, and freshwater had to be hauled up from street pumps or wells and then lugged upstairs. Indoor plumbing was nonexistent, so tenants had to use a chamber pot or outhouses in the alleys behind the buildings. Disease was rampant.

The Mandelbaums probably lived with relatives at first before finding a home of their own. Their new home was probably a single, airless, lightless room in a decrepit tenement house, one of many they would live in over the next ten years. Survival quickly became the name of the game. Fredericka and her husband scratched out a living as peddlers, hawking everything from rags to broken timepieces to scraps of silk. They couldn't afford a pushcart, or a storefront, so they carried their goods on their backs, setting out early each morning. Fourteen-hour workdays often yielded only six dollars a week. Because she was so tall, Fredericka stood out among the horde of street vendors.

After years of eking out a meager existence, Fredericka's luck began to change when the Panic of 1857 plunged the country into a depression. Businesses failed, banks closed, and thousands of people lost their jobs. In the Five Points, ten thousand people were fed by charity in single day. Women and children scavenged in the streets for items that would help them survive, including wood and coal, scrap metal, rope, and glass. They sold these items to junk dealers and individuals like Fredericka.

Fredericka had several mentors, some of the most notorious and successful fences in New York. Kleindeutschland provided New York with most of its leading fences. Her mentors included Joe "Mose" Ehrich, known as the most "successful, adroit, and daring fence known to the police annals of the city"; Ephraim Snow, the "godfather" of fencing; and "Gen," Abe Greenthal, whom the *New York Times* called "one of the oldest and shrewdest criminals in the country."[8] He was one of the country's most successful pickpockets and fences. His entire family was involved in the criminal business. His sons, daughters, and in-laws were either shoplifters or pickpockets. He was also the boss of a loose-knit group of Jewish pickpockets who operated throughout the city.[9]

Snow ran his fencing operation out of his dry-goods store on Grand and Allen Streets, while Ehrich operated out of a shop farther downtown on Maiden Lane. From them, Fredericka learned to bribe politicians and the police to keep them from shutting down her operation. There was no "honor among thieves"; a fair payment to the criminals who worked for her would keep them coming back to her and provide her with an endless supply of merchandise to sell. And finally, she learned to only buy items that she could sell for a profit.

Fredericka soon gained a reputation as a "middleman," willing to buy stolen merchandise and then sell it on to retail business owners looking for a bargain on materials for which wholesalers charged high prices. She didn't care about where the merchandise came from as long as she could make a profit. She was street smart, savvy, and quick to seize any opportunity. She worked with an endless supply of shady sellers as well as legitimate buyers who then resold the products for twice as much. Everyone seemed to like Fredericka; her prices were low, and she didn't ask questions. Moreover, she was a good judge of character, and she was scrupulously honest.

The city was teeming with "street rats," orphaned or abandoned children who were homeless and slept wherever they could find a place. Children roamed the streets, selling bits of rope and slivers of coal, eventually graduating to pickpocketing and looting vendors. Fredericka began cultivating relationships with these urchins, buying their wares and selling them.[10]

She soon became acquainted with a more professional class of thieves: shoplifters, pickpockets, and burglars. Many of the shoplifters were women who trolled the upscale stores in the "Ladies Mile" shopping district, such as Lord & Taylor, Arnold, Constable & Company, and A. T. Stewart. Fredericka would introduce them to the clerks that she had an arrangement with, to look the other way for a percentage of the profits. Cashmere shawls, sealskin purses, and bolts of silk easily ended up in the large pockets sewn under their skirts, as did the contents of the customers' pocketbooks.

Fredericka never purchased anything for more than half its worth and always sold it for twice as much. She learned to speak English almost as well as she spoke German, which made her an asset to adult criminals. Fencing stolen goods soon became her main gig. Her favorite items were bolts of silk and diamonds, both of which she could buy on the cheap and then sell at a considerable markup. She soon became an expert in determining the value of jewelry, silks, and any loot brought to her by thieves.[11]

Fredericka regularly paid bribes to the politicians, police, and judges to turn a blind eye to her criminal operation. Marm made sure she never spoke with more than one crook at a time when negotiating a deal. If no one could corroborate what was said or what took place in a specific meeting, then it was her word against theirs. Marm insisted that sellers remain present and in her sight throughout any transaction, and money only ever exchanged hands after she had the stolen goods safely in her possession.

Fredericka was able to operate so easily because the New York City Police Department was still a relatively new organization. Closely modeled after the Metropolitan Police in London, it had been established in 1845, replacing the old night-watch system. Uniforms weren't introduced until 1853 and cops initially carried nothing but a wooden club to keep the peace. The residents and police themselves had not yet formalized what role the department would play. The one thing that everyone agreed on was that policing social disorder, riots, gang fights, and drunk and disorderly persons on the street mattered more than going after more high-level crime. In 1856, Republican governor John King and the reformers in Albany created a new Metropolitan Police, abolishing the Municipal Police Force. Defying the state, Mayor Fernando Wood and the Municipal Police Force resisted for several months. The city effectively had two police forces, the state-controlled Metropolitans and the Municipals. There was chaos in the city until the State Supreme Court stepped in, leaving the Metropolitan Police the only force in the city.

While the state abolished the rewards systems, the New York Police Department took advantage of a loophole that allowed cops to accept them in special cases whereby the victims of theft paid the police to negotiate the return of their property.[12] This meant that the police only bothered with thieves when they were paid by the owners of the property.[13]

The law also contributed to Fredericka's success. A receiver could be prosecuted only if she or he was clearly connected to a specific theft.[14] For much of the nineteenth century in New York, a receiver could be indicted, convicted, or punished only if the thief connected to the stolen property was convicted.[15] So, for much of Fredericka's career, the law was in her favor. In 1868 the New York State legislature passed a law that to convict someone of bribery, the person who offered the bribe had to testify and show corroborating evidence.[16]

By 1865 Fredericka and her husband were able to sign a two-year lease on a building at Clinton and Rivington Streets, opening a successful dry-goods store as a front and conducting her fencing business in the back. Soon the business occupied three buildings. To suit her new station in life, that of a respectable businesswoman, Fredericka wore her black hair simply dressed in a tight bun, topped off by a feathered fascinator. Her clothes were well cut but only in somber colors of black, brown, or dark blue. She became a regular attendee at her local synagogue.

Although their eldest daughter Bessie died sometime after they arrived in New York, the Mandelbaums soon added four more children to their family: Julius in 1860, Sarah in 1862, Gustav in 1864, and the baby Anna in 1867. Despite her new career, Fredericka was a devoted and loving mother. She was a tad overprotective, never letting her children out of her sight, and she would call off a business meeting if one of her children needed her. Despite her growing wealth, she chose to stay in Kleindeutschland, where she was able to use the crowded streets to expand her fencing operation.

The Mandelbaums lived above their store, in rooms elegantly furnished with stolen goods from some of New York's finest mansions. "Whether 'Marm' Mandelbaum intended to astonish her clients with a display of her wealth, or to show that she lived in a style befitting her position, cannot be discussed. There were chairs which would have attracted the cupidity of an antiquarian; a massive mahogany sideboard, and on it a magnificent display of silverware, which would have been rated as 'A 1 swag' had a client of the old woman called on her to dispose of it."[17] A warm, generous hostess, she held frequent dances and dinners attended by celebrated criminals as well as friendly politicians and cops. They called her "Marm," which was short for "mother," because she hovered over them like a mother hen, guiding and nurturing their criminal careers. "They call me Ma because I give them money and horses and diamonds," she said.

Almost six feet tall and 250 pounds, Marm was rather homely, with small black eyes and plump, rosy cheeks. Most of the contemporary descriptions of her reek of anti-Semitism, describing her as some sort of female Fagin. New York's Police Commissioner George W. Walling wrote that she was "greasy, fat, and opulent," but admitted that she was a "thorough businesswoman." The *New York Times* described her in 1884 as "almost masculine in appearance, restless black eyes, and a dark florid complexion." Robert Pinkerton, co-director of the Pinkerton National Detective Agency, called her "a gargantuan caricature of Queen Victoria with her black hair in a roll and a small bun hat with drooping feathers." While Marm might not have been considered a beauty, she was smart as a whip, and she seems to have had a personal charisma that belied her looks.

She was a regular presence at the Eighth Ward Thieves Exchange near Broadway and Houston Street. Today, the area is prime Manhattan real estate, a location of upmarket condos, trendy eateries, and upscale retailers. But in the late nineteenth century, the Thieves Exchange was the center of the city's criminal underworld, where fences and criminals could get their hands on all kinds of stolen goods.[18]

Fredericka was always looking for new recruits. The story is that she opened a school of crime on Grand Street, which was not far from police headquarters. Here children could learn from professionals the fine arts of pickpocketing, shoplifting, and grifting. Advanced students might then move on to learning safe cracking and burglary, with postgraduate courses in confidence schemes and blackmail. Fredericka supposedly shut down the school when the son of a prominent police official enrolled in the school. However, there is no evidence that this school ever actually existed.

She befriended both crooked cops and judges at the nearby Fifth District Court. Tammany Hall politicians recognized her influence in the neighborhood, stopping by her store to say hello, reasoning that she could help them get out the Jewish vote. As Police Commissioner George W. Walling later wrote,

As a handler of stolen goods Marm Mandelbaum has no peer in the United States . . . We even hired rooms on the opposite side of the street from her store for the purpose of obtaining such evidence as would lead to her arrest and conviction as a receiver of stolen goods. Mrs. Mandelbaum is a very sharp woman, however, and is not often caught napping. Whenever she buys goods off thieves, she appoints a place of meeting where she can confer without suspicion. She will not allow them to come to her store under any consideration.[19]

Fredericka dealt in goods of all kinds: silk, lace, diamonds, horses, goats, carriages, silverware, gold, silver, and bonds, and she could estimate a thief's loot in a glance. She used the money she earned to buy up real estate, not just tenements but also warehouses to hold the stolen goods. She hired goldsmiths to melt down jewelry and coins, women to unpick the marks out of costly cloth, engravers to doctor jewelry, and handsome cab drivers for quick getaways. And most important, she paid the law firm of Howe and Hummel an annual five-thousand-dollar retainer (approximately one hundred thousand dollars today).[20] Her own hands remained clean; she knew that receiving stolen goods was not against the law unless she had a hand in stealing them herself.

Fredericka's husband Wolfe does not seem to have been involved with either of her businesses. Described by one of Fredericka's protegees, Sophie Lyons, as "rather weak-willed for his calling, lazy, and afflicted with chronic dyspepsia,"[21] he seems to have taken a backseat while Fredericka built her criminal empire. He finally died of tuberculosis in 1875, leaving her a widow with four children ranging from eight to fifteen years old. Her oldest son, Julius, soon joined the family business, but Fredericka made sure to keep her other three children out of it. She hired a man named Herman Stroude, who always accompanied her when she went to assess merchandise.[22] On average, Fredericka offered one-fifth of the wholesale price of goods. On silks worth three dollars a yard, she would pay sixty-five cents; for sealskin bags that retailed for three hundred dollars, she would pay seventy; and for camel hair shawls worth between one thousand and twelve hundred dollars, she would pay one hundred.[23] After the transaction, Stroude would cart the goods to one of Fredericka's numerous warehouses or to her home, where she had a series of hiding places. She had a chimney with a false back in her office, behind which was a dumbwaiter that could be raised or lowered with the yank of a lever. If there was a suspicious knock on the door, she could gather up the loot and drop it out of sight.[24] By way of example, Walling noted, "the ramifications of her business net were so widespread, her ingenuity as an assistant to criminals so nearly approaching genius that if a silk robbery occurred in St. Louis, and the criminals were known as 'belonging to Marm Baum,' she always had the first choice of the 'swag.'"

In 1875 the police seized a large amount of goods from Fredericka's premises. Although the police knew that the goods were stolen, none of it could be identified. One merchant who had lost a large amount of silk swore that the silk seized was exactly like what had been stolen from his store, but he couldn't absolutely be sure. The same thing happened with some expensive shawls, and in the end the police had to return the merchandise to Fredericka.[25]

By 1880 Fredericka was the most successful fence in the United States and one of the most powerful figures in professional crime, amassing a personal fortune estimated at more than one million dollars. Over the course of her career, she handled an estimated five million to ten million dollars in stolen property. Many well-known bank robbers and thieves sought her out, and she mentored those she thought were particularly talented.[26] She owned tenements in New York as well as warehouses in New Jersey, where she stored stolen merchandise that she openly bought and sold.[27]

Fredericka not only mentored the notorious art thief Adam Worth,[28] known as the Napoleon of Crime, but also bank robbers like George Floyd and Piano Charley Bullard. She not only bought them the most up-to-date tools, but she also paid for their bail if they were arrested, and even went so far as to break Adam Worth out of jail. Certain favored criminals benefited from her Bureau for the Protection of Criminals, a fund that provided bail money and legal representation. Paying for their defense not only helped keep some of her best thieves out of prison, making sure they were out making her money, but also earned her their gratitude and a nice profit since she required them to pay the funds with interest, giving her a measure of control over their future actions.[29]

Fredericka was involved in planning some of the biggest thefts in the city's history, including the Manhattan Savings Bank Robbery. Planned by George Leonidas Leslie, the heist took three years to plan. Leslie was no ordinary bank robber. He came from a well-to-do family in Ohio and had trained as an architect, but during the Civil War, his father had bought his way out of the draft. After the war was over, Leslie found himself persona non grata in his hometown. He came to New York and turned to bank robbing. At the time, dynamite was often used during bank robberies, which was dangerous.

Or it involved hours of trying to crack the safe using a stethoscope to listen to the tumblers. Leslie invented a wheel that could be inserted into the vault, which made it easier to open but meant breaking into the bank twice, once to plant the device and once to rob it. Unfortunately, Leslie was murdered before the robbery took place. His partially decomposed body was found on Tramp's Rock in the Bronx, near the Westchester County line. His murder was never solved. The consensus is that he was lured to his death, thinking it was an assignation with the wife of one of his fellow gang members.[30] Fredericka paid the funeral expenses of her "poor pet," as she always called him, shedding tears at his death.[31]

Another of Fredericka's favorite associates was a man known as Piano Charley Bullard. He was a classically trained pianist who regularly entertained Fredericka and her guests on the white grand piano at the lavish dinner parties she threw. Piano Charley was also a talented safe cracker, but he was less competent at keeping himself out of jail. In 1869 he was serving time for stealing one hundred thousand dollars. Fredericka recruited some of her criminal crowd and rented a building near the prison. The men tunneled into Piano Charley's cell, bribed a few guards not to notice, and Fredericka's favorite piano player escaped.[32] Marm was incredibly loyal to this motley band of thieves. George W. Walling wrote in his memoir, "She attained a reputation as a businesswoman whose honesty in criminal matters was absolute."

Marm also had an affinity for female thieves and encouraged the ambitions of several pickpockets, shoplifters, and blackmailers, including women with names like Big Mary, Ellen Clegg, Queen Liz, Little Annie, Old Mother Hubbard, Black Lena Kleinschmidt,[33] and Kid Glove Rose. Although they were breaking the law, her crime ring created opportunities that were unavailable elsewhere. Most jobs for women, who were uneducated, involved working in factories for long hours for little money, or as domestic help. Working as a shoplifter or pickpocket, providing they didn't get caught, afforded them the chance to make money and use their skills.

Marm trained them to always work in pairs; one would be the lookout while the other stuffed the goods into a pocket in her petticoat. They only shoplifted from high-end stores such as Lord & Taylor, A. T. Stewart, and

Arnold Constable, and only took the finest goods. Marm had no pity for the wives of criminals, however, especially those who were unfortunate enough to get caught and sent to prison. Marm refused their pleas for money and insisted that they work for it.[34] Most women, she griped, were "wasting their life being housekeepers."

But the good times couldn't last forever, and 1884 was Marm's Annus Horribilis. The year started off with a civil suit that had been initiated back in 1881. A merchant named James Scott claimed that in 1877 thieves stole 26 cashmere shawls worth $780 and 2,000 yards of black silk worth $4,000 from his store in Boston. Scott claimed that the goods were received by Marm, who knew that they were stolen. Why was he so sure of this? Well, the thieves in question were some of Marm's associates, Michael "Sheeny Mike" Kurtz and James Hoey, and both had worked with her for years.[35] When Kurtz was arrested for the crime in Washington, he telegraphed Marm, on his way to Boston, to help get him out of it. Unfortunately, Marm's attempts did not work. Kurtz ended up serving three years in prison. When he got out, he swore an affidavit against Marm. She was arrested, but when the case came up for trial, he was a no-show.

The case was delayed for three years, because Judge Charles Donohue ruled that Scott's original attorneys had to be replaced for unknown reasons. Hoey testified that Marm admitted to him that she had bought the stolen goods from Kurtz. Hoey's wife, Mollie, was threatened with a long prison sentence unless she rolled over on Marm. She appealed to Marm for aid but was refused. In revenge, Mollie told all. Detective Dusenberry, a twenty-five-year veteran of the police, testified that neither Hoey nor his wife could be trusted. Marm testified on her own behalf, denying the whole story. She also denied that she had ever had possession of Scott's property or that she was complicit with Kurtz.[36]

The jury decided for the plaintiff in the amount of $6,666 plus court costs. Marm's attorneys, William Howe and Abraham Hummel, filed a motion for a new trial, which was denied. On January 24, 1884, Marm was ordered to pay Scott the grand total of $7,267.75.[37] Mollie Hoey was eventually pardoned by Governor Grover Cleveland, her reward for betraying Marm.[38] There was one catch, though. She had to be available to appear in court to testify against Marm regarding any indictments that were pending against her.

New York City's new district attorney, Peter B. Olney, had had enough. Olney took his oath of office seriously, and because he didn't trust the police, he hired the Pinkerton Detective Agency to set up a sting operation. A detective named Gustave Frank, using the alias Stein, took lessons from a silk merchant on quality and pricing. Armed with a thousand dollars provided by the Pinkertons, he told Marm that he wanted to buy some cheap silk, but Marm refused to sell to him. Frank/Stein was persistent, coming back again and again. Only when he told Marm that he was an acquaintance of an associate of hers did she agree to sell. Off her game because of the civil suit, Marm was not as cautious as she normally would have been.[39]

Marm eventually began doing business with Frank/Stein. He knew of her generosity toward crooks, particularly those of her own German-Jewish background, confiding in her that he was a thief, and wanted to buy stolen goods. Slowly winning her trust, he was eventually able to purchase "marked" silks from her. Marm gave him advice about the best way to dispose of the goods. "Don't sell this piece in New York, Mr. Stein, because it came from one of the big stores here." It took him three months to build a case against her. Frank ended up buying twelve thousand yards of stolen silk.

On July 22, 1884, Detective Frank approached the carriage in front of Marm's haberdashery shop. Inside was Marm, her twenty-four-year-old son Julius, and her most trusted confidant, Herman Stroude.[40] Flanked by a cadre of Pinkerton detectives, Frank waved the arrest warrant in her face, "You are caught this time, and the best thing that you can do is to make a clean breast of it." Marm responded by punching Frank in the nose and knocking him from the carriage. The other detectives had to grab hold of her to keep her from striking him again.[41]

When the police raided her various warehouses, they discovered more of the stolen marked silk and enough loot to put her away for good. "It did not seem possible that so much wealth could be assembled in one spot," one journalist marveled. "There seemed to be enough clothes to supply an army. There were trunks filled with precious gems and silverware. Antique furniture was stacked against a wall."[42]

Because it was well-known that Marm had any number of judges and police in her pocket, Marm, Julius, and Stroude were transported to the Harlem Police Court, where Marm had no influence. Judge Murray was known to be one of the few honest judges left in the city. The three were arraigned on seven counts of second-degree grand larceny and one count of receiving stolen merchandise. Bail was initially set at thirty thousand dollars, ten thousand for each defendant. Her lawyers argued that it was too high. One of them, William Howe, made a long argument for the reduction of bail. Justice Murray declined to reduce the amount. Bail was ultimately set at five thousand each for Julius and Stroude and ten thousand for Marm.[43] Marm was not allowed to put up bail for her son; a man named John Briggs put up the bail for him.[44] A woman named Susan Chambetta put up the bail for Marm.

The hearing on whether the case should go to trial was held on July 25. Testimony took two full days, the court packed with a colorful array of spectators. Marm's defense was that she was a legitimate businesswoman caught up in a turf war between the district attorney and the police. Howe read her statement to the court: "I keep a dry goods store and have for twenty years past. I buy and sell dry goods as other dry goods people do. I have never knowingly bought stolen goods. Neither did my son Julius. I have never stolen anything in my life. I feel that these charges are brought against me for spite. I have never bribed the police, nor had their protection. I never needed their protection . . . I and my son are innocent of these charges, so help me God!"[45]

Olney was trying to show up the police department for his own political gain. A war in the press ensued with both the police and district attorney in a battle of words. Olney defended his use of the Pinkerton detectives by saying that superintendent Walling had told him that the police had not gotten enough evidence over the past twenty years to arrest Marm. Wisely the two sides decided to end their feud. They needed each other if they were going to put Marm away.[46]

Her arrest was covered by all the major New York papers, fascinated that a such a well-known criminal figure was finally coming to justice. Olney's use of Pinkerton detectives set off a feud between the district attorney's office and the city's police inspector.[47] Jumping to their client's defense, Howe and Hummel argued for her innocence and to discredit Pinkerton detective Gustav Frank, who, they suggested, might well have been a criminal himself.[48]

On August 15, Marm, Julius, and Stroude were indicted by the grand jury for receiving stolen goods. Despite all the legal wrangling by her lawyers, nothing could be done to stop the case from going to court in December. On December 2, the day the trial was scheduled to start, Olney came into court prepared with fourteen witnesses ready to testify against Marm, but Howe managed to get an adjournment to the next morning. He claimed that he still had some details in the case and needed time to clarify. Olney strenuously objected to the adjournment, but the judge granted Howe's motion until December 4.[49]

On the day before the trial, Marm was seen leaving her house dressed in all black. She waved to the Pinkerton detectives, who by now knew that their cover had been blown. Climbing into her carriage, she went to her lawyers' office, with the detectives following close behind. When she arrived, she exited the carriage and went inside. She had made several trips to visit her lawyers during the time she was out on bail, so nothing seemed unusual about it. She stayed for a time, came back out, waved again at the detectives, climbed back into the carriage, and was driven home, still with the detectives following.

But it was Marm's maid who climbed into the carriage and sped off with the detectives in hot pursuit. She was approximately the same height and weight as Marm and was dressed exactly like her, including the tiny hat with the plumes and veil covering her face. Once she realized that the coast was clear, Marm boarded a waiting carriage and made her getaway.[50]

As described by the *New York Times:*

District Attorney Olney sat, sternly imposing . . . Mr. Howe was plumply serene and ponderously gracious . . . The well-dressed gentlemen in the audience folded up their papers . . . directed their gaze to the various doors in the room in the fond anticipation of Mrs. Fredericka Mandelbaum stalking into the room in the manner which is peculiarly her own . . . "Frederika Mandelbaum!" . . . The words seemed to float over the heads of the merchants and lose themselves. There was no answer. Dead silence reigned . . . Then a little sound of something like disappointment was heard in the court, and Lawyer Howe rose to his feet. "The defendants are not here, your Honor."[51]

Marm had jumped bail and fled to Canada allegedly with an estimated one million dollars in cash and diamonds. Upon investigation, it was discovered that she had transferred her properties in the city to a man named George Rettinger.

Initially Marm, Stroude, and Julius registered at Rossin House, one of the leading hotels in Toronto, under the names of C. Newman and mother and J. Pink of Boston. After a few days, they left, taking furnished rooms on Simcoe Street, an aristocratic quarter of the city. With her height of nearly six feet, Marm was hard to miss, and a full description had been printed in the Toronto newspapers. She remained in the apartment, changing her style of dress to try and disguise herself. But Marm decided that it would be better to move on to Hamilton, which is where Chief Stewart and Detective Castel found them staying at a second-class hotel near the Grand Trunk railway station. The police surprised Marm and her companions by calling them by their proper names. Marm, Julius, and Stroude were arrested and charged with bringing stolen property into Canada. Assistant District Attorney Allen said, "It is said that the diamonds found on her were part of the goods stolen by Billy Porter and 'Sheeny Mike,' in a burglary committed by them in Troy."[52]

Hummel came up from New York to defend his client, her son, and Stroude. The case came before the magistrate on December 10. Hummel asked that the case be dismissed, because Marm could not be extradited back to New York to stand trial. The customs inspector examined the diamonds that Marm had brought into the country, along with Fred Marks of the firm E. Marks & Son, but Marks failed to identify any of the diamonds as the ones that were stolen from his firm.[53]

Now settled in Hamilton, Ontario, Marm was a law-abiding citizen who donated to charities, joined a synagogue, and worked long hours in her hat shop. She purchased a large home living an *apparently* crime-free life from that point on.[54] She was reported to have traveled to Albany to sell a house she owned that had once belonged to diamond thief John Curtin, but no effort was made to arrest her.[55] While the authorities knew where she was, there was little they could do to get her back to the United States, where she could be arrested.

In 1885, the *New York Times* ran the headline, "Mrs. Mandelbaum's Visit," with the news that Marm's youngest daughter, Annie, had unexpectedly died while visiting the city from Canada. The reporter recounted that "the thought of having her favorite child buried without taking a last look at her face touched a tender chord in the heart of the hardened criminal, and to gratify their wish she took the chance of falling into the hands of the police and passing her remaining days in prison." The story went on to detail the steps Marm took to return to the city undetected, but also noted the mother's misery at the death of her child, noting, "She showered kiss after kiss upon the cheeks of the dead girl, and her piteous cries brought tears to the eyes of the persons who witnessed the scene."

When a friend asked if Marm would ever return to New York, she replied, "I don't know. I've often thought of coming back, delivering myself up, and standing trial. I am sorry that I ever left New York. I should have faced the music."

She also confessed, "But I will say that if I spent $10,000, I could come back to New York and be a free woman."

But Marm was tired of paying off cops and politicians to stay in the game. "The more you produce, the more they want. If I hadn't been so free with my money, I wouldn't have gotten into this scrape."[56]

In 1888 Julius surrendered to the authorities in New York. He had been studying in Berlin for several years and wanted to be able to practice medicine in the United States.[57] Olney was no longer the district attorney, and the case against Julius was dropped. He returned to Canada while Marm was alive, but then he returned to New York and became the principal in a company that manufactured and distributed various medications.

In the last years of her life, Marm suffered from a series of illnesses. She died on February 26, 1894, at the age of sixty-five, from Bright's Disease.

Although her obituary notice in the *Hamilton Spectator* took note of her criminal past, it called her "a woman of kindly disposition, broad sympathies, and large intelligence."

Her body was returned to New York for burial in the Union Field Cemetery alongside her husband Wolfe in Ridgewood, Queens. Her obituary in the *New York Times* noted, "Her success was in great measure due to her friendship for and her loyalty to the thieves with whom she did business. She never betrayed her clients, and when they got into trouble, she procured bail for them and befriended them to the extent of her power." And the *Brooklyn Daily Eagle* called her "a most respectable and philanthropic receiver of stolen goods in New York."

Her funeral was a spectacular affair; a large crowd of mourners gathered, including old friends and neighbors, police officials, politicians, judges, and newspaper reporters, along with several well-known criminals, who came to pay their respects to their mentor and patron. Following the burial, many mourners were reported to have complained to the police that their pockets had been picked!

SOPHIE LYONS
(1848-1924)

QUEEN OF CRIME

Shoplifter, pickpocket, and blackmailer, Sophie Lyons lived a life full of adventure, excitement, danger, and tragedy. Dubbed the "Queen of Crime" Sophie Lyons lived an outrageous life on both sides of the law. Herbert Asbury wrote that she was "the most notorious confidence woman America has ever produced."[1] Born and raised to be a con artist, she made her fortune through a slew of crimes before turning to a life of reform. Crime was her sole source of income for decades and she was very, very good at it. Although she was born poor, she refused to end up that way. Throughout her life, Sophie was an irresistible subject for newspapers and magazines, which devoted streams of ink chronicling her notorious escapades. She was one of the few to die wealthy instead of broke or in prison, but it was not easy for her to put the past behind her. And her children suffered as the sons and daughters of a known criminal. In the end, as she said in her memoir, "Crime doesn't pay."

Like her mentor, Marm Mandelbaum, Sophie Lyons was an immigrant fleeing the poverty and anti-Semitism of nineteenth-century Germany. She arrived in New York with her two siblings just after Christmas in 1855, when she was eight years old. Her father, Jacob Van Elkan, had already emigrated with his youngest child, Mary. Sophie's mother either died during or soon after giving birth to Mary, as no record of her has ever been found. Jacob soon introduced the children to their new stepmother, Mary Levy. There is no record of an official marriage between Jacob and Mary, which was not

unusual for people who lived outside of the law or had just emigrated from a country and tried not to draw attention from the local authorities.

You might say that Sophie was born into a life of crime. A police chief once referred to her as "a thief from the cradle." Both her father and her stepmother had already had several brushes with the law. Sophie's father started out as a peddler but soon found out that working as a fence was much more lucrative. He opened a clothing store, where he sold the items that his family stole.[2] Her stepmother was already known to the police as a shoplifter.[3] Sophie later wrote about her childhood, "I didn't know that it was wrong to steal, no one ever taught me that."[4]

Sophie was taught to steal by her stepmother. Mary first trained little Sophie to steal from candy shops, drug stores, and grocery stores and to stuff the items into hidden pockets sewn in her dress. Once Sophie had mastered those skills, Mary gave her a knife to slit open pockets, purses, and shopping bags, feeling out the loose money, and getting it into her hands without attracting attention. Sophie was forced to practice over and over, "until my childish fingers had acquired considerable dexterity."[5]

She stole her first pocketbook at the tender age of six. "I was very happy because I was petted and rewarded," she later recalled. "My wretched stepmother patted my curly head, gave me a bag of candy, and said I was a good girl."[6] Her nickname was "Pretty Sophie," but her childhood was anything but idyllic. When the young thief-in-training failed to come home with the requisite number of pocketbooks, she was beaten, kicked, or burned with fire irons.

In Sophie's memoir she wrote that her stepmother dressed her in a different outfit every day before they went out to "work" "in case anybody saw me steal something the day before happened to be around. My stepmother was wise enough to disguise me in this way, and it enabled me to keep working for a long time in the same place."[7]

Occasionally, when Sophie was out picking pockets, she would see a doll in a store window. Unable to resist, she would use the money she had stolen to buy herself the toy. She would blissfully play with her new toy for hours, until her stepmother or brother would come out and catch her, giving her a few hard knocks for neglecting her duty. Later she would say, "A mother's kiss was never known to me, a loving mother's caress was never for me. Many a night the cold flags of New York were my pillow, as I gazed up at the canopy of glittering stars, I wondered if there were any cruel mothers up there."

With no alternative, Sophie was forced to steal every day. She claimed that there were days where she managed to pilfer one hundred dollars,[8] at a time when the average policeman earned six hundred dollars a year.[9] Sophie and her siblings were just a few of the ten thousand street children that lived in the city, a third of them (mostly girls) surviving as thieves. Sophie claimed that she never attended school, and she did not learn to read or write until she was twenty-five. If they were not in school, children had to earn a living, stripping tobacco and rolling cigars. Working in the needle trade was a way for unmarried girls to contribute to the family, for as little as six cents per shirt.

Jake and Mary saw no need for their kids to go to school. Public school taught values like honesty, hard work, and respect for authority, which conflicted with the underworld code. A mark was but a pocket to be picked. Don't worry about the "authorities"; they can be bought off. Officials are more corrupt than the worst criminal. Never rat out a fellow thief. Sophie would write in her autobiography, "I was told that money was the really valuable thing to possess, and that the successful men and women were those who could take pocketbooks."[10]

The most important skill Sophie learned was patience, taking her time to size up a crowd, observing the small details that revealed whether or not a person had something worth stealing. Older men were easier to rob than younger men, who could chase you down. Sometimes a man's wallet was visible, especially on payday. Sophie was taught to observe the quality of the clothing men and women wore and how they carried themselves. A silk handkerchief, a stick pin on a coat, a watch chain dangling from a vest pocket, none of it escaped Sophie's notice.[11]

Large crowds were crucial, easier to slip away unnoticed. A moving crowd was known as a "push," because people were pressed, pushed, or jostled. Crowds gave Sophie the opportunity to sidle up to her target. She could "fan" her mark, run a hand over the front and back of his or her body within seconds, and locate a watch or valuables, without the mark ever being aware.[12] A good thief had to know how to blend in. Sophie had an air of confidence and regality that she used to her advantage. She looked perfectly innocent as she and her stepmother went looking for marks, riding the ferry to Hoboken with the other day-trippers or spending the day in Central Park or at Barnum's American Museum, one of their favorite haunts.

Despite her skills Sophie was arrested many times as a child. For her, jail was the only opportunity to be a normal child. The policemen let her play, gave her candy, and, more important, didn't beat her. Sophie admitted, "More than once when I would dread going home, I would have myself arrested by stealing so a policeman could see me do it. But it didn't help me much, for my stepmother never failed to get me out of jail within a few days after my arrest."[13] Like a seasoned actress, Sophie could cry on cue so that her victims and wardens could not bring themselves to prosecute her. She was an unusually pretty child, with gray eyes, long, curly brown hair and a melancholy expression. No one could believe that such a pretty, well-mannered child could also be a skilled and cunning criminal.

In 1859 twelve-year-old Sophie was arrested picking pockets at Barnum's American Museum on Ana Street and Broadway. This time, instead of jail, Sophie was sent to the House of Refuge, the nation's first juvenile reformatory. It was created in 1825 as a reform school on Broadway and 23rd Street before moving to Randall's Island in 1854. The House of Refuge's officials believed that industry and instruction would instill discipline and self-control in the city's juvenile delinquents. A female wing had just been added in 1860 when Sophie arrived. Most of the five hundred boys and one hundred girls were in their mid- to late teens, making Sophie one of the youngest inmates. Many of the inmates were guilty of either vagrancy or petty larceny, although a few had moved onto arson and manslaughter. Sophie's crime of burglary fell in between.

Upon arrival at the reformatory, children were stripped, washed, and given a uniform, and then housed in a windowless five-by-eight cell. For eight hours a day, boys made shoes, cane chairs, or brass nails, and girls cleaned, sewed, and cooked to prepare them for life in domestic service. It was honest but low-paying work. "They may and can become honest, upright, conscientious and hard-working laborers and merchants . . . but very few will ever attain exalted station."

Years later Sophie looked back on her time at the House of Refuge and Superintendent Jones with fondness. In her memoirs she wrote that Jones would often invite her to his office to play with his two young daughters. He told his daughters that it was not Sophie's fault that "she did wrong." Her mother made her steal.[14] Playtime at the House of Refuge was minimal, and corporal punishment was meted out to anyone who broke the rules. The food was better than Sophie was used to, in both quality and quantity. The biggest lesson she came away with, however, was that crime could give her a better lifestyle than honest work ever could.

Children were classified from one to four. Class Four children were deemed "vicious, bad or wicked," and given very few privileges. Sophie was a Class Three, meaning she was considered redeemable.[15] Her record mentions: "Rumors that the mother lived off the depredations of her children on the public. This we know nothing of, but there seems something mysterious in the case; the child is very quick, nervous and precocious and needs training in a steady way."[16]

Sophie spent a year and a half at the House of Refuge before she was finally released in 1861. She was now on her own; both her father and stepmother were dealing with legal troubles of their own. Now fourteen, she had matured into a young woman, confident in her skills as a pickpocket. She also grew quite bold, as her young, pretty face and her ability to feign innocence meant that when she was caught stealing, she was usually set free. Six months after her release from the House of Refuge, Sophie's luck ran out when she was hauled before the Court of General Sessions in New York City on June 28, 1861. Her conviction for picking pockets alongside a boy named Louis Minot reveals she had clearly made the choice to continue a life of crime.[17] She received a two-month sentence at the penitentiary on Blackwell's Island, located in the East River. Sophie also added married woman to her resume. At the age of sixteen, Sophie married Maury Harris, a professional pickpocket, but on their honeymoon, he was caught by the police stealing a wallet. He was arrested and sentenced to two years in New York State Prison.

In her late teens Sophie came under the protective wing of Frederica "Marm" Mandelbaum, becoming part of a sisterhood of criminals. Mandelbaum acted as a patron and fence to many in the underworld. Her influence was pivotal to Sophie's success. Sophie learned how to manipulate the cops and the court systems. She also upped her shoplifting game including wearing skirts with hidden pockets and carrying a large umbrella to drop items into. It was Marm who taught her to exploit her beauty and sex appeal to con fervent and gullible men out of their money. "You are beautiful my child," she said to her. "You ought to do well. Men will like you and that is the best of all, for you can do with them as you please, and with your face it will not be necessary for you to nip their clocks, they will give you anything you want."[18]

Many of Marm's male associates noticed that seventeen-year-old Sophie had blossomed into a stunning young woman. She was petite, she was only five feet two inches, with a slim figure, gray eyes, a melancholy expression, and masses of dark brown hair.[19] Not only was she intelligent, but she had a fiery personality to match. One of the men smitten with her was Edward "Ned" Lyons. Born in Ireland, Ned and his family immigrated to America in 1849 at the height of the Great Famine. By the time he fell for Sophie, he had already spent time in the Boston House of Correction. Although he claimed to be a jeweler, he more than likely fenced jewelry that he'd stolen.

Ned also took advantage of the three-hundred-dollar enlistment bonus for joining the Union Army during the Civil War. He would then desert and reenlist under a new name to collect another bonus. But his true passion was for robbing banks. Bank robbery at the time took real skill and ingenuity, and bank robbers were part of an elite criminal fraternity. Ned's job was as the "cracksman," handling the explosives used to blow open the safe and bank vault doors. Unlike Sophie, he could read and write.

Sophie never mentions in her memoir how the two met. They were married in 1865, ten days before her eighteenth birthday. Later Sophie admitted that she wasn't even sure if she'd divorced her first husband Maury before marrying Ned. It was probably a shotgun wedding as their first child, George Edward Lyons, was born on July 18, 1866. After their marriage, Ned discouraged Sophie from "working." Despite his profession, he was a traditional kind of guy, and he wanted his wife to stay home to tend to their growing family. But Sophie missed the thrill of stealing.

In her memoir Sophie claims that the family needed the income from her stealing. The couple spent money like it was water. By the end of the decade, they had three little ones to support. Ned had a big score in 1869, when he and his crew robbed the Ocean Bank in lower Manhattan, making off with five hundred thousand dollars in cash and securities, the equivalent of about nine million dollars today.[20] Thanks to his take, they could put a life of crime behind them for at least a while. Unfortunately, he had itchy fingers. Robbing banks was in his blood. He liked the excitement of planning a robbery, and the danger of executing the plan. This time the job would be in Philadelphia. Unfortunately, Ned and his crew were caught in the middle of the job. While the other two men escaped, Ned was arrested. He jumped bail and left the city, but ended up arrested again a month later, robbing another bank. This time Ned ended up sentenced to five years in Auburn Prison.

Sophie began lobbying to get Ned moved to Sing Sing in Ossining, New York, because criminals knew that it was an easier prison from which to escape. Desperate to get her husband moved, Sophie traded sexual favors with the lawyer she hired.[21] Ned was moved to Sing Sing, but now the lawyer also demanded a fifteen-hundred-dollar payment. Back home Sophie returned to shoplifting. She managed to steal for months with no problems, but in September 1871, she was arrested for stealing a forty-dollar cloak from the A. T. Stewart department store.[22] Two weeks later she was convicted and sentenced to five years in the women's prison at Sing Sing. Before heading to prison, she placed her children in an orphanage on Randall's Island.[23]

Ned managed to break out of Sing Sing in December 1872. But he hadn't forgotten about Sophie. Two weeks later Ned was back to rescue his wife. Sophie had gotten herself moved to kitchen detail in the prison's hospital. Just before Christmas Ned and an accomplice drove a sleigh through a blizzard to the prison's entrance. Ringing the bell, a disguised Ned announced that he was delivering an enormous fruit basket to a sick prisoner. Sophie accepted the basket and then handed it to a fellow prisoner to take it upstairs. "I was all ready, of course, when my husband drove up in a sleigh, wonderfully disguised, wearing a handsome fur coat, and carrying a woman's fur coat on his arm."[24] Sophie then ran through the open gate and jumped into the sleigh, which then disappeared into the blinding snow. It was a daring and sensational escape and the only case of a husband-and-wife breakout.[25]

But there was trouble in the marriage. Ned was livid that Sophie had left the children at an orphanage instead of leaving them with a friend. Also, their youngest and his favorite, Eugenia, died while they were in prison.[26] But there was no time to dwell on their sorrow; Ned and Sophie were wanted fugitives. The Lyons family fled to Canada because they had no extradition treaty with the United States. It seemed like the family could finally settle down, but they had little time to enjoy their freedom. Soon after their arrival in Montreal, Ned slipped back into the United States to help an old associate, Langdon Moore, bribe a warden to get out of prison. When he returned, Sophie accused him of having an affair with Langdon's wife, Becky.

Ned was furious when Sophie confessed that she had slept with the lawyer hired to get him transferred to Sing Sing. She, in turn, blamed him for getting arrested and sent to prison in the first place. Their marriage was beginning to fall apart under the strain of their legal and personal problems. When Ned went back to Albany to track down the lawyer, threatening him with violence if he did not return the fifteen-hundred-dollar payment, Sophie left him and went to New Orleans.[27] Their separation was short-lived, however. They eventually reunited and added three more children to their family: Vincent, Charlotte, and Mabel.

The couple eventually slipped back into the United States, settling in Jersey City,[28] across the Hudson from Manhattan. Like New York, the police force was reputed to be corrupt. As long as Sophie and Ned paid them off, they were safe, but the couple could not seem to stay out of trouble. In 1876 they were caught picking pockets at a fair on Long Island. Using aliases, Sophie and Ned tried to bribe the cops, but they were out of luck. These cops were honest![29] Both Sophie and Ned were sent back to prison. While Ned languished in Auburn Prison, Sophie found herself a lawyer who managed to convince a judge that her sentence had passed, so she could not legally be kept in prison.[30]

While Ned was doing another stretch in Auburn Prison, Sophie took up with Hamilton "Ham" Brock, the owner of the Star and Garter saloon on Sixth Avenue.[31] In October 1880, a few months after Ned was released from prison, he headed over to Brock's saloon, determined to kill his wife's inamorata. Instead, Brock shot Ned. One bullet pierced his right lung, another went through his cheek, shattering his jaw.[32] Sophie broke up with Brock a year later when she found out that he had informed the police about a bank robbery in Connecticut.[33]

Looking for a fresh start, Sophie took all her money out of the bank and headed for Detroit, Michigan. During the nineteenth century, the midwestern city drew more than its fair share of shoplifters, con artists, forgers, burglars, pickpockets, hotel thieves, pimps, prostitutes, and murderers. Chased out of one town after another, career criminals sooner or later ended up in Detroit, usually more than once. A big draw of the city for Sophie was its close proximity to Canada, where her children were attending boarding school. The population of the city had also exploded in recent years, now numbering more than 116,000 residents. While not the size of New York City, the city's shopping districts and wealthy citizens were catnip to a career criminal like Sophie. Detroit would now be Sophie's home base.

Sophie needed to expand her criminal repertoire if she was going to stay in the game. Picking pockets and shoplifting would no longer pay the bills, not with five kids in fancy boarding schools. Nor would it pay for expensive lawyers. Sophie had learned early in her career of crime that just as she could ply other tools of larceny, like a shoplifter's bag sewn into her skirt, her beauty was a tool that could be used to her advantage.

One of Sophie's favorite scams was the "badger" game. It was highly lucrative, and it gave Sophie a chance to show off her acting skills. She would entice wealthy lawyers and bankers to her hotel room with the promise of sex. She would have the men disrobe and then quickly lock their clothes in a trunk or throw them out the window. The humiliated patsy would pay her a thousand-dollar ransom for the return of his clothes to avoid the histrionic scene that she threatened to unleash. Sophie chose her victims carefully to ensure that they would give into her demands to protect their good name.

On one occasion, using the alias Louise Sylvan, Sophie charmed a wealthy banker out of his clothes inside a Boston hotel room and then locked them in a trunk, as she demanded a check for ten thousand dollars. Sophie was caught attempting to cash the check, but the embarrassed victim refused to press charges, allowing her to go free.[34] "His money was saved," Thomas Byrnes wrote, "but his character was ruined, and the result was the breaking up of a happy home."

Sophie refused to be controlled by a society that said that women must be pure and virtuous. When she was on trial for blackmailing that same Boston lawyer in 1880, she unashamedly acted the role of the repentant "soiled dove" to play upon the sympathy of the jury and the public. In a newspaper interview Sophie lied and said that she had been having a long affair with the lawyer and that he frequently rewarded her with money, "If a woman is weak enough to submit to a man, I think she has a perfect right to accept money from him if he is willing to give it to her." Seven out of the twelve male jurors voted to acquit her. When the jurors could not agree on a verdict, Sophie was acquitted. But her "badger" game came with a high price. Sophie never went back to Boston after her close call.

Sophie tried her "badger" game a little too close to home when she tried to blackmail a prominent Grand Rapids citizen who had sampled her charms. She would sit on a horse block daily in front of his home hoping to embarrass him into writing a check to get her out of his life. Unfortunately for Sophie her mark was not easily intimidated. Instead, he had his servants turn the garden hose on Sophie.[35]

On February 6, 1883, Sophie was sentenced to four years and eleven months in the Detroit House of Correction for larceny.[36] Convinced she would be acquitted, Sophie brought her youngest son, Vincent, with her to court. After the verdict was announced, Sophie cried out in a dramatic fashion, "I am not guilty! There is not justice for me in Ann Arbor! My child, you have no mother."[37] She then broke down sobbing. The prison, opened in 1861, sprawled over three acres at Russell and Alfred Streets, near the Eastern Market; it was owned and operated by the city of Detroit, and although it was a municipal jail, it housed many prisoners from other jurisdictions, including federal prisoners.

Luckily for Sophie, her lawyer appealed her conviction, and she was released in July 1883. By the time she was released, Sophie was pushing forty, having spent almost half of her life behind bars. She was exhausted, her health poor, and her money almost gone from lawyers' fees. A life of crime was the only thing she had ever known; not only her, but her step-mother, father, and both of her husbands had been criminals. But now it was getting a lot harder. Sophie's notoriety was kicked up a notch when she was one of eighteen women profiled in New York Police Department inspector Thomas Byrnes's book, *Professional Criminals of America,* published in 1886. Thanks to this publication, 204 of the top criminals in the country could no longer hide behind disguises and aliases.

Byrne included photographs, brief biographies, and known aliases, rendering them recognizable not just to law enforcement across the country, but also to the average citizen. Three of Sophie's four husbands were included in the book. Most police stations now had a camera to take mug shots, and then there was the new technology of fingerprinting to contend with. And then there were the Pinkertons, private detectives hired by banks and department stores to keep thieves like Sophie Lyons out.

If there can be said to be one regret in Sophie's life, it would be her children. Sophie was determined to do better by her children, to keep them away from a life of crime. That meant enrolling them in convent and boarding schools outside of the country. But with Ned and Sophie's growing notoriety, it became harder and harder to keep the truth from their children. They were now known as the offspring of a notorious criminal. Before Sophie's arrest in Detroit, her four youngest children were under the assumption that she was an actress, constantly on tour. In 1882 her youngest daughter, Mabel, died from scarlet fever.

Florence and Charlotte (Lottie) remained at St. Mary's Academy until Sophie was incarcerated and stopped paying tuition. Sophie's case had received a great deal of publicity, and parents complained about their children fraternizing with the offspring of a criminal. The two girls were sent to a Roman Catholic orphan asylum. Lottie, the youngest, was soon adopted by the Doyle family. Sophie, incensed, went to the Doyle home and brought Lottie home, despite the girl's protests. Poor Florence remained at the orphanage until she was fifteen and old enough to leave on her own.[38] She eventually ended up working as a domestic at a Catholic charity home for young girls.

Despite Sophie's best efforts, her oldest son, George, followed Sophie and Ned into a life of crime. In 1880 Sophie dragged her fourteen-year-old son into Essex Market Court. She appealed to the judge to commit her son to the Catholic Protectory in Westchester, because he was disobedient, refused to attend school, stayed out all night, and kept bad company. George, in his defense, called his mother a thief, said she was living with two husbands and that she just wanted to get rid of him.[39] In front of the courtroom, Sophie slapped him. The judge committed him to the House of Refuge instead, even though Sophie begged him to send her son to a place where he would be educated and raised right. She was prepared to pay five years' tuition and board in advance. Later, George tried to commit suicide in his cell by tying a handkerchief to his neck and around the cell bar.[40]

A year later George was caught robbing houses with two other teenage boys.[41] He had inherited his father's passion for burglary but not his skills. Although he was only fifteen, he claimed to be seventeen. He was sent to a reformatory in Elmira, where he would be held until the warden decided he was reformed and could be released. After almost five years there, he was sent to Auburn Prison, where he died of typhoid fever. Neither Sophie nor Ned could afford to pay for a cemetery plot or burial for their son. Another inmate, Jim Brady, generously offered to pay so that George would not end up in a prison grave. Sophie was grateful for his kindness, and so George was buried in Saint Joseph's Cemetery, seven miles south of the prison.[42]

Clearly Sophie had a predilection for bank robbers, hooking up with Jim Brady after his release from prison. Things were getting too hot in the United States and Canada, so she and Brady traveled across Europe pulling various con jobs, with Sophie posing as a wealthy society woman named Madame de Varney.[43] Dressed in silks and lace, she would assume an aristocratic air to mingle with wealthy patrons in hotels and at the theater and the opera. Brady was also the father of her youngest child, Sophia, who was born in London in January 1891. Baby Sophia was a little late-in-life surprise, given that Sophie was forty-three and Brady also in his forties. Sophie soon dropped Sophia off with a nurse in France with instructions that she be placed in a French Catholic school when she was old enough.

Sophie was now famous on both sides of the Atlantic. She was credited with a number of "firsts." She was first to employ the "kleptomaniac defense," getting charges dismissed by tearfully explaining to a New York judge that her compulsive stealing was something that she had no control over because of her upbringing. It was also said that she invented the "sliding drawer panel" trick, where a victim that she lured to her room would place jewelry into a dresser drawer for safekeeping only to discover later that Sophie had previously cut a hole in the wall of the adjoining room, allowing an accomplice to slide open the panel, reach into the drawer, and remove the goods, with her victim being none the wiser. She also used to hollow out her heels and use a false trunk to smuggle jewelry from Amsterdam to New York.[44]

At the dawn of the twentieth century, Sophie Lyons had reached her mid-fifties. After years of skirting the law, Sophie was tired of the game. Her taste for the criminal life had turned sour. Detroit was growing rapidly. Sophie realized that the best way to provide for a comfortable old age was to go into real estate. But she needed capital, so she headed back to Europe with Billie Burke. Whatever crimes they committed are shrouded in mystery but probably included stealing money and jewelry from the wealthy. After a year and a half, Sophie returned with "seven trunks full of grand Parisian gowns and a jewel box choked with diamond rings, brooches and other gems of value."[45] She bought several rental properties on the city's west side, including a three-story brick mansion.[46] Eventually she owned eighty thousand dollars' worth of property in her Detroit neighborhood.

Sophie stirred up controversy in 1909 when she rented one of her houses to Mary E. McCoy, an African American philanthropist and activist, who planned to open a maternity hospital and orphan asylum for African American women and children. The neighbors objected and took Sophie to court. It was bad enough having a reformed criminal in the neighborhood, but now she was trying to drive down their property values! Sophie successfully fought the injunction, because the judge ruled that he could not force

Sophie to turn out her tenants.[47] Sophie always enjoyed thumbing her nose at her middle-class neighbors.

Sophie eventually settled down with Billy Burke, a jewel thief who was twelve years younger than her. After finally divorcing Ned Lyons, they were married, but in 1908 Sophie said that "rings and ministers don't make a marriage."[48] When Burke was arrested in Sweden in 1911, in the company of another woman, Sophie told the *Detroit Free Press* that she didn't care if Burke "lavishes a little attention on other ladies occasionally,"[49] because there was only one Sophie Lyons. When Burke was released, Sophie offered him seven hundred dollars a month to stay out of trouble.

Meanwhile Sophie was busy writing her memoirs. The book was published in 1913 with the title *Why Crime Does Not Pay*, a cautionary tale of the life of "the cleverest crook in the world." In the book Sophie claimed to have completely put her criminal past behind her. "There is something I want more than property," she said. "That is the respect of good people. Maybe I can get some of it by showing that I am not all bad and am sincere."[50] The memoir was a somewhat fanciful tale of Sophie's life and crimes, part fact, part fiction with some of the names changed to protect the guilty. To appease her associates who were still in the business of crime, she kept the details vague. She was also careful to keep the criminal activities of her current husband, Billie Burke, out of it, or her other husbands, focusing mainly on her life with Ned Lyons. For a brief moment, Sophie was known more for her literary efforts than her criminal ones.

Sophie told reporters that she was now dedicated to helping other criminals turn straight, especially first offenders. "You know how hard it is for a man or woman to secure permanent work after leaving prison?" she asked, citing her own experiences of being shunned for having a criminal record. "I am going to help some of these. They will find a friend in Sophie Lyons." And she was true to her word.

Sophie began to visit the Detroit House of Correction to share stories of her criminal past and encourage the inmates to stay on the straight and narrow path after they were released. "There was never a friendless girl who came to my grandmother and did not receive a welcome, there was never a tenant who was out of work who was asked for his rent," Sophie's granddaughter Esther Bower said. Sophie spent tons of money on shoes, clothing, and groceries for desperate families, finding them a place to live as well. Sophie even provided holiday meals for prisoners in jail and helped struggling ex-convicts get back on their feet.

Sophie publicly offered to provide rent-free homes for any criminals with families who were brought to Detroit by the Pathfinders' Club reform group. On February 2, 1916, she announced at the Pathfinders' annual dinner that she would be donating land worth $35,000 to establish a building for juvenile delinquents. She specified that the gift was offered on the following condition: "The home is to be devoted to the work of convincing children who have begun to be criminals that they have chosen the wrong path, and also to training them so that they will have the strength to go alright. A secondary purpose is to provide a place in which adults who have fallen into crime may get a new start in life."[51] There were some cynics who questioned whether Sophie was sincere. After all, they pointed out, she had found the righteous path only after a lucrative career as a criminal. While she may have made her money in real estate, the seed money came from dubious means.

She also could have written that crime does not leave much time for motherhood. Sophie wrote that she had tried to do better by her children than her parents did for her. "Whatever I have done in my life it has been only that my children might have the advantages that I never possessed, an education and proper training for the battle of life." But Sophie's relationship with her remaining children continued to be strained. Charlotte/Lottie grew up to be an opera singer in Paris, but she ended up dying in poverty. Her favorite child, Vincent, changed his name to Carleton Mason and joined the navy. After he left the navy, ironically, he ended up working for the Internal Revenue Service in Seattle. Sophie barely knew her youngest daughter, Madeline, who spent most of her life in France. After World War I she ended up in a mental hospital.

Only Florence, the child who most resembled Sophie, ended up settling in Detroit. Their relationship was frequently on-again, off-again. Sophie disapproved of Florence working as a nanny or a maid, believing that the work was beneath someone of her intelligence, yet she was not willing to help her daughter out financially. Florence also had to use an alias so that potential employers would not realize that she was related to Sophie. Those who did, fired her on the spot.

Florence fell on hard times after she left her abusive alcoholic husband, reduced to playing a hand organ on the street with her five-year-old daughter.[52] Sophie told the press that she refused to give her any money, because Florence had married without her knowledge or consent. But the truth is that Sophie held a grudge against her daughter for telling her young sisters that Sophie was a criminal.[53] The two women finally reconciled before Sophie's death, and Sophie left Florence fifty thousand dollars in her will.

A few years before her death, Sophie teamed up with a male ex-convict and spoke before the Michigan House Judiciary Committee to defeat a bill to impose the death penalty in the state. She argued that death was no deterrent for impulsive criminals. Ex-prisoners committed murder because of the brutality exacted upon them inside prisons. Despite her best efforts, the bill passed.

Because Sophie had lived the life, she could tell the difference between ex-convicts who were serious about turning their life around and career criminals. Big hearted and a little naive, despite her former profession, Sophie made little effort to hide her wealth, freely wearing her jewelry, even while navigating shady neighborhoods. Having been married to several bank robbers, Sophie kept her money hidden inside the walls and floor of her house. Her husband Billie Burke's presence was a bit of a deterrent, but he passed away in 1919. Now seventy-one years old, Sophie finally hired a live-in housekeeper.

Now the criminal became the victim. Sophie was robbed at least twice. The first time, she was mugged as she shopped at the neighborhood grocery store.[54] The second time, she returned from an outing to find that thieves had broken into her home while she was away and stolen $20,000, $13,000 in diamonds, and $6-7,000 in bonds.[55] She commented to reporters, "I have no idea who did the 'job,' and I am unhappy to think that men would do such a thing to an old woman who devotes a large income to prison relief work."

On May 24, 1924, Sophie Lyons passed away at four thirty in the afternoon at Grace Annex Hospital in Detroit. She was seventy-five years old. Following the viewing, Sophie's casket was taken by hearse to Woodmere Cemetery, where a service was held in the cemetery's chapel. Florence and her daughter Esther were the only family members present for the service. They were joined by a small group of Sophie's closest friends, including Ira Jayne, a justice of the Wayne County Circuit Court known for his work on behalf of troubled children. Inmates at the Detroit House of Correction participated in a memorial service in Sophie's honor led by her old friend, Pathfinders' Club founder J. W. Wright. After the service was over, Sophie's body was cremated. Her ashes were buried in the grave of her son, Carleton Mason.

When her will was read, she left bequests to the total value of her estate, which fell far short of the rumored half million dollars, but it was still an impressive amount: $241,766 (more than $3.5 million in 2018 dollars). The inmates at Sing Sing, the Detroit House of Correction, and several other prisons where Sophie had been an inmate were to receive yearly gifts of magazines and holiday treats. Sophie also left $1,000 for a new Steinway piano for the House of Correction.

Sophie wanted two of her properties to be used as a home for children whose parents were incarcerated. The balance of the estate was to be used to create the Sophia Lyons Memorial Trust Fund, with income from the fund going to pay the children's home's expenses. Through her charity, Sophie hoped her name would live on in Detroit. Unfortunately, Sophie's wish was not fulfilled; the children's home was never built.

ROXALANA DRUSE
(1847-1887)

THE LAST WOMAN TO BE HANGED IN NEW YORK

December 18th would be the last day that anyone in Herkimer County saw William Druse alive. At first no one thought anything of it; Druse was known to be eccentric. He would disappear and then return just as mysteriously. But some of the neighbors became suspicious that Druse had met with foul play. They noticed that the little house was boarded up, the windows covered with newspaper, a dense black smoke poured from the chimneys, and a foul stench filled the air, as if meat were burning. That was odd. When Alonzo Filikins went to the Druse house to have a knife that William borrowed returned, he knocked on the door, but there was no answer, although he could hear people talking inside.

When she was asked, Roxalana Druse at first said that her husband had gone to see his sister Sabrina in Van Hornsville, five miles away. When Jeremiah Eckler stopped by on the pretense of buying a load of hay, Roxalana told him that William had gone to New York City with a patent right to sell. He would probably be gone two to three weeks. In fact, she was just as anxious to know what might have happened to him. She even sent telegrams to friends and relatives asking after William, but no one in the town was convinced.[1]

Already unpopular with some of the town's residents, Roxalana soon found herself under suspicion. People in Warren began to compare stories. By this time almost a month had passed since Druse had been seen. Then Fred Vrooman found an ax in a mill pond, near the bridge, wrapped in a copy of the *New York Tribune*. District Attorney A. B. Steele was sent

for, and after he was acquainted with the facts, he immediately decided to interview Roxalana's nephew, fourteen-year-old Frank Gates, who lived with the family.[2] After severe questioning, Frank cracked, admitting that William Druse had been murdered. He also told them where, why, and how it had happened and where vital evidence could be found.[3]

According to Frank, on the morning of December 18, there had been an argument between Roxalana and William Druse over an unpaid grocery bill. Roxalana ordered him and her son George to leave the house without going too far away. While they were outside, Frank heard a shot and rushed back in to find out what had happened. When he walked into the kitchen, he found Druse slumped on the floor. Roxalana and William's daughter Mary had a rope pulled tight around his neck. Roxalana then handed him the recently fired .22-caliber revolver, threatening to kill him if he didn't fire the remaining bullets into Druse. Frank tearfully admitted that he had done what she had asked, firing two or three shots into his uncle. Roxalana then went further. If he did not "finish him up," she would kill him and George.

She would also kill them if they didn't help her cover up the murder and if they told anyone what had happened that morning.

Thinking quickly, Roxalana grabbed an ax that Druse had owned. In front of her daughter, son, and nephew, she hacked Druse's body to pieces with repeated blows, not stopping until his neck was entirely severed. When Druse first met Roxalana Telft in 1863, he was struck by her attractive figure and completely lost his head over her. Twenty-one years later he was struck again, this time by the ax she brandished as she beheaded him. But now Roxalana had a problem. What to do with the body? According to Frank Gate's confession, her solution was to burn it, which explained the smoke and stench reported by the neighbors. While Frank and George played checkers in the next room, Roxalana and Mary set about dismembering the late William Druse.

The house had two stoves, both of which were put into use to get rid of the body. Ashes and bones were found in both stoves. Unfortunately, Roxalana had been less than thorough when disposing of the evidence. She and Frank threw the ash, bone pieces, and murder weapons into a nearby swamp and well in Richfield Springs. The ax and revolver were both wrapped in paper and later found in a nearby pond. The ax was later identified as belonging to Druse. There were rumors that Roxalana had fed her husband's organs to the family hogs, but that was later disproved. Roxalana and her daughter Mary were arrested, along with Frank Gates.

Steele at once contacted Dr. L. O. Nellie, one of the three coroners in Herkimer County. A coroner's inquest was quickly convened on Saturday, January 17, held in Jeremiah Eckler's cheese house, to assess the evidence, but there were so many spectators that the inquest was moved to the town hall at Little Lakes. Human remains, the ax, and the revolver were all entered as evidence, along with the contents of a small box, a mass of dirt, wood ashes, and small pieces of bone, all frozen together in a solid mass. There were about eighteen to twenty small pieces of bone, from one inch to two inches long. Two patellae, or kneecaps, were found, as was the upper end of a left tibia, or lower leg bone, showing two articular surfaces, thereby proving conclusively that the bones were human.

The coroner's jury was taken to the Druse farm to view the scene of the murder. The walls of the kitchen were newly covered in paper and the doors and casings were newly painted green. The painting was done on New Year's Day, and the paint and brush still sat on the floor of the downstairs bedroom. In the kitchen where the murder was committed was a small box stove; the cook stove had been moved to the buttery. Near the door and window were spatters of blood. The jury tore paper off the walls looking for bullet holes. They found only one, about five feet from the floor, in the wall opposite the outside door, which opened into the kitchen.[4]

When Frank Gates was called to testify, he told the coroner's jury that Roxalana and Mary had tried to hire him to kill Druse the previous summer, but he told them he wouldn't do it. This would mean that Roxalana had been planning to get rid of her husband for a while. George Druse corroborated Frank Gates's testimony. "Ma told us to get out around the corner of the house; we went out there and then we heard a revolver go off. Then Ma called Frank. She told him to shoot; he shot. Later Ma went out and got the axe and the head was cut off; she cut off the head from father." He also testified that he and Frank went out to the woodshed to get more shingles, and then to the woods to get the ax that his father had left near the woodpile. He said he wasn't sure what happened after. When they returned to the house, he and Frank were told to go upstairs.

When Roxalana was called to the stand, she declared that her brother-in-law, Charles Gates, had assisted in the murder. She refused to answer any other questions on the grounds that it might incriminate her. Gates was arrested but he had an alibi. He was working in Major Rathburn's woods all day. James Miller corroborated his statement.[5] Gates did testify that he bought Mary Druse a pistol at her request. It cost three dollars at Crim's store. "Mary gave me the money. She said they wanted it as they were alone so much. It was a pearl-handled seven shooter."[6]

On January 28, the coroner's jury found that William Druse was shot and killed by Roxalana. Her children Mary and George and her nephew Frank were charged with giving comfort, aid, and abet to Roxalana in committing felony and murder.[7]

The *New York Times* reported that District Attorney Steele was not satisfied with the verdict of the inquest. He still believed Roxalana must have had male accomplices to help her dispose of the body. A human head was found in the maple-sugar house on the farm of Palmer Wood, near the scene of the crime. A man named Casler, working on the farm, went into the woods to prepare for maple-sugar making, and while clearing out the furnace of the evaporator, he allegedly found a human with the hair cut off, which might have been William Druse's head.[8]

The rumor turned out to be false. Will Elwood came to the house the night of the murder to get three bags of buckwheat. He and Charlie Gates took a load of hides to Little Falls a few days later. Although it couldn't be proved, reporters speculated that this was actually how William Druse's head was moved.[9]

At the conclusion of the inquest, Sheriff Valentine Brown placed the four prisoners in a close-covered sleigh to take them to the Herkimer County Jail. During the almost four-hour trip, Roxalana remarked that "whether it turned out to be state prison for life, or hanging, she would never have to live with William Druse again." Boys being boys, Frank and George amused themselves by making funny comments about anything they saw that piqued their interest on the ride. When they arrived at the jail, they were met by a curious crowd, but they were hurried through to the general waiting room.

After a few moments' rest, they were informed that their quarters were ready, and as Roxalana rose to accompany the jailer, she remarked in an off-hand manner, "Well, I hope I may be able to procure tonight what I had not had before in two years, a good night's sleep." The two women were placed in a warm and comfortable room in the upper portion of the building, and the two boys on the upper tier, in the general quarters assigned to prisoners.

On January 30, 1885, Roxalana and Mary were formally arraigned. Brought before Justice T. C. Murray, the two women, accompanied by their attorney H. D. Luce, entered a plea of "not guilty." Given the severity of the crime, the courts established bail at two thousand dollars for each woman. They were taken back to jail to await the action of the grand jury. The courtroom was crowded, but Roxalana and Mary betrayed not a hint of emotion. Frank and George were arraigned next and were also committed to jail until the grand jury convened. Charles Pett, a resident of the town of Warren, was appointed Mary and George's guardian and administrator of the estate.[10]

When journalist W. H. Tippets came to the jail to interview Roxalana and her daughter, he found that she appeared cool and unconcerned, that it was evident there was no love lost between her and her husband. She insisted that her brother-in-law Charles Gates had been there on the day of the murder, that he had assisted in getting rid of the body. As far as Roxalana was concerned, he should also be held. Tippets came away from the interview unsettled. It was clear to him that Roxalana thought she had done the world a service by killing her husband, that people would sympathize with her as a victim of circumstance and not see her as a cold-blooded murderer. Mary was silent during the interview; she kept her eyes focused on the floor, only raising them at intervals to watch her mother.

Tippets questioned Frank Gates about his father. Frank adamantly told Tippets that his father had not been there during the murder. Charles Gates did come by the house that day, but he knew nothing about the murder. Frank also told the journalist that his aunt had "scared the life out of him," that he was afraid that she would kill him if he did not do as she ordered; that during the time his aunt was cutting up the body, she repeatedly threatened to kill him if he breathed a word in relation to the murder. He said that the terrible scene made him so deathly ill that he ran outside where he fainted dead away from the shock.[11]

In April 1885, a grand jury formally indicted Roxalana Druse and Mary Druse for first-degree murder. Both Roxalana and Mary pleaded "not guilty." Luce asked that the trial be scheduled for September to give the defense adequate time to prepare.[12] As separate indictments had been handed down, Roxalana would be tried first, and then Mary. Neither George nor Frank was charged with aiding or abetting, and eventually the charges against both boys were dropped.

To pay for Roxalana's defense, an estate sale was held. Sheriff Brown had completed a detailed inventory of items in preparation; the list of farm equipment took two pages. Roxalana didn't object to the sale of the farm, but she made it clear that there were certain items that belonged to her that she didn't want to sell. These included a table, stand, a half-dozen chairs, a bureau, a spinning wheel, and a sewing machine, along with the family Bible. The sale took place on June 6th at Thorp's Hotel.[13] All told, the sale brought in almost six thousand dollars, before the debts were paid. The only item that didn't sell was a small box organ that belonged to Mary; it was brought to her at the jail.

On September 21, Roxalana's trial began at the Herkimer County Courthouse with Judge Williams presiding. Joining her defense team was Amos H. Prescott, a former New York assemblyman and brigadier general in the National Guard. The trial lasted only two weeks, and the courtroom was packed with spectators every day. People had come from miles around to observe the proceedings. It was the hottest ticket in Herkimer County. The *Utica Daily Observer* noted that there appeared to be more women than men among the spectators: "What any lady can find interesting in the recital of these details of one of the most horrible crimes ever committed is difficult to imagine."

The trial started off slowly, with an uninspiring opening statement by William C. Prescott; it was so boring that none of the reporters in the courtroom bothered to take it down. It wasn't until District Attorney Steele called Frank Gates to the stand that a buzz of excitement ran through the courtroom. Everyone was eager to get a first glimpse of the witness. Fourteen-year-old Frank was the prosecution's star witness. Despite defense attorney Luce's frequent objections, Frank was able to give his testimony, not leaving out any of the gory details, despite the presence of ladies in the courtroom. He identified the ax and the knife that was used in the murder. Throughout Frank's testimony, Roxalana displayed little emotion, apart from an icy glare at her nephew. Seated next to her mother in the prisoner's box, Mary was clearly uncomfortable; she continued to stare at the floor.

During his cross-examination, Luce tried to discredit Frank's testimony, pointing out any inconsistencies between the statements he had made at the coroner's inquest and his testimony at the trial. He needed to shift some of the guilt for the murder from Roxalana onto her nephew. He found an opportunity when Frank testified that while he fired the gun at William Druse, he didn't intend to hit him. At the coroner's inquest, Frank had testified the opposite. This was the opening that Luce was looking for. Did Frank carefully aim the pistol at William Druse or simply point it in the general direction? Luce also pointed out to the jury that despite Frank's confession to his part in the murder, he was granted immunity from prosecution by the district attorney.

Luce took a more hands-off approach with Roxalana's young son George. Now eleven years old, he had been separated from his mother and sister for more than nine months. And now he had to testify in front of a room full of strangers. Luce knew that it wouldn't help his case or his client if he ruthlessly went after a nervous and frightened young boy who had witnessed the brutal murder of his father.

Instead, he questioned George about the toxic nature of his parents' relationship. George gave his testimony in such a low tone that it was almost impossible for the court and spectators to hear. He was frequently admonished to speak up. He told the court that his parents had frequent rows, mainly quarreling about bills, that his father would call his mother "a Goddamned bitch," and that once he drew an ax and threatened to knock Roxalana's brains out a month before the shooting. He also told the court that there was never enough to eat, that sometimes when William was away working at other farms for two or three days, they had nothing to eat at all.[14] During his testimony Roxalana openly wept as her son described life on the farm.

One by one, the neighbors testified about the terrible smell and the black smoke coming from the Druse house. A cornerstone of the people's case was provided by Dr. A. Walter Suiter. A pioneer in forensic science, he had been hired by District Attorney Steele to make a thorough study of the remains, to establish whether or not the fragments of bone that were found on the farm were human. Suiter testified that the fragments were indeed human. He also produced a floorboard from the house that was stained in human blood. Suiter also produced microscopic slides to show the bone fragments he picked out from the "chaotic mass" he had found at the farm.

Roxalana's lawyers argued justifiable homicide. Unfortunately, they couldn't claim temporary insanity. Roxalana had been examined by Dr. John Perdue Gray as well as Suiter. Both men judged her to be sane and competent to stand trial. Her lawyers no doubt hoped to garner sympathy from the jury with the "battered woman" defense. They couldn't hope to justify her actions but hoped that attacking William Druse's character might explain them. Luce opened the defense on September 30, 1885, to an overflowing crowd in the courtroom, two-thirds of whom were women. He said that William Druse had attempted to kill his wife with an ax and that she had shot him in self-defense.

Roxalana Druse and her husband William were not in what you would call a happy marriage. During their twenty years of marriage, William had subjected his wife to both verbal and physical abuse. Their fights had become legendary throughout the area, from screaming to what sounded like acts of violence. Gossip around the county was that the two had not slept in the same bed for ten years. William, George, and Frank slept upstairs, while Roxalana and Mary slept downstairs in the parlor. Roxalana later testified that the only time her husband had been nice to her was on their wedding day.

The major witness for the defense was Mary Druse. Luce led her through a laundry list of the abuse her mother had endured. Once, Mary testified, he had hit her mother with a horsewhip and then gave a neighbor five dollars to keep quiet about the incident. On the morning of the murder, her father had complained about the tea, punching Roxalana in the face with his fist. Then he grabbed a knife from the table and threatened to cut her throat. That was the last straw for her mother. Soon the first shot was fired.

Unfortunately for Roxalana, the jury didn't buy it. Local feeling had never been warm, even before the murder. It was firmly against her after it, particularly given the gruesome nature of the crime. To many she was not an abused spouse but a violent, dangerous woman. Sneaking the revolver into the house beforehand looked like premeditated murder. Threatening her son and nephew with death unless they helped her commit and conceal the murder made her seem cold and calculating, not desperate and fearful.

If the jury saw anyone as deserving of sympathy, it was her son George and her nephew Frank, both of whom turned state's evidence. Mary, having pled guilty to second-degree murder, received life imprisonment in Onondaga County Penitentiary.[15] For the two boys, the trial must have been a nightmare. Not only did they witness the murder, but they were also forced to participate on pain of death. Frank, having already confessed to the crime, was forced to relive the ordeal all over again at the trial. Even at his young age, Frank must have known that his testimony had the potential to send his aunt to the gallows.

With all the evidence stacked against her, it was almost a foregone conclusion that Roxalana would be found guilty. Judge Williams instructed the jury to take note of the serious controversy in the case, not that William Druse had been killed, but whether the act was "justifiable or excusable." He informed the jury that he did not believe that the dead man's disposition and cruelty were legal justifications for murder. Rather, he said, the jurors had to decide if Roxalana was in "some great personal danger."

The jury deliberated for more than five hours. Just after midnight on October 3, 1885, the jury rendered their verdict: guilty of murder in the first degree. Roxalana, who was sitting beside her lawyer, heard the verdict apparently unmoved, but afterward said that a great wrong had been done her, that she was not guilty of premeditated murder and had been unjustly convicted.[16]

Sentence was passed down on Tuesday morning, October 6th. Judge Williams sentenced Roxalana hanged "by and under the direction of Herkimer County by the neck until you be dead," on Wednesday, November 25, 1885. Asked if she had anything to say, Roxalana answered simply: "I have nothing to say." She showed almost no emotion when Judge Williams solemnly pronounced the sentence, but after passing out of the courtroom, she burst into tears.[17]

The first hanging date was not kept. Roxalana's lawyers immediately appealed the verdict. A stay of sentence was granted by the governor's office during October because an appeal had been filed. Roxalana spent the first anniversary of the murder in her cell in the Herkimer County Jail. The next July, Roxalana and her lawyer appeared before a judge in Utica, and Luce argued his appeal. He admitted that his client's greatest mistake was trying to cover up the murder by burning the body. Roxalana, when asked by the judge, said that she did not think that she'd had a fair trial.

Initially confident, Roxalana's morale took a beating in court. The judge, George Hardin, ruled that her trial had been fair, the evidence sufficient, and her guilt clear. He resentenced her to be executed on August

19, 1886. There was yet another respite as Luce filed an appeal of Judge Hardin's judgment with the New York Court of Appeals. The ruling did not come down until October 26. The judges agreed with the lower court; they saw no reason for setting aside the verdict. This set the stage for yet another resentencing by Judge Williams in Herkimer County Court. It took place on November 8. Wearing a black suit, Roxalana stood before the judge, her eyes downcast, looking pale and nervous. The court asked the usual question of Roxalana, as to why the sentence of death should not be passed upon her, her response was, "I have nothing to say."[18]

She was set to hang on December 20, 1886, two years after the murder. Roxalana broke down and wept bitterly at the news. Only the governor or an act of the legislature could save her from the hangman's noose. Governor David B. Hill promptly denied clemency, but then he changed his mind on December 22, two days after she was supposed to hang. A bill to abolish the death penalty for women and substituting life imprisonment was before the state legislature, and Hill wanted to know the result before her execution.[19] Unfortunately for Roxalana Druse the bill was defeated on February 18, 1887, and a new date was set for her execution, February 28. On February 25, the *Franklin Gazette* reported simply, "It is understood that Governor Hill will not take further action in Mrs. Druse's case, and that she will be executed at Herkimer next Monday."

The case aroused much public debate for and against her execution and executing women in general. One man offered to go to the gallows himself, in place of Roxalana; another offered ten dollars if he could act as executioner. Women's rights groups were strongly opposed, stating that an all-male jury wasn't exactly a jury of her peers. Also, since women lacked the right to vote, they couldn't control their own destinies. Letters and petitions about the case began to arrive at the governor's office in early November 1886, asking the governor to commute her sentence. The governor sided with the law, saying that he found no grounds for clemency.[20]

A team of medical experts, Dr. Andrews of the Buffalo Insane Asylum, Dr. MacDonald of the Asylum for Insane Criminals at Auburn, and Dr. Lewis Balch, Albany secretary of the State Board of Health, were sent to the jail by the governor to verify whether Roxalana was sane or not. The commission visited the jail at Herkimer to conduct their investigation. On February 15 they submitted a report in writing to Governor Hill that they unanimously found that Roxalana was sane and was sane at the time she murdered her husband.

To the Hon. David B. Hill, Governor of the State of New York.

Albany, February 15, 1887

Sir: The undersigned, Commissioners appointed by you to examine Roxalana Druse, now confined in the Herkimer County Jail, under sentence of death, and to report their conclusions as to her present sanity and their opinion as to her sanity at the time of the commission of the act for which she was convicted respectfully submit;

That they have carefully examined the said Roxalana Druse and have arrived at the conclusion that the said Roxalana Druse was sane at the date of the commission of the act for which she was convicted and is now sane.

We have the honor to remain, Sir, your obedient servants,

Judson B. Andrews, M.D., Charles F. MacDonald, M.D., Lewis Balch, M.D.[21]

Governor Hill asked for Judge Williams's opinion as well. His response was that a criminal's gender should not make a difference.

When it was explained to Roxalana that all hope of saving her life was lost, she turned alternately moody and frightened. She lost her appetite, claiming that she couldn't eat. She shivered when she heard hammering in the jail yard and asked what it was. Because her cell faced the south side of the jail, she couldn't see the gallows being built in the yard on the opposite side. For three nights before the execution, Roxalana slept only a few hours.

Roxalana had only two wishes: She wanted to see her children one last time, and she wanted her funeral to be held immediately following her execution. Unfortunately, Mary Druse was not allowed to see her mother. She sent a telegram to Governor Hill requesting permission to visit her mother before her December 28 execution date, but her request was denied. Reverend Powell also begged the governor to allow mother and daughter to be reunited, but his request went unanswered.[22]

However, George Druse was given permission to visit his mother on February 26, two days before her execution. He hadn't seen her since the trial, nor had he spoken to her in two years. Since the trial he had been living with his aunt and uncle, Phoebe and Newton Chamberlain, on their farm. No one knows what they spoke about that day, but it couldn't have been easy. As George was about to leave, his mother presented him with a present, a camp chair. Clutching it with both hands, he looked back one last time and said quietly, "Good-bye, Ma."[23]

Herkimer County's sheriff was already preparing for the execution. The county had never hanged anyone before. Then, as now, executing a woman brought increased public and press attention. Roxalana was the fifth woman to hang in the state and the first to be executed in thirty-nine years. With the increased attention came increased pressure to see that everything went as planned. The scaffold used to carry out the court's sentence had been built at Fort Plain for the hanging of Charles Eacker at Fonda in 1871. It was constructed so that it could be dismantled, stored, moved, and erected again. Sheriff Cook ordered it painted glossy white and striped, black. It was simple gallows, consisting of two uprights and a crossbar. On one of the supports ten notches were cut. Ten people had been hanged on the scaffold. One of the men who had charge of the scaffold said, "I will cut another notch on Monday."

Public hangings were outlawed in New York State in 1835, but people could still be near a hanging even if they could no longer watch. They had to be held in closed jail yards with a limited number of witnesses. Twelve "citizens of Herkimer County" were listed officially as witnesses. There had been a blizzard the day before the execution; snow had to be removed from the walkway to the jail and the area immediately surrounding the scaffold. The local militia, the Remington Rifles, was instructed to keep order among the crowd outside the jail. Throughout the morning, reporters hoping to gain admittance to the courtyard had been arriving, only to be detained by the sheriff's office.

Roxalana wore a black satin dress to the gallows, with a small bit of white ruching threaded with silver about the neckline and hem. In front and at the top of her bodice she wore a bunch of roses taken from a bouquet sent to her by Mary through Superintendent Terry along with a letter.[24] The *Herkimer Democrat* noted that the dress had been made for the occasion by a local dressmaker, Maggie Clark. At Roxalana's cell Sheriff Cook announced that he was required to read the death warrant issued by Judge Williams on November 8, 1886, aloud. As he read in a shaky voice, Roxalana cried softly.

A few hours before her execution, she had written a final statement that was published in the *Herkimer Democrat* after her execution. In the statement, Roxalana claimed that her daughter Mary had nothing to do with the killing of William Druse, or the deposing of his body.

State of New York,

County of Herkimer

I, Roxalana Druse, in my last moments, do hereby solemnly swear and affirm that my daughter, Mary Druse, who is now confirmed in the Onondaga Penitentiary, had nothing whatever to do with the killing of her father, William Druse, or with the disposition of his body. This statement I have repeatedly made, and always adhered to it at the inquest and since my confinement. My daughter, Mary Druse, is absolutely innocent and was in no way connected with her father William Druse's death.

Mrs. Roxalana Druse

By signing this document, Roxalana hoped to guarantee that Mary would one day receive a pardon. Stating that her daughter was innocent wasn't the truth but trying to save her daughter from a lifetime in prison was a noble gesture on Roxalana's part.[25] Roxalana said good-bye to her friend Mrs. Waterman, and thanked her husband for his assistance as well. She had also left letters for Sheriff Cook, Mrs. Cook, and Deputy Mason, thanking them for their treatment of her during her captivity. She also wrote a final letter to her daughter Mary:

I shall have this letter buried with me if I die, but hope that a kind, tender one from above will whisper softly in the Governor's ear and let me live. Dearest child, if no such message comes, do not grieve for me; be brave, for I have suffered everything but death for what others ought to, and if I die, I shall be at rest. Weep not, dear child, for me when I am gone, for life has so little pleasure at the best and none for me. It is nearly 3'oclock at night. I have willed my body to Mr. Powell, and he will take care of it. He will write to you in a day or two . . . Farewell is my last dying words, is all I can say to my dear daughter that I love so well.[26]

Leaning heavily on the arm of Reverend Powell, together they walked out of the cell for the last time. In her left hand she clutched the bouquet sent by her daughter. Her eyes were red and glassy from weeping. Entering the courtyard Roxalana shook visibly when she saw the white gallows, trimmed in black crepe, for the first time. Sheriff Cook and Rice gently eased her to the platform and placed her directly beneath the noose.

Roxalana and Reverend Powell knelt on the plank floor of the scaffold to pray. Sheriff Cook asked Roxalana if she had anything to say. Trembling, tears streaming down her face, Roxalana turned to the one person who had given her steadfast support for the past sixteen months. Then Powell spoke briefly for her, thanking those who had befriended her and asking her enemies to do as she had done, forgive. He then lashed out a final time to denounce capital punishment. Taking Roxalana by the hand, he intoned, "Go to thy fate, trembling child of sorrow, Go to thy loving Father, God!"

Two deputies stepped forward and stood on either side of the condemned woman. While one lashed her legs together, the other tied her wrists in front of her. When the black hood was placed over her head, she let out a shriek, and then cried out again when the noose was placed around her neck. Cook dropped his hand, the signal for the hangman to release the pin. The counterweight fell, sending Roxalana's body upward three feet in one violent motion. Dr. Cyrus Kay noted the time as 11:50 a.m. There was one convulsion of the body, and then the body hung quiet.

After five minutes Drs. Kay and Suiter stepped forward onto the platform and made a gruesome discovery. Her neck had not been broken; she was still alive! Roxalana slowly strangled to death before mercifully dying. It took fifteen agonizing minutes for her to die. Sheriff Cook had decided on "suspension hanging" for Roxalana's execution. This meant that Roxalana wouldn't stand on a trap door but under a noose connected to a counterweight. When the signal was given, the mechanism would drop, and Roxalana would be jerked violently upward, her neck instantly broken. At least that was how it was supposed to go.

She was officially pronounced dead of asphyxiation three minutes past noon and cut down almost a half an hour later, while a wagon containing her coffin was brought into the inner yard. It was only after lowering her body into the coffin that the hood was removed. The casket had silver-plated trimmings and an ornament consisting of a hand grasping a bunch of flowers on top. The undertaker placed the remains in the coffin, the lid was nailed shut, and the hearse and two sleighs slowly led out of the yard.

The procession reached Oak Hill Cemetery where Roxalana's coffin was brought to the vault where it would remain until the spring. Roxalana Druse, the first and last woman to hang in Herkimer County, was finally dead and buried. The gallows dismantled, it was returned to Oneida County, the rope that had been used already cut up into souvenir lengths.

When Mary Druse was told that her mother was hanged she broke down, and the feelings she had been keeping inside manifested themselves in an outpouring of grief. Her grieving was so prolonged that authorities at Auburn Prison were worried that she was in danger of losing her mind as the result of the strain she'd been under since the trial.[27]

Roxalana's death raised the question of finding a more humane way to execute criminals. Newspaper editorials condemned her hanging as cruel and barbaric. A "Death Commission" had been formed in 1885 to evaluate possible replacements for hanging. The commission included Elbridge Gerry, a wealthy philanthropist who had founded the Society for the Prevention of Cruelty to Children in 1874. The commission considered modern methods currently in existence, including the guillotine, firing squad, lethal injection or some form of gas chamber, as well as the Spanish garrote.

While Gerry preferred the idea of a morphine injection, another member of the commission, a former steamboat engineer named Alfred Southwick, enthusiastically promoted the idea of electricity as a method. A letter from Thomas Edison changed Gerry's mind. Edison promoted the idea of electricity, and the best equipment for the job was that of George Westinghouse and his alternating current (AC). As a result of Edison's advice, Gerry threw his weight behind the electric chair. The "Electrical Execution Law" was debated in 1888 and formally became law on January 1, 1889. Hanging was officially abolished in favor of electrocution.

Mary Druse was pardoned by Governor Morton after serving ten years of a life sentence. The pardon was favored by District Attorney Steele, who conducted the prosecution as well as Justice Williams, the presiding judge at the trial. Williams said, "I said to Mary when I sentenced her that if she changed her character and became a good woman, she might, after years, hope for Executive Clemency." She was released from Auburn Prison on June 25, 1895.[28] She was not told of her pardon until the papers were received. Overcome with the news, she couldn't speak for some time. She told a reporter that she had been praying for a pardon and had faith that it would eventually come.[29]

Mary was now twenty-nine years old; her time in prison had profoundly affected her. Her pardon did not come without controversy. Several New York City judges were opposed to the pardon. One of the harshest critics was Judge John Goff. In the *New York Times,* Goff said, "In the Druse case, of course, we revolt at the thought of liberty for such a woman, but it is very possible that her confinement should not be in a penitentiary. This suggests a fault in our system. They do these things better in England . . . We don't need Mary Druses in our midst."[30]

Mary moved in with a couple who had visited her in prison. At their home she slowly became used to being back in society and began thinking about her future. A few years after her release, in 1899, she married John Ganon, a harness maker. They lived in Syracuse, where Mary worked as a domestic. The marriage was not happy, and Mary was separated from her husband when he died in 1915. Not long after, Mary came down with pneumonia and died on August 15, 1915. She is buried in an unmarked grave in the family plot of her employers in Syracuse.

George Druse apparently never visited his sister while she was in prison nor after her release. He remained with his foster family, the Chamberlains, for several years. Changing his name to George William Stewart, he found a job with the Remington Arms gun factory. He married in 1896 and had a daughter named Florence. He died of a heart attack at the age of six-ty-eight in 1944. His wife altered his death certificate, inserting the names of her parents for Roxalana and William Druse. George is buried in Utica, New York.[31]

LIZZIE HALLIDAY
(1859-1918)

THE WORST WOMAN ON EARTH

In September 1893, a few months after the Lizzie Borden trial ended, another Lizzie was arrested for multiple murders. Her name was Lizzie Halliday, and her crimes were considered so appalling that newspapers branded her "The Worst Woman on Earth." She was charged with murdering three people and was suspected of killing many more. Her trial in 1894 "will almost, in interest, be as famous."[1] Within a few years she had been mostly forgotten, while Lizzie Borden became one of the most famous alleged murderers in true-crime history, with multiple movies, a nursery rhyme, books, a ballet, and a bed and breakfast in her former home.

Lizzie Halliday was born Eliza Margaret McNally in 1864. She emigrated from Ireland with her parents at the age of eight. Once in America, the McNally family settled initially in Newburgh, New York. Going by the nickname "Maggie," by all accounts the first few years of Lizzie's life in America were normal; she went to school, performed chores around the house, and played with her siblings and neighbors. Lizzie's sister Mary later claimed that Lizzie once attacked their father, beating him with her fists, and that she once attacked their sister Jane in a rage. Soon her family was done dealing with her behavior.

Having left school at fourteen, Lizzie was expected to either seek employment or find a husband. Her prospects for work were limited to employment as a household servant for those families who could afford it or as a washerwoman. Initially Lizzie would work hard, but then something would go wrong, and she would erupt into a fit, using vile language. She

MRS. HALLIDAY IN HANDCUFFS.

would threaten to have her employer arrested and accuse him of abuse or not paying her wages. One woman known only as Mrs. M later said that Lizzie had threatened a child with a knife while alone in a dank cellar; strangely she was never punished for this assault.[2] Her brother John later stated that Lizzie "was inclined to quarreling that the family all disowned her for years. She could not stay in a place any time when working on account of her violent temper, and as for late years we know nothing of her only hearsay."[3]

In 1879, when she was fifteen, Lizzie married her first husband, Charles Hopkins, who was living under the alias Keetspool Brown after deserting from the British Army. Hopkins was considerably older than Lizzie and had been involved in some shady dealings when Lizzie first met him. A carpenter, Hopkins had worked for a wealthy farmer in the area who had a housekeeper named Mrs. Campbell. Although she was married, the two began an affair while her husband was working in Vermont.

Hopkins convinced Mrs. Campbell to steal money from her employer so that they could run off together. After Mrs. Campbell had stolen around two hundred dollars, Hopkins broke off the relationship. During this time, he'd met and courted Lizzie. Despite being unceremoniously dumped by her lover, Mrs. Campbell still tried to woo him back. Lizzie was not pleased at the attention Mrs. Campbell was giving her new husband. Before long Mrs. Campbell was found dead in her bed. On her nightstand was a small bottle of poison, which seemed to suggest that the poor woman had committed suicide, although there was no note. Lizzie later claimed that Hopkins had given Mrs. Campbell the poison, telling her that it was medicine to cure her ailment.[4]

Nine months after the marriage, Lizzie gave birth to her only child, a boy she named Charlie, after his father. Her sister Martha later claimed that Lizzie probably suffered from what we now call postpartum depression after her son's birth; she was moody, irritable, and suffered from delusions.[5] Lizzie and Charles Hopkins were married just under two years before he died suddenly in 1881 of typhoid fever. Local residents, however, had no problem believing that Lizzie had killed him.[6]

Over the next few years, Lizzie would marry four more times, several of them bigamous. Most of her husbands were much older men with army pensions. Her second husband, Artemas Brewer, was described as a broken-down veteran from Greenwich Village in Washington County. Wounded in the Civil War, he suffered greatly from rheumatism and heart problems.[7]

No one could figure out why she married Brewer. He was not much to look at. He was unusually short with a disproportionate head; long, straggly whiskers; and very large feet. Brewer, on the other hand, must have thought he had hit the jackpot to have such a young, pretty woman marry him despite his infirmities and lack of looks. Lizzie's description of her marriage was that he was "a bad old man. He was inclined to let me support him. Brewer was always chewing opium, same as Chinamen smoke, so he died shortly after I married him."[8]

Brewer didn't last a year married to Lizzie. One night he unexpectedly died in his sleep. The local doctor, Dr. Bartlett, confided to many in Greenwich that he thought Brewer had died from opium poisoning. Brewer's brother Albert, who sat with him just before he died, claimed that Lizzie frequently threatened his brother's life and that she often used vile and profane language. Despite what Dr. Bartlett and Albert Brewer claimed, Artemas Brewer's death was ruled as complications brought about by his various ailments. Although there was no proof, many who knew the couple were firm in the belief that Lizzie must have given her husband a fatal overdose of opium, causing his death.[9]

Husband number three, Hiram Parkinson, was already married when he met Lizzie, but he claimed to be a widower with grown children. He met Lizzie when she came to do his laundry at the local hotel. Soon he was spending more time at Lizzie's flat over the blacksmith's shop than he did at his hotel room. The marriage fell apart after five months, when Hiram informed Lizzie that he was heading back to Greenwich to see his children. Lizzie fought with him physically, removing his clothes when he tried to get dressed. Parkinson informed Lizzie that they were through, that when he returned from his trip to Greenwich, he wanted her gone. When he returned, he discovered that Lizzie had stripped the house of all the furniture, clothing, and housewares, which she had sold, pocketing the money and leaving him with nothing.[10]

Husband number four, George Smith, was an old army buddy of Artemas Brewer. Town gossip informed her that not only did he have an army pension, but he was also the caretaker of a horse farm where he lived. Lizzie showed up on his doorstep, offering to work as his housekeeper in exchange for room and board for herself and her son. Soon Lizzie and George were married. It wasn't long before Lizzie began to make life difficult for her husband with her violent temper and mood swings, similar to her previous husbands. During one fight, she threw a flatiron at him; another time, she tried to stab him with a pair of scissors. After a few months Lizzie grew bored with her new husband. She began sneaking around behind his back with Hiram Parkinson, who seemed to have forgotten the bad blood between them.[11]

After a few months, Lizzie tried to kill George by giving him a poisoned cup of tea. George managed to call for help before collapsing, and a neighbor called for a doctor. When the doctor arrived, he gave George an emetic to cause him to expel the tea. After a half hour, George was pronounced out of danger. They searched for the cup of tea, but it had disappeared, and so apparently had Lizzie. After two days she returned, begging for forgiveness. He would regret being so forgiving. Several months later George came home one night to find that the house had been stripped of everything that could move and his wife gone.[12]

Now calling herself Lizzie instead of Maggie, she wasted little time in marrying husband number five, a man named Charles Playstel. Unlike her other husbands, Charles was closer to her own age. Not much is known about him, other than he was a painter and paperhanger by trade. "He was a lovely husband. He always gave all his money to me. He was good to my boy, too, I'll say that for him." Lizzie left him shortly after he told her that he'd pounded his first wife to death.[13]

In 1886, Lizzie moved to Philadelphia with her son Charlie. She looked up an old acquaintance from her childhood, John McQuillan, who was running a tavern on North Front Street. The McNallys and the McQuillans had been neighbors in County Antrim in the north of Ireland. The families became reacquainted in Newburgh, New York. When Lizzie was a teenager, she'd kept company for a while with one of the McQuillan boys, Nathaniel.[14]

At first, John thought Lizzie was his sister, whom he was expecting to arrive from Canada. He hadn't seen his sister since they were children and wasn't sure what she looked like. Lizzie, of course, didn't bother to correct his mistake. Why would she since it was free room and board? He soon realized his mistake but couldn't figure out how to get rid of her. His wife took an immediate dislike to Lizzie, insisting that John get rid of her as soon as possible.[15]

Lizzie worked for a brief time in a gingham factory, but it didn't last long. Deciding that she'd be better off going into business for herself, she decided to open a shop. She bought new furnishings on credit for the flat upstairs and proceeded to take an insurance policy out on her newly acquired furniture. Although the furniture cost thirty-seven dollars, Lizzie insured it for six hundred. In March 1888, during one of the worst blizzards in history, Lizzie's house mysteriously burned down. The fire destroyed not only her own store, but also the buildings on either side. When the firemen entered her building, they noticed that there were no furnishings apart from several pots and kettles in the middle of the room containing burning rags doused in oil. There was also no Lizzie. Lizzie and her young son were nowhere to be found.

Lizzie was found several days after the fire in a hospital in Camden, New Jersey, claiming that she was suffering from mysterious ailments. Although she claimed to have been in the house the night of the fire, the doctors found no apparent burns or evidence that she suffered from smoke inhalation. The staff at the hospital soon realized that there was nothing wrong with Lizzie. They contacted the authorities, who took Lizzie and Charlie into custody. Charlie was quickly remanded to the custody of the Pennsylvania Society to Protect Children from Cruelty. She never saw her son again.

Despite the evidence against her, Lizzie blamed unknown assailants for the crime, claiming that she dared not tell the authorities who did it, because her life would be in jeopardy. Convicted of arson in April 1888, she did two years in Eastern State Penitentiary. Now a historic landmark and no longer a prison, Eastern State Penitentiary had been in existence for almost sixty years by the time Lizzie became an inmate. The prison was co-ed, with 980 individual cells. All prisoners were held in solitary confinement, and no interaction was allowed between inmates. If inmates needed to leave their cell for any reason, they were hooded to prevent knowledge of the complex and interaction with other inmates. They were fed in their cells and allowed supervised time indoors in the small exercise yard, but time was scheduled so that no two prisoners were ever in the exercise yard at the same time.[16]

Two months before she was due to be released, Lizzie was deemed insane and sent to a state asylum. In 1891 she was released and sent to a halfway house from which she promptly fled. Making her way as far from Philadelphia as her money could take her, she ended up in Newburgh, New York, where she began calling herself Lizzie Brown. She met Paul Halliday at the local employment office. A twice-widowed farmer just shy of his seventieth birthday, Halliday had a substantial spread, a military pension, and a severely disabled son named John, who lived with him. Paul was delighted to discover that Lizzie came from the same part of Ireland as his family.[17]

Not long after Lizzie went to work for him, the old man proposed marriage, apparently to avoid having to pay her wages. Lizzie, forty years his junior, accepted. The groom was certainly no prize. Halliday had rheumatism, he liked to drink, and most of his money came from making and delivering coal, which was a dirty business. He had also had a hard time keeping a housekeeper. The couple were married on March 26 in Middletown, New York. Paul Halliday would be Lizzie's sixth and last husband.

His children didn't think that Lizzie was good enough for their father and they didn't hesitate to tell him to get rid of her, but she seemed to have Paul Halliday wrapped around her little finger from the start. Then there was the fact that no one knew anything about her past, where she had come from before she'd turned up in Newburgh. Within two weeks of the wedding, Lizzie's terrible temper reared its ugly head. She hinted that she had killed her first husband back in Ireland, crushing his head with a stone. Robert Halliday, one of Paul's sons, later told reporters that Lizzie claimed that she was too sharp for the authorities and could fool the best doctors into believing that she was insane. Paul explained away her behavior by telling his family that she suffered from a woman's illness.[18] None of his neighbors liked Lizzie either. There were rumors that she was a gypsy, that she had roamed the countryside with a band of ruffians.[19] But the twice-widowed Halliday was smitten.

In May 1891, a series of fires destroyed the Halliday's house and barn. A third fire razed the old mill where the family had moved after the loss of their house, killing Paul's son John. Lizzie claimed that John helped her from the house and then ran back in to rescue some of the furnishings. He was overcome by smoke and never came back out.[20] Lizzie was suspected of setting the fires, and there were even rumors that she had murdered John with an ax, dragged the body into the cellar, and then set the house on fire to cover her crime. But there was not enough evidence to prove that Lizzie was the culprit for the fire, much less John's death.[21] "The entire neighborhood was convinced that Lizzie had set the fire that had killed John, who she was known to hate," the *St. Louis Post-Dispatch* later reported.[22]

The next month, Lizzie, according to a report in the *New York Times,* "eloped with a neighbor, stealing a team of horses in order to accelerate their flight. In Newburgh, her companion deserted her, and she was arrested for grand larceny. Her counsel entered a plea of insanity, and she was sent to an asylum." According to Paul's son Robert, Lizzie "hired a horse and buggy in Newburgh, claiming that she was a poor Irish servant who wanted to visit her sick mother. The man let her have the horse and buggy. She drove out of town, got an old man to go with her as she did not know the country and within twenty-four hours had sold the rig and horse to some gypsies."[23]

Lizzie was initially incarcerated in the Newburgh jail. Deemed insane, she was sent to Auburn Asylum in February 1892; later she was moved to the new Matteawan facility. If she had been faking her insanity, as some of the press and the public believed, she could have had a career on the stage. Discharged as cured in May 1893, she returned to the waiting arms of her husband. Neighbors reported that the couple were inseparable. Paul seemed never to let Lizzie out of his sight.[24] None of the neighbors had liked Lizzie before, but after her release, they avoided her like the plague.

Paul Jr. visited the farm after neighbors reported that they hadn't seen his father in a couple of weeks. Lizzie informed him that Paul had gone out for the day to visit property he had bought in Bloomingburg.[25] Paul Jr. was immediately suspicious; his father hadn't said anything to him about buying property. The neighbors watched the house night and day, but Halliday never came home, which made Paul Jr. suspect foul play. He went to the local constable for help. He was persuaded to do everything by the book. A search warrant was needed so that any evidence found could be used against Lizzie in court.

On the morning of Monday, September 4th, Constable Joseph Scott and Justice Abram Thayer arrived at the farm with the warrant, but Lizzie refused to let them in, blocking the doorway. Her actions clearly indicated that she had something to hide. When they tried to force the issue, she struck Constable Scott on the hand with a board and threatened to "cut his heart's blood out."[26] Needing to get Lizzie out of the house, Scott asked Lizzie to please travel with them to Bloomingburg to find Paul at his new property. Her anger subsided, Lizzie agreed to go with Scott and Thayer to Bloomingburg to find her husband. After they left, the neighbors searched the property.[27] In the barn, they discovered the decomposing corpses of two females, one older and one younger, covered in hay. Who were they, and why were they buried in the Hallidays' barn, the apparent victims of violence? It would take several days to learn their identities. The "why" has never been answered.[28]

While searching the house, they discovered more evidence. One of the quilts was badly stained with blood. The rough floorboards were badly stained and showed evidence that they had recently been washed, which seemed to make the blood stains more visible. One of the neighbors said that only a day or two before, Lizzie had asked what she could use to remove blood stains from the boards. Two shovels and a crowbar that had been used were found. In the bedroom, a .32 caliber bullet was picked up from under the bed.[29] A telegram was sent to Bloomingburg for Constable Scott and Justice Thayer to return as soon as possible with Lizzie.

A coroner's jury was quickly assembled, and several local physicians arrived at the farm to examine the bodies, which were laid on a crude dissection table made from a barn door laid between a pair of chairs. The older woman appeared to be in her late forties, and she was wrapped in a black dress, a bonnet tied to her head. Her hands, knees, and feet were bound by rope. Beneath her clothing, she wore only a thin cotton shift, which led the authorities to deduce that she had been murdered in her sleep. The clothing had no bloodstains or bullet holes, while the cotton shift had been seared by gun powder from the murder weapon. Eight bullet wounds were found in the chest, near the heart.

The younger woman was no more than twenty. She was similarly tied up, wrapped in clothing, and wearing only a thin nightgown. Her body, too, was riddled with bullets and she was less decomposed than the other woman's remains. By this time, a curious crowd of hundreds had arrived at the farm, every last one of them had a theory about the case, but no one was able to identify the bodies.[30] Post-mortem photographs were taken, and District Attorney Hill had an illustration made from one of the photographs of the younger woman to accompany a newspaper article that would hopefully lead to identifying the victims.

Meanwhile, Justice Thayer and Constable Scott had arrived in Bloomingburg with Lizzie to look for Paul Halliday when they received the telegram about the discovery of the bodies. Lizzie was immediately arrested and taken by Constable Scott to his home for holding until they could make the trip to the county seat and the jail there. Lizzie did not resist arrest, but she denied knowing who the women were and how they came to be buried in the barn on the property.[31] The search for Paul Halliday continued. At first it was believed that he had either participated in the murders or that he had run off to save himself.

When Lizzie was approached that night by a reporter from the *Middletown Times-Press,* she began to act in a bizarre manner, babbling about seeing her "old man in heaven" and accusing him of wearing her petticoat. She began to scream loudly and tear at her clothes, claiming that potato bugs were crawling on her. It was the same thing she had done two years before, when she had been arrested for stealing horses. She refused to tell them where Paul was or who the women were. Instead, she continued to pick at the imaginary bugs that were crawling on her.[32]

On September 7th, a neighbor, William Grieves, discovered Paul Halliday's remains beneath the kitchen's floorboards. He had been dissatisfied that the search for Halliday's body had been abandoned, so he went to look for it himself.[33] As the *New York Times* reported, "His head had been battered with a club or gunstock, for there was a contusion on the left side of the face and the eye hung down upon the cheek."[34] Paul had been shot in the chest three times, and like the two women, his ankles and wrists were bound.

The murder weapon was a .32 caliber pistol that had been given to Paul by a friend. It was later found tossed in Justice Thayer's outhouse along with two boxes of ammunition. Later a woman's gold watch with the initials SJM, a chain, and two rings were also found in the outhouse.[35] Even after the discovery of Paul Halliday's body, the search continued for additional bodies. A young boy named George Cline, who lived near the Hallidays, had been missing for two years. It was suspected that he might have been another of Lizzie's victims. They didn't find any bodies, but they did discover several bottles of whisky, which they polished off, after they made sure they weren't poisoned. Charley Higham found an old memorandum book near the Halliday house. Flipping through it, he discovered that Halliday had marked entries "Lizzie Halliday's crime." On the other side of the entry was written, "Burnt barn May 26, 1891. May 6, 1891, the house was burned. Paul Halliday, May 21, 1891."[36]

A crowd came from miles around looking to take a souvenir from the site of the grisly murders. There was no one on guard at the property to stop the hordes from satisfying their morbid curiosity. "Wagon load after wagon load drove over from Middletown and there were scores of carriages from every town in this part of the country," the *Middletown Times-Press* reported. They took everything that wasn't nailed down: plates, dishes, knives, forks, cooking utensils, remnants of clothing, and pieces of furniture. Women could be seen carrying these articles in their arms and stowing them away in carriages. They even hacked up an old wagon.[37]

Once the female victims were identified as Margaret and Sarah Jane McQuillan, authorities determined that Lizzie must have chloroformed Margaret and her daughter Sarah Jane after they went to bed, and then shot them at close range. The theory was that Paul was murdered first on August 28th, Margaret on August 30th, and Sarah Jane on September 2nd, two days before Lizzie was arrested. The *Middletown Times-Press* speculated that Lizzie killed Margaret McQuillan because she feared the woman had realized she had killed her husband. Having accomplished a second murder, she realized

that there were two members of the McQuillan family who would be suspicious if Margaret did not return. She had to lure the daughter and then
dispose of her. That only left Thomas McQuillan, Margaret's husband. No
doubt if Lizzie hadn't been arrested, the poor man might have suffered the
same fate as his wife and daughter.[38]

By late September, Lizzie was indicted by the grand jury for murder
in the first degree, for the murders of Margaret and Sarah Jane McQuillan
and her husband. When Lizzie was asked for her plea, everyone in the small
court leaned forward so as not to miss a word that she said. "I'm not guilty,"
she sheepishly replied. If she was found guilty, she faced the electric chair.
Lizzie had to wait more than a year for her trial while incarcerated. During
this time she did her best to present herself as insane, ranting, raving, and
refusing to keep herself clean; her hair grew matted and filthy.

Twice Lizzie tried to commit suicide, once by cutting her throat with a
piece of glass from the window of her cell,[39] and the second time she tried
to strangle herself with her garter.[40] She even managed to set a fire in her
cell. When she tried to strangle his wife, sheriff Beecher had had enough; he
secured her to the floor of her cell with a chain.[41] Lizzie responded by refusing to eat. If she had hoped to starve to death, her wishes were thwarted by
her jailers who force-fed her.

During her time in the county jail, Lizzie became something of a
national celebrity. The story of the killings was quickly picked up by the tabloid press in New York City and beyond. The strange and shocking details
of the crimes continued to hold the nation's interest day after day. "From its
circumstances, origin, conception and execution; its unique characteristics,
the abnormal personalities and the peculiar localities it involves, and, above
all, in the strangeness and mystery of its great central figure, it is unprecedented and almost without parallel in the annals of crime," *New York World*
wrote about the case.

Interest in Lizzie was so high, ground-breaking journalist Nellie Bly
scooped her male colleagues by getting Lizzie to tell her life story. Her goal
was to try to get Lizzie to not only talk about her crimes but also to determine whether Lizzie was truly insane or faking it. She had experience living and talking with the clinically insane. Nellie had successfully feigned

madness to get thrown into the asylum on Blackwell's Island. The resulting articles exposed the inadequacies of the care given at the asylum.

She made two trips to Monticello to interview Lizzie, the first in October, where she worked to gain Lizzie's trust. The second interview was in November at Lizzie's request. Before the interviews, Nellie had done extensive research on Lizzie. She knew far more than the sheriff's office did, and she used that information to get Lizzie to open up to her. Her first impressions of Lizzie were that she was perfectly sane, and that conviction never wavered. "There was nothing insane about her actions. They were the actions of a very shrewd person, who was thoroughly conscious of her danger, and was carefully considering all chances before venturing to commit herself in any way."[42]

Although Lizzie was cunning, she lacked the intelligence to put one over on Nellie. Lizzie probably saw Nellie Bly as a way to get her version of the story out. No doubt she was flattered that a celebrated journalist like Nellie Bly would travel all the way from the city to interview her. But she wasn't going to make it easy for Nellie. It took a bit of time for Lizzie to talk about the McQuillan murders; at first Lizzie was only concerned about the valuable livestock and possessions at the farm that needed to be retrieved and sold to pay for her defense.

Finally, she began to share, sort of. On Nellie's first visit, Lizzie told her a bizarre story, that Thomas McQuillan drugged her with chloroform, that three men showed up with revolvers, and that when she woke up, Margaret, Sarah Jane, and Paul Halliday were missing. On her second visit, Lizzie changed her story. This time she had been drugged by a band of gypsies who she knew, who forced her to watch the murders take place. She told Nellie that she was too frightened to name the real killers.

She also claimed that this same band of gypsies not only set the fires that burned down the house and barn, but they also killed Paul's son John by locking him in his room. According to Lizzie, they would waylay unsuspecting peddlers and desolate women, stealing their wares and valuables, and then murdering them and disposing of their bodies in an old lead mine. Nellie was not buying it, and she asked Lizzie why she hadn't noticed the bloodstains or the bullet holes in the floor, or the fact that something had been buried beneath the floorboards. Lizzie claimed that she hadn't seen anything.

Despite Nellie offering her two hundred dollars for her defense if she confessed to the murders, Lizzie wouldn't budge. Nellie noted that not once did Lizzie express any sorrow over her husband's death. Nor did she express any emotion over the fate of Margaret and Sarah Jane McQuillan. Nellie eventually grew annoyed with Lizzie's lies and decided to push the issue. "Lizzie Halliday, do you know what I believe? I believe that you alone and unaided killed your husband and the McQuillan women and buried them. I don't believe you were ever insane for a moment in your life, and that you are the shrewdest and most wonderful woman criminal the world has ever known."

Lizzie just sat smiling at her. Nellie pushed harder. "Did you or did you not kill those people?"

Lizzie insisted on sticking to her story. "I have been crazy, I was drugged."[43]

Lizzie was not merely likened to Jack the Ripper; Sullivan County Sheriff Harrison Beecher speculated that she was the Ripper. "Recent investigations show that Mrs. Halliday is in all probability connected to the Whitechapel murders," he announced to the press, "It has been proved that she was in Europe at the time. She frequently refers to the subject, both when she is in possession of her mental faculties and when she is raving." The grisly details of Jack the Ripper's five 1888 murders were still fresh in the public's mind in December 1893 when Sheriff Beecher made his announcement.

The *New York Herald* reported Beecher's assertions, and the dispatch was picked up by newspapers from Frederick, Maryland, to Marion, Ohio. "We suspect that this mysterious creature was connected with the horrible Whitechapel Murders," the *Middletown Times-Press* reported on December 4th, 1893, noting that Sheriff Beecher had asked the suspect point blank about her involvement. Beecher additionally said, "I said to Mrs. Halliday, 'Lizzie, you are accused of the Whitechapel murders. Are you guilty?' 'Do you think I am an elephant,' she replied. 'That was done by a man.'"[44]

The *Middletown Times-Press* report continued, "Mrs. Halliday is constantly speaking of these murders. She also talks of many women brought up from New York who have been robbed, killed, cut up in small pieces, and dumped in the Hudson River."[45]

It is no surprise that Lizzie Halliday denied involvement in the Ripper murders. For one thing, she was incarcerated in Eastern State Penitentiary at the time. Lizzie always managed to portray herself as the victim not the perpetrator, from the arson in Philadelphia through the murders of her husband and the McQuillans, often claiming that she was drugged by a brutal band of gypsies and forced to watch while they committed the crimes. This was also her defense regarding the arson in Philadelphia: Someone else did it while Lizzie watched. The residents of Sullivan County had no doubt that Lizzie murdered her husband and the McQuillan women. They also believed that she was faking insanity, and that her actions were those of "an unusually cunning and crafty woman."[46]

Lizzie refused to speak to her court-appointed attorney, George Carpenter.[47] Carpenter was not pleased at being selected to defend Lizzie and tried to get out of it, but his request was denied. Based on her refusal to cooperate, he had no other choice but the insanity defense. His plan was to call as witnesses the professionals who had deemed Lizzie insane in the past, as well as have her examined by psychological professionals before the trial started.[48]

The insanity plea was a relatively new defense. One of the most famous cases using the insanity plea was the trial of former congressman Daniel Sickles, who was acquitted for the murder of his wife's lover after claiming temporary insanity. It was often referred to as the insanity dodge, and prosecutors believed that some prisoners feigned madness as a "get out of jail free" card. There was a fear that there would be widespread abuse of the plea, used by shady lawyers to get their clients off.[49] "Public delusion is that the insanity dodge is a thing which succeeds very frequently," said Dr. Carlos J. MacDonald in 1895, discussing Lizzie's case at a meeting of the Medical Society of New York. "It is wrongfully put forth in a certain number of cases, but it is a well-known fact that it seldom succeeds where it is wrongfully offered."[50]

District Attorney David S. Hill was sure that he had an open-and-shut case. But one thing was nagging him: Did Lizzie have an accomplice? Lizzie was a petite woman; Paul Halliday was taller and of a heavy build. How would Lizzie have had the strength to drag the body and bury it the way that it was placed? He was not alone in his suspicions. The *Sun* speculated that Lizzie must have had an accomplice to help her dig her husband's grave. Neighbors reported seeing Lizzie with an unidentified man in late August, but by the coroner's account, Paul Halliday was already dead when this man was spotted with Lizzie. Who was this man?[51]

Hill was also lacking a motive for the murders of Margaret and Sarah Jane McQuillan. If he could prove a connection between Lizzie and the two McQuillan women, that she harbored a grudge against them, it would help prove that Lizzie was not insane when she committed the murders, that they were entirely premeditated.[52] It was *The World* that first reported the connection between Lizzie and the McQuillans.

The trial finally started on June 18, 1894, presided over by Judge Samuel Edwards. Lizzie pleaded "not guilty" in the deaths of her husband and the McQuillans. The courtroom was packed with spectators, demands for seats at the trial had been received by court officers from journalists from the major newspapers across the country.[53] Many of the spectators had come long distances to catch sight of Lizzie. Those who couldn't find a seat were standing shoulder-to-shoulder in the back of the courtroom. Jury selection, normally a lengthy process, had been completed in only three hours the previous day. They were all seated in the jury box waiting for the prisoner's arrival.

Wearing a plain brown dress that Sheriff Beecher's wife had made for her, Lizzie was brought into court between two officers, her eyes firmly directed at the floor. She appeared nervous and uneasy, exceptionally thin and very pale after her months of incarceration. Lizzie sat with her head down, chin resting on her chest, as District Attorney Hill described the crime as it occurred. He spoke for thirty minutes, telling the jury that the case would be proved by the circumstantial evidence since there were no eyewitnesses to the crime.[54]

A series of witnesses were brought forth to testify that Lizzie had lured the McQuillans, one by one, from their home under the pretense of employment, cleaning a large boarding house for which Lizzie was willing to pay double the going rate. Mrs. Caroline Wright, a neighbor of the McQuillans, testified to this fact. She positively identified Lizzie as the woman who called herself Smith, who came with a buckboard wagon asking for the McQuillan family by name. Mrs. Wright had overheard much of the conversation between Lizzie and the McQuillans that day, which she now recounted for the jury.

Wright testified that Sarah Jane hadn't wanted to go work at this time. She had been working for a family on Grand Street and had been granted vacation by her employers during the time they were out of town. She declined the offer, saying she preferred to enjoy her vacation. Her mother Margaret offered to go instead. Wright testified that she hadn't liked the look of "Mrs. Smith." "I leaned forward," she said, "I leaned forward and said right out to Margaret. Don't go with her, I said, she was a procuress or something of that sort!" Mrs. McQuillan laughed at the idea. Packing a few belongings, she accompanied Lizzie back to the Halliday farm.[55]

With tears streaming down his face, Thomas McQuillan recalled the events that led to the demise of his wife and daughter. He clearly identified Lizzie as the woman who had offered employment to his wife and then later came back to pick up his daughter. She told him that his wife had fallen and was seriously injured. When he said that he would immediately come and fetch her, Lizzie told him that the doctor wouldn't allow Mrs. McQuillan to be moved. Instead, she suggested that he send Sarah Jane to attend her mother until she recovered.

In the courtroom, District Attorney Hill showed Mr. McQuillan property that they believed belonged to his daughter. He positively identified her dress, cloak, watch, ring, and hat. Thomas McQuillan admitted that the McNallys and the McQuillans had known each other back in Ireland and in Newburgh, but that the last time he had seen Lizzie, she'd been fourteen and called herself Maggie.

Several witnesses were called to testify to Lizzie's sanity prior to the discovery of the crime. Justice Abram Thayer testified that Lizzie had been perfectly rational the day they went to her home until after they discovered the bodies. He told the court that she then began to act queerly, complaining that potato bugs were crawling on her.[56]

When defense attorney Carpenter made his opening statements, he made it clear to the jury that he was only defending his client because the court ordered him to do so. He then moved on to make the point that Lizzie had no motive for committing the crimes, and that she was clearly insane. He called a series of witnesses to testify that Lizzie was mentally unstable, including James H. Goodale, the deputy sheriff of Orange County, who had arrested her for horse theft, and three doctors. Goodale told the court that Lizzie used to yell "Ma! Pa! Nancy!" from her cell. "Wild as a hawk," he said. "She was insane then and is insane now."[57] Dr. H. E. Allison, the superintendent at the Matteawan Asylum, where Lizzie had only recently been an inmate, agreed. During the trial multiple physicians stopped by Lizzie's cell to examine her for madness.

During the examinations Lizzie would chatter constantly. She claimed that one of the physicians was the Holy Ghost and that she didn't recognize Dr. Allison. Dr. Edward L. Mann was appointed to give Lizzie an examination several times a day to determine her physical and mental well-being. Lizzie flew at him, kicking him viciously in the stomach.[58] Dr. Mann testified that he thought that Lizzie was not insane, that her actions over the past year proved that she was a pretty good actor. Her actions in concealing and then throwing away the watch, rings, and the gun were clearly the acts of someone sane, he pointed out.

Carpenter, in his closing argument, informed the jury that this was his first case involving the death penalty, and that it was the first case ever tried in Sullivan County where the counsel was unable to get his client to speak. He tried to show that since Lizzie had chosen her victims haphazardly and without a motive, she had to be insane. He also asked the judge to charge the jury that Lizzie's failure to speak in her own defense shouldn't be held against her.

On June 21st, after deliberating for three hours and ten minutes, the jury found Lizzie guilty of murder in the first degree. Carpenter asked for a poll of the jury. Each juror was asked if his verdict was that of guilty, and all answered in the affirmative. Lizzie covered her face with her handkerchief while her lawyer wept. He knew that a guilty verdict meant that Lizzie Halliday would die in the electric chair. The following morning, Judge Edwards sentenced Lizzie to die on August 6, 1894.[59]

On the way out of the courtroom, Lizzie attacked Sheriff Beecher, biting his hand through the gloves that he wore. He developed a serious infection as a result of the bite. In two different versions of the story, the resultant wound became so badly infected that he either needed to have the hand amputated, or he contracted a fatal poisoning of the blood. Newspapers reported that Lizzie's bite was poisonous, speculating that she was so crazy, so full of hatred and rage, that she could convey this through her teeth to her intended victim.[60]

Lizzie was taken to Dannemora prison to await execution, but she wasn't there for long. Governor Flowers granted Lizzie clemency based on the recommendation of a group of physicians, who after examining her, declared her to be insane.[61] Instead, her sentence was changed to incarceration for life in Matteawan State Hospital for the Criminally Insane.

Lizzie continued to exhibit dangerous behavior, and the other inmates generally gave her a wide berth. In 1897 Lizzie took offense to her treatment by Kate Ward, one of the attendants. Together with a second inmate named Jane Shannon, considered even more dangerous than Lizzie, they isolated the attendant in a bathroom. Shannon knocked Ward to the ground and jumped on her. After Lizzie stuck a towel in her mouth, the two women proceeded to pound the victim with their fists. Lizzie pulled out Ward's hair and scratched her face with her fingernails. When Ward was finally rescued, she was unconscious. She did, however, manage to survive the attack. Lizzie and Shannon were moved to isolation.[62]

After nine years of relatively stable behavior, Lizzie turned feral again when her favorite nurse, a young woman named Nellie Wickes, informed her that she had gotten engaged and was resigning. Only twenty-four years old, Nellie had been promoted to be the head of the women's unit, due to her ability to relate to the inmates. In her new position, she had shown Lizzie more kindness than any other person, giving her certain privileges in the group. On her part, Lizzie seemed to bloom under her kindness, developing a sort of maternal affection for the young woman.

When Lizzie heard the news that Nellie was leaving, she threw herself at Wickes's feet and begged her to stay. Over her last few days, Lizzie made verbal threats, saying that she would kill the young nurse rather than see her leave. As Lizzie had often made threats of this nature, those around her ignored her ultimatums. It was a decision they would later regret.

On her final day in the institution, at eight in the morning, Wickes entered a bathroom. Lizzie slipped in behind her and knocked her to the floor. Before the nurse could react, Lizzie took her keys and locked the door from the inside. She then turned to the defenseless woman, seized a pair of scissors attached to a chain at Wickes's waist, and stabbed her more than two hundred times in the neck and face. Her screams alerted the other attendants, who eventually managed to come to her aid, but the young woman died a few minutes later, just as her fiancé arrived at the hospital to pack up her belongings. While being taken to a cell in solitary confinement, Lizzie said, rather calmly, "She won't leave me now."[63]

Beyond her acute mental derangement, it is impossible to know what drove Lizzie Halliday to perpetrate the crimes that secured her reputation as a female Jack the Ripper. She was still incarcerated at Matteawan when she died of natural causes on June 18, 1918, at the age of fifty-eight.[64]

MARY ALICE
LIVINGSTON (1861-1948)

CLAM CHOWDER MURDER

In the spring of 1896, all of New York was riveted by the trial of Mary Alice Livingston Fleming. The story was salacious in the supreme. The story had everything: murder, sex, and greed, and it involved one of the first families of New York State. The alleged murderer, Mary Alice Livingston, was accused of murdering her own mother. The bizarre instrument of death was a pail of clam chowder, delivered to the victim one hot summer day by her own granddaughter. Matricide was considered a particularly heinous crime in the Victorian era, and the arrest of Mary Alice in her mourning clothes at her mother's funeral drew special notice from the press. If she was convicted, she faced the real possibility of being the first woman in New York State to be executed in the electric chair. And then there was the little matter of Mary Alice's juicy personal life. Unmarried at thirty-four, she was the mother of three illegitimate children, a fourth was born just before the trial.

The People vs. Fleming received prominent coverage in all the New York newspapers, but especially in Joseph Pulitzer's *World* and William Randolph Hearst's *Journal*, which were in an all-out circulation war. News of the trial was rarely off the front pages during the seven weeks of the trial. Only three events knocked the trial off the front page: The Republican Convention in St. Louis, which nominated William McKinley for president, a tornado that killed two hundred people in the same city a week later, and the crowning in Moscow of Tsar Nicholas II. The *World's* September 1895 issue announcing the arrest of Mary Alice sent circulation to over 580,000.

MRS. FLEMING.

Money and New York society were always guaranteed headline grab-
bers, especially during the Gilded Age. Mary Alice's family, the Livingstons,
were included on the list of Mrs. Astor's Four Hundred, those who were
considered acceptable in fashionable society. In 1686 Robert Livingston was
granted one hundred thousand acres of Livingston Manor, which ran from
the Hudson River to the Massachusetts border, and today corresponds to
the lower part of Columbia County. Philip Livingston was a signer of the
Declaration of Independence; William Livingston signed the Constitution
and was the first governor of the State of New Jersey.

On August 31, 1895, Evelina Bliss returned home to her apartment on St. Nicholas Avenue in upper Manhattan, after running errands. She was on her own for the weekend. Her two younger children were on vacation; Florence was in New Jersey and Henry in Massachusetts. Henry Bliss, her estranged husband, who she was still on friendly terms with, was staying at the Colonial Hotel on West 125th Street and 8th Avenue. Her daughter Mary Alice Livingston also lived at the Colonial Hotel with her three children, and she was six months pregnant with her fourth. Henry Bliss was paying for Mary Alice's rooms, but he was getting tired of supporting her and her children. Mary Alice had an inheritance from her late father, but the courts had decided that she could get that money only after her mother's death. She had recently petitioned to gain access to the money and had been denied.[1]

Evelina had recently visited her eldest daughter and was very upset that she kept having children without the benefit of marriage. Mary Alice was emotional and high-strung, and she responded angrily to her mother's complaints. Mary Alice was in a desperate financial situation. If only she could get access to the eighty-thousand-dollar inheritance (approximately three million in today's dollars).

Mary Alice's eldest daughter, Gracie, who was ten, had been playing with her friend Florence all day, along with Gracie's baby brother, Averill, who was fourteen months old. In the early afternoon Mary Alice ordered a cup of clam chowder and a piece of lemon meringue pie from the hotel's restaurant, which were delivered to her room. When Gracie and Florence returned from playing, Mary Alice asked Gracie to take the clam chowder, now in a small tin pail, and pie over to Evelina.[2] Gracie and Florence walked the five blocks uptown to Gracie's grandmother's building. Evelina was happy to see them. She poured the chowder into a pitcher and put the pie on a plate. After a short visit Gracie and Florence left. When they got back to the Colonial to give the pail back to Mary Alice, she said to the children, "I hope you didn't eat any of it."[3]

"No, Ma," Gracie replied.

Mary Alice ordered dinner from the hotel restaurant, and after they had eaten, the two little girls took Averill to play in Mount Morris Park. They played there until after dark, and then Florence walked Gracie and Averill home before returning to her own building on Manhattan Avenue. Augustus Teubner, an old friend of the Bliss family, stopped by to visit Evelina at around five o'clock that evening. He found Evelina in great distress. She complained of intense abdominal pains, and she was vomiting violently. After alerting a downstairs neighbor, Teubner left to find a doctor, finally locating Dr. William Bullman, whose office was at 135th Street. Bullman arrived at the building at six-thirty and found Evelina in great pain, trying to make herself throw up the rest of what she had eaten. She blamed her illness on the clam chowder she had eaten. While he was examining her, she told him "Doctor, I have been poisoned by a relative who in the event of my death will come into possession of a large sum of money."[4] When he pressed her to reveal the name of the person who poisoned her, she replied, "Oh never mind. Perhaps it was an evil thought." Dr. Bullman gave her an injection of morphine and returned later with a nurse and further medication. Her condition continued to deteriorate during the night.

By the time Dr. Bullman returned the next morning, it was too late. Evelina was dead. From the beginning Dr. Bullman suspected that the death was suspicious. The pitcher that held the clam chowder was found to have white residue at the bottom, and Dr. Bullman ordered the pitcher to be saved. Portions of vomit were also preserved for further examination, and an autopsy was ordered. The doctor reported his findings to the Harlem police station, that Mrs. Bliss had been poisoned. If Augustus Teubner had not stopped by to see Evelina that Friday night, she might have died alone in her apartment. Dr. Bullman would not have been called, and no one would have heard Evelina's suspicions that she was poisoned.

The police informed Henry Bliss that his wife had died and that an autopsy was being performed. Henry then told Mary Alice of her mother's death.[5] They both arrived at Evelina's apartment to find it crawling with doctors and cops. Florence and Henry, Evelina's younger children, found out the news when they arrived back from their vacations that afternoon. Florence was asked by a reporter from the *New York Herald* about her mother's death. "I don't know why the newspapers want to make such a scandal of my mother's death," she said. "She has had heart failure for some time, and her death was natural."[6]

Evelina's funeral and burial were scheduled for Tuesday morning, September 4th. The previous day, Mary Alice had a brief interview with Captain Thompson of the 30th Precinct at her hotel. Mary Alice told Captain Thompson that her mother was her best friend, and that she was entirely innocent.[7] Dressed in deep mourning, and closely veiled, Mary Alice, accompanied by two detectives in plain clothes, took a cab to her mother's apartment at 397 St. Nicholas Avenue, where the funeral was being held. Only Mary Alice's stepfather, her siblings, and a few friends attended the service. After the funeral Evelina was buried alongside her parents at Green-Wood Cemetery in Brooklyn, the largest and most fashionable in the New York vicinity. Samuel Morse, the inventor of the telegraph; DeWitt Clinton, governor of New York; and Horace Greeley, newspaper editor and presidential candidate were all buried at Green-Wood.

Mary Alice was formally taken into custody after her mother's funeral. Because she was accused of a capital crime, bail was not a possibility, so Mary Alice was committed to the Tombs, the main city prison. She gave her age as twenty-nine, shaving off five years.[8] It was noted that throughout her interview with the police that Mary Alice remained outwardly calm, betraying no emotional response to her mother's death, or being arrested for her murder.[9] Indeed, the *Sun* reported that when Mary Alice was told that she was under arrest, she exclaimed, "How annoying!"[10]

Her stepfather later denied to the press that he thought Mary Alice was guilty, that she poisoned the chowder that she sent to her mother. But he also stated that he thought that she was out of her mind, that she hadn't been sane in years.[11] Her half-brother Henry E. Bliss told a reporter, "I cannot believe that she could do such a thing. I have asked her if she sent that clam broth to my mother, and she said that she did not."

By the time Mary Alice was arrested, a preliminary analysis by Walter T. Scheele, the chemical expert assigned to the case by the coroner, hadn't been completed. However, some information was leaked to the press and "Poisoned By Antimony," was the top headline in the *New York World* on September 4th. A few days later the report was completed and released to the press. Scheele had indeed found some antimony in the contents of Eve-lina's stomach and the dregs of the clam chowder found in the pitcher, but more important was what else he found: arsenic, tartar emetic, and sugar. Detectives made inquiries at all the drugstores in Harlem to discover who had purchased the poison. Thus far, they were at a loss to find any druggist willing to admit that he sold any poison to Mary Alice or to any member of her family.[12]

From the beginning the New York press could not get enough of the story. The *Tribune* explained the intense public interest in the case as "a manifestation of a morbid craving for the unclean." Reporters clamored to interview Mary Alice during her stay in the Tombs, but she refused to speak on the advice of her lawyers. Instead, they began digging into her back-ground and were surprised to discover the many skeletons in the Livingston closet. Her father Robert Swift Livingston, the grandson of the last lord of the Manor of Livingston, had been a judge in Duchess County. Mary Alice was the youngest of his eleven children.

Her parents had a May–December romance; Evelina Davis was eighteen and Livingston eighty when they married. There was some nasty gossip that Evelina was more attracted to his wealth than the man himself, but their marriage appeared to be a love match, despite their considerable age differ-ence. His many children were concerned about what effect this marriage would have on their portion of the estate, but they could do little to stop the marriage from going forward.

For the first few years of her life, Mary Alice lived at Almont, a two-hundred-acre estate in upstate New York. Soon after her father's death, when she was five years old, Mary Alice and her mother moved back to Man-hattan, as ownership of Almont passed to one of Robert Swift Livingston's sons. On her father's death, his estate of two hundred thousand dollars was held for her in trust. Her mother had the use of the interest during her life. One year later, Evelina remarried, to Henry Hale Bliss.[13] Mary Alice was given a good education, attending private schools in the city, and although they were not Catholic, she attended the Academy of Mount St. Vincent in Riverdale (now the College of Mount St. Vincent),[14] where she was second in her class.

From the time Mary Alice was eighteen, her love affairs gave her mother and stepfather a good deal of concern. Attractive, lively, and intelligent, Mary Alice fell in love easily and often. She had a brief but intense affair with Archibald Cornelius, the family gardener and coachman. As soon as her mother became aware of the liaison, Cornelius was fired but not before Mary Alice wrote him many love letters that were later used against her in court. Her next love affair was with Henry Fleming, an oil merchant and president of the Central Refining Company. In June 1881 Evelina went to Philadelphia on business, leaving Mary Alice alone. She and Henry had a night on the town, which resulted in a night at a hotel in Greenwich Village. By all accounts Mary Alice was a willing participant in her ruin. She assumed that Henry would marry her, but Fleming had other ideas.[15] He told her mother that he doubted that Mary Alice had been a virgin, and he denied that he had seduced her.

By August Mary Alice was obviously pregnant, and Fleming began paying a weekly sum of thirty dollars for her support. Fleming paid the rent on an apartment, as well as the doctor's bills after Mary Alice gave birth prematurely in February of 1882.[16] Fleming continued to visit and support her and baby Walter, but matters came to a head in the summer of 1882 when Mary Alice finally wised up and realized that Fleming wasn't going to put a ring on it.

In June 1882, she filed a suit for breach of promise.[17] Her lawyer thought she would have a better chance of succeeding in the Brooklyn courts than in Manhattan, where Fleming might be able to influence the judge, and the glare of publicity would be less. If that was her hope, she was soon disappointed. The news quickly reached the New York newspapers and drew considerable interest. When the case came to trial in January 1883, the Bliss family lawyer, Merritt E. Sawyer, represented Mary Alice. Henry Fleming was to be defended by the ethically questionable law firm Howe and Hummel, who would become famous for defending Marm Mandelbaum a year later. When the trial started in January 1883, hundreds turned up at the courtroom every day, and thousands had to be turned away.

Mary Alice's letters to Fleming were used against her in court, especially the one where she claimed that she would rather be his mistress than the wife of another man.[18] These letters suggest that she was not an innocent victim seduced by an older, sophisticated gentleman and ruined.

When Fleming got up on the stand, he suggested that it was Mary Alice's idea to go to the hotel, and he implied that both mother and daughter had been his mistresses.[19] He declared that an attempt was made to blackmail him.[20] When the verdict came in, Mary Alice was awarded $75,000 in damages,[21] which was reduced to $25,000 on appeal, but the damage to her reputation was irreparable. Evelina and Henry Bliss's marriage was also a casualty of the trial. They had argued over how to deal with Mary Alice's situation. Money was also a problem; Evelina was not happy with the way that Henry was spending her inheritance from her late husband.

Despite being a single mother, Mary Alice did not lack for male attention. In the year following Livingston vs. Fleming, she had a new beau, a lawyer named Henry R. Willis. Once again, Mary Alice became pregnant, this time with a daughter, Gracie, who was born in July 1885. Mary Alice's breach of promise suit against Willis filled newspapers in October 1886 and vied for readers' attention with the dedication of the Statue of Liberty, the final construction of the Brooklyn Bridge, and a mayoral election in which Theodore Roosevelt placed a distant third. Relying on her diary in court, Mary Alice testified that when she discovered that she was pregnant, Willis gave her twenty-five dollars to have an abortion, but the operation was unsuccessful. That was the only money that he ever gave her.[22] Her mother's testimony corroborated Mary Alice's story that Willis had given her money for an abortion. When she found out her daughter was pregnant again, Evelina confronted him at his office.

When the judge asked Mary Alice about her financial situation, she claimed that she had no property, no income, no money of any kind. Apparently, the money that she had won from Henry Fleming was gone.[23] When Fleming passed away in 1887, he left thirty thousand dollars to his new wife, but nothing to his son by Mary Alice.[24]

Willis testified that Mary Alice seduced him, not the other way around. He admitted that they had sex but claimed that he never proposed marriage. He told the court that he had no other means than from his practice as a lawyer.[25] The case was tried in Manhattan this time and in front of two judges instead of a jury. One was in favor of Willis providing support for Mary Alice and Grace, the other was not. In the end, no award was given. Mary Alice, twenty-five and the mother of two children by two different men, could no longer claim to be the innocent victim. Perhaps the admission that she had attempted to have an abortion worked against her.

With this second trial Mary Alice's chances of making a respectable marriage were basically over. Despite this, neither her interest in men nor theirs in her had diminished. By 1893 Mary Alice gave birth to her third child, a son named Averill. The father was a man named Ferdinand Wilckes, a handsome German businessman whom she had met through her brother Henry.[26] The judge in the Fleming case had given her the right to use the last name, and she had begun to call herself Mary Alice Fleming. No doubt the Livingstons were relieved that Mary Alice, the black sheep of the family, would be indicted under that name. They had been deeply embarrassed to have the family name so prominently displayed in her two well-publicized breach-of-promise cases in the 1880s.

On September 10, Coroner William O'Meagher held a public inquest in the Criminal Courts Building to determine the cause of Evelina's death. All the publicity led to a crowded and excited courtroom. Charles W. Brooke led Mary Alice's defense team; Assistant District Attorneys John F. McIntyre and Seaman Miller led the prosecution. Mary Alice was brought from the Tombs in the custody of a policeman. Dressed entirely in black, with a crepe hat and a black veil trimmed in crepe, she smiled and chatted with her lawyers. The stares of the spectators in the courtroom made Mary Alice uncomfortable, and she turned her chair around and sat with her back to the audience.[27]

Dr. Bullman testified regarding Evelina's death and the statement she made that she had been poisoned by relatives for her money. He also testified that the cause of death was acute gastritis caused by poison. Dr. Philip O'Hanlon, who performed the autopsy, testified to the same thing, but neither man mentioned a specific poison.[28] Detective Joseph Sawyer testified that he had learned that Mary Alice had ordered clam chowder on the day in question, and that the chowder had been taken by her daughter Grace and her friend Florence King to Evelina at her apartment.

Her brother Henry nervously testified that yes, he believed that there was a provision in Robert Swift Livingston's will for Mary Alice that was to be kept in a trust until her mother's death.[29] He also said that he had not seen or spoken to his sister for five years because he did not approve of her lifestyle, but he didn't believe that she had killed their mother. Assistant District Attorney McIntyre surprised the court by announcing that "the People will not offer further proof." The audience in the court was surprised when the coroner delivered his charge to the jury. The prosecution was holding its cards to its vest, not ready to expose its case to the defense quite yet.

Before the coroner's jury, Mary Alice pleaded "not guilty." Dressed in mourning, she returned to the court to learn that she had been indicted on the charge of murder in the first degree.[30] The jury of nine men took fifteen minutes to come back with their verdict. Mary Alice's lawyers called for her release based on the coroner's jury. Assistant District Attorney McIntyre asked for a brief recess and came back with a bench warrant from a judge for Mary Alice to be held until the action of the grand jury in a hearing not open to the public or to Mary Alice's lawyers.

Mary Alice applied to gain access to a portion of her inheritance from her late father to pay for her defense. Her inheritance stood at about $82,937.00[31] (about 2 million in today's dollars), and Mary Alice sought $25,000 of it. Her cousin, Robert S. Livingston, opposed the motion. His reasoning was that if Mary Alice were convicted, she would be debarred from all interest in the estate that was to come to her on her mother's death. Referee Lawrence Godkin ruled in February that she could not have her share until she was acquitted of the murder charge.[32] The case moved to the Appellate Division, and on May 8th, the Godkin order was reversed.[33]

Mary Alice gave birth to her fourth child, named Robert Livingston Fleming, in the maternity hospital on Blackwell's Island.[34] After the birth she was returned to the Tombs along with her baby, who became a favorite of all the other women who were incarcerated. Nicknamed Robin by his mother, he became the "baby pet of the Tombs." The women loved to play with him and sometimes gave him his bottle. The female prisoners, unlike the male prisoners, were usually only locked in at night. During the day they could sit in the halls of the prison. In addition to her bed, Mary Alice's cell contained a small bookcase, a washstand, two chairs, and a second bed for her son.

Recorder John Goff was the judge presiding over Mary Alice's trial.[35] The top judge of the city's Court of General Sessions was the recorder, a title held over from the days when a judge had the responsibility of keeping a record of various happenings in the city. John Goff had been elected in November 1894 as part of a reform-minded ticket organized to defeat Tammany Hall.[36] Goff was a noted reformer, but he appeared to have difficulties in his transition from prosecutor to judge. Five appeals had been filed against his rulings, and four had been reversed.[37]

Mary Alice's chief lawyer was Charles W. Brooke, who proved to be very combative in the courtroom. He had defended numerous clients on the charges of assault, arson, and embezzlement, as well as in several murder trials. There was speculation that Brooke planned to use the insanity defense in Mary Alice's trial. He was short and stout and looked his age. Balding, with a thick gray mustache and heavy eyes, he wore a small pince-nez, which gave his face a rather owlish look. But when he got going, he was a different man, full of energy with vivid facial expressions.[38] He could command a courtroom with his booming voice and dramatic arm movements. His team consisted of his son Lex Brooke, Gatz Nathan, Howard Okie, and John C. Shaw.

The prosecution was a team of three lawyers. Assistant District Attorney John F. McIntyre was a native New Yorker who had many years' experience as a prosecutor and an enviable record in obtaining convictions.[39] In court McIntyre was the opposite of Charles Brooke; he was calm, cool, and dignified. Seaman Miller was relatively new to criminal court, and it showed. He was timid, nervous, and lacked confidence. The third member of the trio, Andrew O'Sullivan, who was there to provide medical expertise, had been on the defense side during the inquest.[40] Brooke was not pleased to see his old colleague on the prosecution team.

Over a thousand men had been summoned and over six hundred questioned on the stand before twelve jurors were picked. Many of the prospective jurors were dismissed because they admitted that they had already formed an opinion of the case because of the newspaper coverage, they did not believe in capital punishment, or they opposed capital punishment for women.[41] Brooke continually emphasized the idea that the law presumes the defendant innocent until proven guilty and stressed the concept of reasonable doubt. Whenever a potential juror passed the examinations of both lawyers, Brooke would turn to Mary Alice to see if she approved. Usually she nodded, but a few times she overruled Brooke and asked the juror to be excused.

The dozen men chosen worked in real estate, construction, dry goods, shoes, wine, tools, coal, and ice. As required, each juror was a man under the age of seventy, and the owner or the husband of an owner of personal property worth $250. McIntyre, on the other hand, spent his time questioning potential jurors as to whether they were personally acquainted with Mary Alice. It took many days to fill the jury box because of the existence of the death penalty. Jurors had to be willing at the end of the trial, if they voted for conviction, to send a mother of four, including a newborn, to the electric chair.

The trial began on May 11, 1896 and lasted until June 23. That morning William Randolph Hearst's *Journal* ran a lengthy article about the trial of Mary Alice, calling her "the strangest woman ever charged with crime in the courts of New York." The article not only questioned the paternity of her four children, but also her own paternity, after noting that her father had been over eighty when she was born. Rumors abounded in the papers that Mary Alice was the daughter of a man of considerable prominence in Wall Street circles.[42] But this man was never identified in any of the newspapers.

Mary Alice wore black throughout the trial, and because she was petite, she was frequently referred to as "the little woman in black." Her demeanor throughout the trial was frequently remarked upon, including how she smiled and chatted with her counsel and half-sister Florence. "She came into court yesterday with cheerful nonchalance exactly as if she were compelled to witness a performance which she feared would bore her."[43] When they weren't commenting on her manner in court, they focused on her unmarried state and the fact that she'd had four children out of wedlock. Mary Alice's younger sister Florence Bliss was at her side during the trial, her presence at the trial clear evidence that she did not believe that her sister had killed their mother. The newspapers noted that Ferdinand Wilckes, the father of her two youngest children, was also in regular attendance in the courtroom.[44]

Now that the trial was about to be underway, Mary Alice felt able to talk to journalists. She spoke with a reporter from the *New York World*. In the article, Mary Alice not only had nice things to say about the judge, jury, and her own lawyers, but she also said favorable things about the prosecution team. The interview conveyed to the reader that she was a well-brought-up young woman who was kind, someone who always had a nice word to say about others. She was not the picture of a cold-blooded killer. Mary Alice shared that she was aware of the criticism of her past. When she was asked if there was anything she would like to say to the public, she said "with a charming smile. 'Nothing, except to ask them not to judge me too harshly or without consideration of my position.'"[45]

There were behind-the-scenes shenanigans going on as well—at least according to the *Sun* newspaper. The paper reported that one of the witnesses, Florence King, had to be sent out of town because Mary Alice's sister Florence had allegedly made persistent efforts to reach the girl, and that through an intermediary, "various inducements had been offered to influence her testimony." They also reported that a member of Mary Alice's defense team, Howard P. Okie, had gone to Rawlin's drugstore on 135th Street to see the book in which Dr. Bullman's prescriptions were kept. He allegedly tried to leave the store with the book. Of course, Mary Alice's defense team denied all insinuations.[46]

During the jury selection, the demand for seats in the courtroom lessened, but when the prosecutors opened the People's case on May 26th, the Criminal Courts Building was once again besieged by eager spectators. Between five and six hundred people begged to be admitted to the courtroom.[47] Court attendants were required to turn away many of the people who were eager to see the now infamous defendant and to hear the evidence against her. "If all the people who tried to get into Part II of the Court of General Sessions yesterday to attend the trial of Mary Alice Fleming for the murder of her mother by poison had succeeded," wrote one reporter, "they would have been piled three or four feet deep."

A steady stream of prosecution witnesses testified about the events in Evelina's apartment the night of her death. Augustus Teubner testified that when he went to visit her that afternoon, he had found her very sick and decided to find a doctor. The nurse, Hannah Phillips, testified about Evelina's final hours. The most important part of her testimony concerned the pitcher that held the remains of the clam chowder, that Dr. Bullman had asked her to save for chemical analysis. It turned out that she had placed the pitcher on the fire escape overnight. Mary Alice's lawyer Charles Brooke pointed out that anyone who climbed the fire escape that night could have tampered with the pitcher.[48]

The next witness was Dr. William Bullman. Dr. O'Sullivan took over questioning for the prosecution since Bullman's evidence would be medical in nature. Brooke tried to keep out Evelina's last words to the doctor, that she had been poisoned by a relative who was trying to get her money, a statement that had already appeared in all the newspapers. Judge Goff instructed the jury to disregard the statement. Brooke had won the legal argument, but the jury had heard Evelina's statement. The doctor was given permission to testify that it was his opinion that Evelina had died of acute gastritis caused by an "irritant poison."[49]

Brooke was tough on Bullman during his cross-examination, in part because Bullman had announced to the papers back in September, after Mary Alice's arrest, that he thought she was guilty. Brooke was determined to raise doubts about Bullman's judgment. He was able to get Bullman to admit that he was unaware of Evelina's medical history because he had never seen her before that evening, and that on his first visit, he did not realize that Evelina was dying. His main point was that if Evelina had been treated by a better doctor, she might still be alive.

Charles Anderson, the manager of the Colonial Hotel, testified that clam chowder had been a regular item on Fridays at the hotel for several years. But the main thing that came out of his testimony was that the contents of Mary Alice's apartment at the hotel had sat in storage for almost a month before police inspectors came to remove several items that would be tested for poison and placed into evidence.[50] Among those items were a black tea tray and a small broken Japanese vase, along with a piece of stained carpet that seemed suspicious. Anderson admitted under cross-examination by Charles Brooke that the storage facility was accessible to many employees of the hotel. The long delay in obtaining these items weakened the later testimony about poison being found. There was also no explanation as to why the police had waited so long to decide that Mary Alice's apartment might contain incriminating evidence.[51]

The next step was testimony of the analytical chemists about the identity of the irritant poison that killed Evelina Bliss. The first of the prosecution's expert witnesses, Dr. Henry Mott, was a respected chemist who had written widely on poisons. But his lengthy testimony about chemistry bored the jury and the spectators in the courtroom; several jurors started to doze off. The next expert witness was Walter T. Scheele, a German chemist who owned a pharmacy on Whitehall Street, in lower Manhattan. Brooke went after Scheele hard, because like O'Sullivan, he had worked for the defense in recent trials. When it was his turn to cross-examine, he ignored Scheele's chemical analysis, instead focusing on whether Scheele had allegedly told people that he would fix the case so that the defendant would be convicted whether she was guilty or not. The chemist was totally unprepared for this line of questioning, as were McIntyre and Dr. O'Sullivan. Scheele angrily denied the charges.[52]

Eleven-year-old Florence King was called to the witness stand. After being questioned by Recorder Goff to see whether she was competent to give her testimony under oath, McIntyre proceeded to question her about the events of August 30th. Florence dutifully recited that she and Gracie had played together early that Friday morning at the Colonial Hotel before heading back to Florence's house to have lunch. When they returned to the hotel, Mary Alice asked them to take a pail of clam chowder and a piece of pie to Mrs. Bliss, Gracie's grandmother. When they brought the pail back to the hotel, Gracie told her mother that the clam chowder was very nice. Gracie's mother then said, "I hope you did not eat any of the chowder." Brooke was very gentle with the young girl during his cross-examination. He simply asked her how many times she had told this story to the police and the district attorney. "Lots of times," she said. Clearly Brooke was trying to establish to the jury that Florence had been coached on her testimony.[53]

Over the two weeks of testimony, the prosecution had linked Evelina's death to the arsenic-laced clam chowder and now definitively linked the clam chowder to Mary Alice. Mary Alice's stepfather, Henry Bliss, was called as a hostile witness. However, he also admitted that he had asked Mary Alice if she had poisoned her mother the day of the funeral. He also reluctantly testified that he had told Mary Alice that she would have to move from the Colonial Hotel because her expenses there were too much, but he claimed not to remember what the two women had fought about two days before Evelina's death, that his hearing was not too good. His memory also failed him with many of the other questions from the prosecution, despite Assistant District Attorney McIntyre reading from his statement to the police made the previous year.[54]

When Ferdinand Wilckes, the alleged father of Mary Alice's two younger children, was called to the stand, he too seemed to have suffered a memory loss regarding what he had told detectives the previous September. McIntyre brought up the fact that Wilckes had once worked in a chemist's shop, and that he had been able to obtain medicine from a local drugstore without a prescription, insinuating that Wilckes may have obtained the arsenic used in the murder.[55] Dozens of Mary Alice's love letters to Wilckes were put into evidence and read to the jury to help establish her motives for murder, including her need for money and her anger toward her mother, which contradicted her statements to the press that she and Evelina were the best of friends.[56]

The prosecution had planned to close their case with the testimony of Mrs. Sarah Reynolds, Mary Alice's friend. This testimony, they claimed, would be important to the People's case. McIntyre stated that on the night of the murder, Mrs. Reynolds was given a package by Mrs. Fleming, with instructions to take it to her home and deliver it to a man who would call for it, and in the event of his failure to appear, to throw it into the Hudson River. The mysterious Mrs. Reynolds never materialized, despite detectives looking for her.[57] On Monday, June 15, after three weeks of testimony from over two dozen witnesses, McIntyre announced to the court, "The people rest."

During the trial, the *New York World* announced that they were forming a jury of "twelve well-known, brainy New York women" to follow the case and pronounce a verdict. The paper wished to provide "a conspicuous experimental justification of the theory that a woman should be tried by a jury of her peers." The jury included a minister, a doctor, an author, a playwright, three women with law degrees, and a "woman otherwise distinguished." One of the women chosen said, "Every woman who is tried should have the benefit of a woman jury. Women have certainly shown their capacity to act as lawyers, and to plead cases with marked success. If they can do this, I cannot see why they should not serve as jurors."[58]

Mary Alice was very aware of the huge circulation of the *New York World* and took every opportunity to present her case to the readers through her letters to the editor. Upon learning about the twelve women jurors, she told the paper: "I am grateful to the *World*, and to its woman jury for the interest which they have taken in the trial. I know the jury is composed of twelve more than usually intelligent women, and I know that they will be impartial enough to give me a fair verdict. It seems to me to have been an excellent idea on the part of the *World*, and I realize the generosity of the women jurors in giving up their time to a consideration of the case."[59]

While the burden of proof was on the side of the prosecution, the goal of the defense was to create enough doubt in the jury's mind so that they could not possibly convict Mary Alice. The defense did not have to come up with an alternate theory as to how Evelina died; they only needed to suggest alternatives that could help with that reasonable doubt. Brooke had already raised the possibility that Evelina had died because Dr. Bullman was incompetent, and in questioning Dr. O'Hanlon about the autopsy, Brooke had seized on the fact that Evelina's heart and kidneys showed signs of aging. Mr. Anderson, the manager of the hotel, testified that Evelina had borrowed fifty cents from him that morning, therefore perhaps she had committed suicide because she was in dire financial straits. He also suggested that Evelina had taken arsenic for her complexion.[60] Brooke had even suggested that perhaps Evelina had died from food poisoning, that the clam chowder had been bad.

John C. Shaw, Mary Alice's mild-mannered family lawyer, was chosen to make the opening address when the defense case started on the 16th. Although he had never participated in a criminal case, he told the jury that he had known the defendant for many years and that he was firmly convinced of her innocence. In fact, the very fact that she had sent her daughter Gracie with the clam chowder meant that she could not possibly have done it. He also declared that if the chowder had been poisoned, Mary Alice would have warned Gracie not to eat any of it before she left, instead of after she returned.

Shaw informed the jury that the defense would show that Mrs. Bliss had been depressed the week of her death, and that her thoughts had turned to suicide. While they couldn't prove that she had committed suicide, they could prove that she was addicted to the habitual use of arsenic. And there were gaps in the prosecution's case; there was no proof that Mary Alice had purchased arsenic, and the items in which arsenic was found, like the tea tray and the Japanese vase, had remained in the hotel until nearly a month after the arrest. Shaw even insinuated that Walter Scheele had put the arsenic in the victim's stomach.[61]

The defense called several witnesses to discredit Walter Scheele, the most effective being a young medical student named Albert Heppner, who claimed that Scheele told him that he wanted to return to Germany and secure a good position there, and that he realized the way to do that was to work with the prosecution and get a conviction in a high-profile case and that the Fleming case was fixed for that purpose.[62]

The next four defense witnesses were expert witnesses called to offer alternative explanations of Evelina's death. Dr. William Thompson stated that Evelina had died from shock and heart failure. He also stated that he had once gotten very sick from eating clam chowder. Dr. Rudolf Witthause thought that Evelina had died from ptomaine poisoning.

After the closing arguments, the jury went off to deliberate. While the jury was out, Mary Alice appeared very calm as she awaited her fate with her sister Florence. Florence, however, appeared on the verge of tears as she nervously waited for the jury to come back. Florence told a reporter that her sister was "just as nervous as I am but is trying hard not to show it." She also expressed regret that Brooke had not called on her to testify on behalf of Mary Alice, because she was sure she could have proved her sister's innocence.

After five hours of deliberation, the jury returned to the courtroom, but only because they had questions. They wanted more details about the history of the tea tray and Japanese vase. They also wanted clarification of the claim in the defense's summary that Scheele had found more arsenic in the victim's stomach than Mott had. The jury returned to the jury room for more deliberation.

At almost one o'clock in the morning on June 24, word came that the jury had reached a verdict. As they filed into the courtroom, two of the jurors appeared to be holding back tears, which some thought suggested that they had reached a guilty verdict. Mary Alice was visibly shaking and supported by one of the matrons of the Tombs. This was the first time that the defendant had shown fear during the six weeks of her trial. When the foreman of the jury answered, "Not guilty," and the other jurors nodded in agreement, the courtroom erupted into loud cheers.

Everyone except for Goff and the prosecution team leapt to their feet. Mary Alice was hugged by her lawyers and surrounded by dozens of reporters offering their congratulations.[63] Goff then announced, "Mary Alice Livingston Fleming, you are discharged." She crossed the Bridge of Sighs back to the Tombs for the last time. She was greeted by loud cheers from the other inmates and the warden. "I was so glad to hear that she had been acquitted," said the warden, "that I had not the heart to stop the cheering."[64]

Both the *Journal* and the *World* carried large illustrations of Mary Alice on her first day of freedom, picking up her daughter Gracie at the Gerry Society (New York Society for the Prevention of Cruelty to Children), where she had been since her mother's arrest. Mary Alice informed her daughter that she had a new baby brother. After picking up baby Robin from the Tombs, they went to John Shaw's summer home in New Jersey to pick up Walter and Averill, who had been staying in private homes during the trial. The reunited family spent the summer in New Jersey.[65]

After her acquittal Mary Alice was portrayed very differently in the media. In the first few weeks after her arrest, the newspapers had portrayed her in a negative light, but in the subsequent months, during the long trial, they had gradually grown more sympathetic toward her. With this, and their frequent references to her baby and her children, and by publishing her letters, they had influenced the public, and perhaps some jurors, in her favor.

Several jurors talked to the *Journal* about their deliberations and attempted to explain their verdict. The initial vote had been nine for acquittal and three for conviction. After several hours of deliberation, one juror changed his vote, and the count became ten to two. At midnight they informed Goff that they were deadlocked, but he urged them to continue to deliberate. Within an hour the two holdouts gave in. The general conclusion from the jurors was that there was not enough concrete evidence to convict Mary Alice.

The *World* reported that their woman jury was three for conviction, seven for acquittal, and two "not proven," which at the time was legally equivalent to acquittal. Several of the jurors voting for acquittal said that they had a hard time believing that Mary Alice would have taken the risk of letting her ten-year-old daughter carry a pail of poisoned chowder. Two of the women who voted Mary Alice guilty argued that the defense had not adequately answered the evidence presented by the People. "I have attended the trial for a week and heard every word of the defense," one said, "I must confess that it seems weak and adequate."[66]

The trial and the verdict also continued the discussion about capital punishment, especially as it pertained to women. One woman who had attended the proceedings throughout the trial wrote to the *Tribune*, "The evidence would have been sufficient to have convicted the accused woman if the punishment had not been death." "The death penalty is virtually abolished for women," argued an editorial in the *World*. Assistant District Attorney John McIntyre declared to the *Journal*, "It is almost impossible to get a jury to convict a woman of murder in the first degree," and he announced plans to draft a bill for the legislature to abolish the death penalty for women. On the other hand, there were many people who believed that the death penalty should apply equally to both sexes. "I don't think there should be any discrimination on the part of justice toward women," said one woman. "They should be held accountable and amenable to all laws, with exactly the same rewards and punishment as men."

Charles Brooke, the head of Mary Alice's defense team, died from intestinal cancer in February 1897, just eight months after her trial. Shortly after the trial, he told the *New York Times* that he had not been fully paid for his legal services, and he was contemplating suing Mary Alice. After Brooke's death, his son Lex did sue Mary Alice, on behalf of his father's estate, seeking

$12,500 in addition to the $7,500 he had already been paid by John C. Shaw. Shaw claimed that Brooke had been paid all that had been agreed upon, and the court agreed.

Although the *World* had portrayed Ferdinand Wilckes as the man who was to marry Mary Alice as soon as she was acquitted, he denied the claims. "It has been reported that we were to be married as soon as Mrs. Fleming was discharged," he said to the *Journal*, "but there is not a word of truth in the report. Not a word on that subject has passed between Mrs. Fleming and myself." However, he added, "We are still good friends." Clearly from Mary Alice's letters, nobody believed that they were just friends. Mary Alice, however, felt differently. Perhaps she hoped that if she announced it to the papers, it would become reality. She was quoted in the *Boston Daily Globe*, "He is the father of my children, and to be frank with you, I am very proud of him . . . he wants to make me his wife. His nearest friends approve. Is it not a natural sequence that we should marry?" But Mary Alice and Ferdinand Wilckes never plighted their troth. Perhaps Ferdinand was wary of Mary Alice despite her acquittal.

When gold was discovered in the Klondike, Mary Alice and her teenage son Walter decided to head north to seek their fortunes. She left behind her other three children in the care of her sister Florence and a nurse. While she probably wasn't planning on panning for her gold herself, no doubt she was looking for a potential husband who had, one who might not know of her reputation or the murder trial.

There she met a man named Harry Frey, whom she married in 1898. By 1899 Mary Alice and her new husband returned to New Jersey from Alaska, and she purchased her old home in Toms River. She had two more children, but, in a few years, her money was all gone and so was her husband. Mary Alice appeared in the papers again in 1902 when she sued her former attorney John C. Shaw, claiming that he had not given her all the money from her Livingston inheritance. Mary Alice did not win this case, and soon the house in Toms River was in the hands of the mortgage company. She spent the rest of her life in New York City, with a few brief sojourns to San Francisco to spend time with her half-brother Clarence Livingston, who was nineteen years older than she was. She died in a nursing home at the age of eighty-seven in 1948.

MARY FARMER
(1880-1908)

The sleepy village of Watertown is the county seat of Jefferson County, New York. It is located approximately twenty-five miles south of the Thousand Islands, and just thirty-one miles south of the Canadian Border. Named after the many falls of the Black River, the city developed early in the nineteenth century as a manufacturing and industrial center. Today it is the home of the Little Trees Air Fresheners, but in 1908, Watertown was a bucolic, quiet city. No one suspected that it would one day be known as the site of one of the most gruesome murders in the history of Jefferson County, what one newspaper called "a particularly fiendish crime,"[1] all due to one woman's envy of another woman's home.

On the morning of April 23, Patrick "Paddy" Brennan woke up at six in the morning, had breakfast, and then went off to work at the Remington Mill. His wife Sarah was due to go into Watertown for a dentist appointment that day. At nine thirty-five that morning Sarah Brennan was seen walking across the lawn to the Farmers' house. She was never seen again. What happened to Sarah Brennan, and the events that led up to her death would not be out of place on an episode of "Women Who Kill."

Patrick and Sarah Brennan had lived in their home on "Paddy's Hill" in Hounsfield, just outside of Watertown, for twenty-five years. It was apparently a nice home, and the land was able to support an additional residence, known as the Barton house, where the Farmers moved in as tenants sometime in 1907. From all outward appearances, the arrangement seemed to be working out. The Farmers paid the Brennans approximately two dollars a

Watertown Times

week for rent. The Brennans were good landlords, and the Farmers were good tenants.

The two couples were also friends. Patrick had known James Farmer for many years. James had grown up in Watertown, and they would both spend their lives working in the paper mills. The Farmers were often at the Brennans' house, eating and drinking. A veteran of the Spanish-American War, James and his wife Mary had recently had a child, a boy named Peter. Patrick and Sarah had lost their only child, a daughter named Mamie, at the age of sixteen in 1901. No doubt Sarah often helped Mary out with the baby.

No one knows what led Mary Farmer to take the actions that she did or what led up to her planning a murder; she never explained what led her down this path. Like many Irish immigrants, Mary struggled. She had emigrated from Ireland in 1900, and like many Irish women, she had worked as a domestic, first in Binghamton and then in Buffalo. She met James Farmer, a millworker, in Buffalo and married him in 1904.

Was it simply envy that the Brennans had a good life and were no longer struggling, while Mary was stuck living in a hovel, with an infant and unemployed husband who was a little bit too fond of his beer? The couple were so poor that they'd had to take a mortgage out just to buy groceries. Was Mary so desperate that she thought that if only she had the Brennan house, her life would be better? Did she conceive her plot after James lost his job at the same factory where Patrick had been his immediate supervisor?

It all began when Mary stole the deed to the Brennan house. She knew that Sarah kept the deed in a black oilcloth purse. It would have been easy enough to steal it on one of her many visits to see Sarah. On October 31, 1907, Mary went to the office of Burns & Burns to see Francis Burns, claiming to be Sarah Brennan. There, she transferred the deed to the Farmers, for the sum of twenty-one hundred dollars (roughly fifty thousand dollars today), forging Sarah's signature. On January 7th, 1908, the Farmers then deeded their illegally gained property to their ten-month-old son. And then the Farmers did nothing.[2] Some speculated that the delay was due to "timidity to commit the deed and the presence of relatives."[3]

Rumors, probably originating from Mary, had been heard around Brownville for several weeks that Sarah had deeded her property to the Farmers. This way it would more easily explain the ultimate disappearance of Sarah and the Farmers moving into her home. When Patrick heard the rumors, he asked Sarah about them, who dismissed it as fictitious gossip.

Thursday, April 23, 1908, started out just like any other day for the Brennans. Patrick woke up at six o'clock, had breakfast, and then left for his job at the Globe Mill where he ran the boiler. Sarah had an appointment that morning to see her dentist in Watertown. When Patrick returned home that afternoon, he found the front door locked, which was odd. He looked for the key that Sarah had always left behind one of the shutters, but it was nowhere to be found. Fetching tools from the barn, he decided to take down the front porch storm door while he waited for her to come home. As he started to work, James Farmer came over and waved him off, telling him that he had no right to take down the storm door, since he, James Farmer, owned the place now.

Patrick was astounded. Had James been drinking? What in the world was he talking about? This was *his* home!

James informed Patrick that the house was his, that he had bought it in October and that the deed was at the county clerk's office. Furthermore, Sarah had agreed to pay the Farmers two dollars a week in rent, and she was in arrears. Patrick couldn't believe what he was hearing. Sarah had never mentioned anything to him about selling the house. It must be a mistake. He sat on the front porch for some time waiting for Sarah to come home and explain, but she never arrived.[4]

Brennan took the ladder from the barn, opened a second-floor window, and spent the night in what he still considered to be his house. Friday morning, he went to work as usual. After work, he went into town to find out what had become of his wife. When he went to the dentist's office, he was told that she never showed up for her appointment. Patrick was convinced that something had happened to Sarah, so he went to the police but was told that nothing could be done if Mrs. Brennan wanted to leave.

In the meantime, the Farmers went into Watertown, to the offices of attorneys Field & Swan, to prepare the legal documents ordering Brennan off the property, which were served to him that afternoon by Constable Asa Sherman. Patrick ignored them and continued living in what he still considered to be his home.[5] He soon noticed that Sarah's clothes were still in the wardrobe, so she could not have gone far.

However, when Patrick returned home from work on Saturday, he found that the Farmers had moved into his house. Brennan later testified that Mary told him that he could live with them for free if he was good to them. Meanwhile Sarah still hadn't returned. According to the Farmers, Sarah was visiting a friend in Watertown, but when Patrick went into Watertown, calling at the places where his wife usually visited, he was unable to find any trace of her.

After spending the night in the Riverside Hotel, Patrick consulted an attorney, Floyd C. Carlisle. Carlisle was concerned enough that he told Patrick to contact Sheriff Ezra D. Bellinger. On Monday morning, April 27, Bellinger and Patrick went to see Francis Burns. He remembered that a woman named Sarah Brennan had come to his office, where she registered a deed for the transfer of her house and property to James and Mary Farmer. When Bellinger asked for a description of the woman who called herself Sarah Brennan, Burns told him that she looked to be in her late twenties. His description matched that of Mary Farmer, not Sarah Brennan, who was fifty-five.

That afternoon Sheriff Bellinger, along with Detective E. J. Singleton, attorney Floyd J. Carlisle, and Patrick Brennan, arrived at the Brennan house and asked Mary Farmer to produce the deed proving that the Farmers now owned the house. When James Farmer told the sheriff that he couldn't come in, Bellinger produced a search warrant. Unable to deny the sheriff entry, they reluctantly let him in. Mary produced the deed from a black oilcloth envelope and showed it to him. When Sheriff Bellinger questioned Mary regarding Sarah Brennan's disappearance, he noticed that she turned pale, but she said that she knew nothing about it.[6]

The men proceeded to go through the downstairs of the house thoroughly but could find nothing suspicious. The Farmers stood by, watching with great indifference. The men then proceeded to the bedrooms. At this point Patrick must have been frantic: Where was his wife? In the back kitchen Bellinger found an old black trunk covered with rope. He asked Patrick if the trunk belonged to him. Mary waved her hand. "That's just an old trunk full of rags. We've even forgotten what's in it. The lock is rusted and we've lost the key."

James Farmer told Mary that there were some keys in a dish on the table, that maybe one of those might fit. Mary got the keys but none of them fit the trunk. James then told the sheriff and his men, "Boys, why don't you smash it open?" He gave them a hammer, and the sheriff broke the lock.[7]

When Bellinger finished, he opened the lid to find a horrific sight, the bloody and mangled body of Sarah Brennan. Her skull had been crushed with a blunt instrument and wounds covered her body. The sickening odor of decaying flesh pervaded the room. It was impossible to immediately identify the body stuffed inside the trunk. A black skirt had been draped over it, but the stocking feet poking out from the edges of the covering suggested that it was a woman. A removal of the cloth dispelled any doubt of the victim's fate.

Although the body was already in the first states of decay, the body mutilated beyond recognition, Patrick Brennan recognized his wife's clothing at once.

"My god, Jim, did you do this?" he exclaimed.

"As God is my judge, I did not," answered James.

James and Mary Farmer were immediately taken into custody. The Farmers were taken to the police station and booked for first-degree murder. While James remained silent, Mary sang like a bird. "She came to my house for a visit. Somebody was passing by and she went to the window to look out. While she had her back turned, I got the axe and raised it and brought it down on her head as hard as I could. It was the only way to get such a nice house. I had wanted it for years." According to Mary, James had helped her with the fake deed, the cleanup, and the move into the Brennan house.

One newspaper reported, "When a deputy remarked that her dreams in the same room as the trunk must have been bad, she replied with a smile that they were not so bad."[8] Mary was given permission to keep her son Peter with her in her cell. She immediately asked for a mop and a pail of water to clean her cell, scrubbing to get it sparkling. This seemed odd given the state of the Farmers' home. Rubbish of all kinds littered the rooms. The yard around her home appeared to be a dumping ground for all kinds of unsightly material. When she wasn't taking care of her son, Mary spent her time writing long letters of wifely devotion to her husband, who occupied a cell on the floor below in the county jail. James never received the letters, however; they were kept by the sheriff.

The coroner of Jefferson County, Dr. Charles E. Pierce, took possession of the grisly remains in the trunk to the local undertakers, Box, Donaldson & Co., in Watertown, where a postmortem was conducted. They found that the left ear had been hacked off, there were three defense wounds on the left wrist, both lips had been cut straight through, and a long gash was made on the forehead over both eyes where the ax had broken through the skull. The left jaw was fractured, and it appeared that the victim had been struck from the side first and then "blows had been rained down upon the face to finish the job."[9] This contradicted Mary's version of sneaking up behind Sarah Brennan and hitting her with an ax.

The crime shocked everyone in the community when they heard the gory details. People wracked their brains to try and understand what motivated James and Mary Farmer to murder their neighbor, a woman who, as far as anyone knew, had shown them nothing but kindness. "How many sleepless nights they experienced in concocting this devilish deed may never be known to the public; what other schemes they had in mind for the taking of the life of Mrs. Brennan, whose little property they sought, before they hit on the idea of striking her with an ax and placing her body in a trunk may go down into the history of the case as unknown."[10]

Yet Mary didn't look like a depraved murderer or at least what one presumed one would look like. "Mary Farmer little looked the part of the fiendish act of chopping to pieces the body of her who had befriended her. Slight of frame and with pleasing features, little of the devilishness inner nature seems to have delineated on the woman's physical makeup, and yet these very deceiving qualities are what enabled her to gain the confidence of Sarah Brennan."[11]

Mary continued to confess, and confess, and confess, although she changed her story repeatedly. After telling the police initially that she had done the deed, she then turned around and claimed that her husband was the sole perpetrator. "I may as well tell the truth: Jim did it. I found him leaning over her body in the sitting room. He had the axe in his hand, and said to me, with an oath, 'That's the end of her.'"[12] She later claimed that she and Sarah Brennan had a quarrel in which her and her husband's character were called into question. Did Sarah perhaps confront Mary about the rumors about the house?

On the morning of May 1, 1908, four days after Sarah Brennan's body was discovered, James and Mary Farmer were arraigned in court in front of Judge George W. Reeves. The couple had separate lawyers. Brayton A. Field represented James, who pled "not guilty." Mary's lawyer, E. Robert Wilcox, also pled his client "not guilty." The *Re-Union* said, "As far as expression goes, she was as immobile as a statue and looked straight ahead, never shifting her glance. During the time that she sat there, not a muscle moved, and she was motionless. Her face was neither flushed nor pale, but it was easily seen that a terrific struggle was going on in her mind."

The coroner's inquest was being held under the direction of Coroner Pierce at the Brownville Hotel. It drew a large crowd; thirty-eight witnesses were to be called to testify. Coroner Pierce himself questioned all the witnesses. During the inquest, the police searched for a lath hatchet; the hammer in the Farmers' possession did not have blood on it. In her various confessions, Mary told the police that the murder was committed in certain rooms in the Farmers' home, but so far, the police had only found tobacco stains and small traces of blood, but nothing that was consistent with such a bloody crime. A stain found on the door frame of the bedroom didn't match Sarah Brennan's blood. Another room, where the walls were covered in wrapping paper, were examined but no bloodstains were found. The police also looked for a bottle of chloroform, which may have been used to subdue Sarah Brennan, but they could not find the chemical in the Farmers' house.

Peter Farmer, James's elderly dad, was called to testify at the inquest. The *Watertown Daily Times* reported, "The elder Mr. Farmer is a fine-looking old gentleman and won the sympathy of nearly all. Several times his voice broke as he told different parts of his story. He said that he lived with his daughter Mrs. Alice Doran, near the 'Barton house.' He testified that on the night of the fatal Thursday, Mrs. Farmer came to his house with a long black pocketbook which she concealed under the cushion of the Morris chair."[13] When Patrick was recalled, he was shown the pocketbook in question. He said that it looked exactly like one Sarah had owned.

The coroner's inquest reached a verdict that Mary Farmer had murdered Sarah Brennan and then took over her home. They concluded that the murder was committed in a back room in the home in which Mary Farmer had formerly lived, into which the deceased was last seen to go.

On May 6, the grand jury was empaneled. James Farmer was brought into court first, shackled to Undersheriff Charles Hosmer. Dressed in a brown pair of trousers and a dark blue coat and vest, Farmer appeared disheveled and in need of a shave. A moment later Mary was brought into the courtroom by Sheriff Bellinger. She had on a blue skirt and wore a heavy short plush coat with a knit shawl over her head. As far as expression, she was as immobile as a statue, looking straight ahead, never shifting her glance.[14] Both Mary and James Farmer pled "not guilty" to the charges.

Mary's lawyer, E. Robert Wilcox, moved to have the charges against his client dropped, because there was no proof that Sarah Brennan died from her wounds or that Mary Farmer caused them. The motion was denied, and Mary Farmer was held over for trial. James's lawyer, Brayton A. Field, moved to have the charges against his client dismissed due to lack of evidence. There was no proof that James Farmer was connected with the murder or that he knew about it. This motion too was denied.

On Thursday, May 14, the grand jury handed down indictments charging James and Mary Farmer with one count each of murder in the first degree. If they were found guilty, it meant the death penalty. They were also charged with stealing the property of the Brennans. When they were informed of the indictments, Mary gasped, while her husband continued to remain silent.[15]

The trial was set for the second week of June. The prosecution was ready, armed with damning evidence against the couple, including Mary's confessions. As the trial began, the *Syracuse Herald* reported, "The only motive that the prosecution could uncover was one involving pure, unadulterated greed by the couple."[16]

Mary's trial was scheduled first, with Justice Watson M. Rogers presiding. A graduate of Albany Law School, Rogers had "become the acknowledged leader of the Jefferson County Bar." District Attorney Fred B. Pitcher led the prosecution, assisted by Floyd L. Carlisle, who had been at the Brennan home on the day Sarah Brennan's body was discovered. John B. Coughlin had joined Mary's defense team along with E. Robert Wilcox. Wilcox conducted much of the defense for the Farmers. He had a reputation as a tough defense attorney. Mary Farmer was the first woman ever put on trial in Jefferson County. One hundred people were crowded in front of the courthouse to see her arrive for her trial.

The jury was selected two days later. A Watertown newspaper noted, "Farmer, the accused, raised her eyes from the carpet which she had studied so intently for the three days previous and . . . scanned the faces of the twelve who had her life in their keeping."

The burden of proof was on the prosecution, but as attorney Floyd Carlisle said in his opening statement, they had plenty of evidence. He detailed for the jury how the Farmers had schemed to forge the purchase of the Brennan property and then reregistered the deed to their infant son Peter. The couple didn't immediately seize the property. Instead, they waited until April to set their fiendish plot in motion.

Patrick Brennan was the first to testify for the prosecution. He told the court that he had known James Farmer for years but had only recently gotten to know his wife Mary since they had moved back to Brownville. After the Farmers moved into the Barton place, Mary Farmer had regularly called on Sarah Brennan. He identified the black oilcloth pocketbook that had been in Mary Farmer's possession as belonging to his wife. It was the one that she kept important papers in, including a passbook from the Jefferson County Savings Bank that had a balance of $540.10.

The prosecution called several witnesses to establish that there was no way that the Farmers could have afforded to buy the Brennan property. They'd had to take a mortgage out for $51.99 to pay for groceries and provisions. Louisa F. Reinwald claimed that Mary had an outstanding debt of $312.01. The defense objected to this line of questioning, and the court ruled that it was inadmissible.

In the little settlement of "Paddy Hill" everyone knows everyone else, and the chief event of the day is a trip to town. Many of the neighbors testified as to the comings and goings of Mary Farmer and Sarah Brennan on the day of the murder. They all agreed that they had seen Mrs. Brennan enter the Farmers' home around nine that morning but never saw her leave, although they did see Mary Farmer coming and going all day. Mrs. Charles Baker swore that she saw Mrs. Farmer "running back and forth from her house to the Brennan's a dozen times," beginning around nine twenty.[17] A neighbor, Ann Collier, testified that Mary Farmer possessed a small hatchet the size of a hammer. Mabel Blake, a former boarder, said that Mary Farmer had told her the previous winter that she had bought the Brennan home for $1,200.

More incriminating was the testimony of twelve-year-old Edith Blake. Edith testified that she had gone to the Farmers' and cared for their son on the day of the murder. Her answers were clear and concise, sticking to her story despite cross-examination. Edith told the court that James Farmer swore and took some keys from his pocket and passed them to his wife, saying he did not want them. Mrs. Farmer then said, "To hell. You won't get a d—[sic] cent of money." Her testimony gave the impression that the Farmers quarreled at the noon hour. Edith then told how Mrs. Farmer had gone to Doran's and returned, getting some paper from a drawer and again returning to Doran's, where her husband was at work. Once at home again, Mrs. Farmer told Edith to tend the baby while she cleaned the back room, taking some clothes from the bedroom. Mrs. Farmer then sent her to a store for some camphorated oil. It developed during the questioning that Mrs. Farmer was very careful to shut the door to the room that she was cleaning so that Edith was unable to see what was going on.[18]

Philip Smith, who lived one house to the east of the Brennan house, agreed to help the Farmers move their belongings into the Brennan house on the morning of April 25. Smith said that he first saw the black trunk sitting near the window in the east room of the Farmers' home. Smith also testified to getting a gallon jug replenished with ale three times while the moving was going on, Mary Farmer furnishing the money for the beverage. All the men drank the ale, but Smith could not say whether Mary drank any. Mary told Philip that she would ask Mr. Tierney to help him carry the trunk, because her husband and Mr. Callahan were drunk, and there was something in the trunk she wanted to be very careful with. The trunk was heavy enough to require two men to carry it, and while it was being moved from one house to the other, Mary followed close after it.[19]

William Tierney corroborated Smith's testimony "of how the trunk was carried and followed in close succession by Mrs. Farmer." Tierney said that Mary Farmer told him there was something breakable inside the trunk and to be very careful while carrying it. The testimony affected the jury greatly, as did seeing postmortem photos of Sarah Brennan's brutalized body, which was brought in as evidence, shocking the court.

James Farmer's sister, Alice Doran, told the court that back in November 1907, James Farmer had asked her to take the deed into town to be recorded because he couldn't take the time off from work. When Alice arrived at the house, Mary Farmer had given her the deed, along with two dollars to file it at the county clerk's office. She took one look at the deed and recognized that the signature was Mary's not Sarah Brennan's. She told her brother of her suspicions, but he denied them. Alice refused to record the deed, so James did it.

She testified that Mary had told her that she had purchased the property from Sarah Brennan for twelve hundred dollars, far less than what the property was worth.

"The woman must have been crazy," said Mrs. Doran.

"Crazy or not, I have the property," replied Mrs. Farmer.[20]

Alice Doran also told the court that Mary Farmer had shown up at her house on the day of the murder at about two o'clock to speak with James, who was helping that day. Doran testified that Mary Farmer handed her husband a bunch of keys and said, "There are your keys. Go and see Paddy Brennan and tell him his wife has gone and he has no home." She said that her brother was apprehensive over his wife's demand, which was very upsetting for Alice to see.

Mary's defense lawyers realized that they were going to have a tough time proving that she was not guilty. Their only hope was to prove that either Mary Farmer was insane or that she had killed Sarah Brennan in self-defense, but there were very few witnesses to prove their theory. Wilcox tried to suggest in his opening argument that Sarah Brennan had sold the property to Mary Farmer because of her fear of a slander suit being brought by Mrs. Albert Baker. The prosecution immediately objected, claiming that any such evidence was hearsay and couldn't be admitted.

Mary McDermott, who once boarded with the Farmers, told the court that Mary once cut off a chicken's head with a pair of scissors, daring it to live. John Farmer, one of James's nephews, claimed that Mary once denied knowing him, even though they had known each other for several years. Under cross-examination by the prosecution, he admitted that Mary owed him money, and that by claiming she did not know him, she could avoid paying him back. Father Pontier testified that the Farmers had asked him to bless the Brennan house after they moved in, because Mary was worried that the "Protestants would burn it down."

The defense called Dr. Robert Gates, who had been Mary Farmer's physician for three years, delivering her son. He testified that Mary had suffered a difficult birth and that she suffered from what is now known as postpartum depression, had trouble sleeping, and was nervous all the time and often heard noises and smelled things. She had told him that being home alone with her son all the time made her feel suicidal. Normally a tidy housekeeper, Mary had become sloppy, and the house looked unkempt. Mary also had told Gates that she had begun having fits when she was thirteen.[21]

The final witness was Dr. Royal Amidon, an expert in nervous diseases, who had been brought in to examine Mary Farmer to ascertain her sanity on May 23rd. He testified that Mary had told him that both of her parents had gone insane. Amidon concluded after a physical examination that Mary suffered from hereditary insanity going back generations. On cross-examination by the prosecution, Amidon admitted that killing another human being for money indicated sanity. He explained that while Mary's actions of concealing the body and stealing the Brennans' property were rational, blaming the murders on her husband was irrational. He also stated that it was possible for someone insane to act with great cunning.

The jury deliberated for about three hours before returning with a guilty verdict. The *Oswego Daily Times* reported, "Mary Farmer appeared to be unmoved by the announcement." Justice Rogers moved quickly to sentence Mary to death in the electric chair, setting the date of execution for August 2, 1908. Mary was sent to the death house at Auburn Prison. One paper reported that "owing to the fact there are no vacant cells in the condemned row, Mrs. Farmer will be held in solitary confinement in the women's prison until additions are made to the number of cells in the condemned ward."

Several newspapers pointed out that thus far Mary Farmer had shown no empathy for either the victim, Sarah Brennan, or her widower Patrick. "The only sign of feeling displayed by her from the time she left Watertown until her incarceration was when the big gate at the prison swung open to permit the party to pass. On the threshold, she shuddered and took a last hasty look outside."[22]

Mary Farmer's lawyers quickly announced that they would file an appeal on her behalf if Governor Charles Evans Hughes denied the application to commute her sentence to life imprisonment. Patrick Brennan immediately began legal action to have the forged deeds declared null and void so that he could regain possession of his property. The Farmer's infant son Peter was put in the care of John Conboy, a member of the Farmer family, and then sent to the Ogdensburg orphanage in St. Lawrence County.

While Mary Farmer sat on death row, her husband's trial got underway. The local newspaper called it "the final act of the tragedy, which had its prologue in a little house in Brownsville one stormy day in April."[23] Six months in prison had given James Farmer time to dry out. The *Watertown Daily Times* noted, "James D. Farmer has been in the county jail since his arrest on April 25. In court, dressed neatly and soberly, clean, and sober, and much lighter in weight after six months imprisonment . . . In that respect his is a great disappointment to the crowd of morbid sensation seekers who pack the courtroom every day, many of whom would be much better employed doing their housework and taking care of their families."[24]

The big question in James Farmer's trial was what was his alleged role in the murder of Sarah Brennan? When did he know about Mary's scheme of forging the deed? While James was involved in the property transactions, it seems possible that Mary duped him by claiming to have saved up the money for the Brennan house from his paychecks. As far as District Attorney Pitcher was concerned, James was as guilty as Mary. "Never in the history of Jefferson County has there been a crime which could measure to this in cold deliberation and in a cruel and relentless pursuit of a criminal purpose." Farmer's attorneys insisted that their client knew nothing about the murder until the trunk was opened.

The same witnesses who were called upon to testify at Mary's trial also testified at James's trial. Poor Patrick Brennan was once again called upon to repeat the story of how he came home from work to find his wife missing and that he was being kicked out of his own home by people he had considered friends and the search for and then the gruesome discovery of his wife's battered body in the trunk. Alice Doran testified that Mary Farmer asked her to take the deed to Watertown to have it recorded. She repeated her suspicions that the signature on the deed was not that of Sarah Brennan but Mary's. Alice became very concerned that something criminal was going on. Alice told the court that she had asked her brother several times if he had ever spoken to Sarah Brennan directly about transferring the deed, and he admitted that he had not.

The defense vigorously argued that James Farmer could not have murdered Sarah Brennan, because he was at his sister's house the entire day working. James Farmer took the stand in his own defense. He testified that he believed that the signature on the deed belonged to Sarah Brennan and that his wife had paid for the property. He emphatically stated that he did not help murder Sarah Brennan or cover up the crime.

Despite his testimony, James Farmer, like his wife, was found guilty of first-degree murder and sentenced to die in the electric chair the week of December 13 pending an appeal. On November 2, James Farmer was taken to Auburn Prison, where his wife was incarcerated. For the next year James Farmer sat on death row while his lawyers frantically tried to find a way to save his life.

In January 1909, the New York State Court of Appeals heard Mary Farmer's appeal. The *Auburn Citizen* reported, "It is stated on pretty good authority that both Warden Benham and Superintendent Collins consider the woman insane." A month later the Court of Appeals denied her appeal unanimously. The Court of Appeals declared it was "clearly a deliberate and intentional act" and that there were no circumstances that "mitigated against its heinousness."

The decision of the court was not unexpected given that Mary Farmer confessed to the murder. E. Robert Wilcox, her attorney, gathered additional materials, including letters from a prominent physician and alienist who had examined Mary and found her to be insane, to present to the governor in the hopes that he would commute her sentence to life imprisonment, but there would be no reprieve for Mary Farmer. On March 22, Governor Hughes denied Mary clemency.

Her date with the electric chair was now set for March 30, 1909. The *Oswego Palladium* reported that "Mrs. Farmer received her death sentence with blank indifference, soon recovering with a slight start as the Warden and the others left. She sat on the edge of her bed and efforts to learn her wishes regarding the offer of strangers for the adoption of her infant were fruitless."[25]

Despite the knowledge that she was going to her death, Mary still hadn't shown an ounce of empathy or remorse for her crime, her husband, or her child. In her last hours Mary was visited by her spiritual adviser, Reverend John J. Hickey, of the Holy Family Church, the Catholic chaplain of the prison. Hickey counseled her to make a statement to exonerate her husband before her death. When he told her that she could see her husband before her execution, Mary finally showed some emotion. "I would like to see Jim."[26] Mary and James were given the chance to see each other twice, but they were never allowed to touch or to speak in private.

James Farmer was moved to another part of the prison on the day of his wife's execution to spare him from hearing Mary as she was led to the execution chamber. She would be accompanied by Reverend Hickey, who prayed with her in the days leading up to her execution, and the two female attendants who had remained constantly by her side since she had first arrived at Auburn.

Mary wrote a simple statement that was notarized, with instructions that it should be released only after her death. She also left an additional statement with her lawyer, to be given to her son when he was old enough to understand. The *New York Times* wrote, "It is said to be full of endearing terms, good advice to the boy to live as he should live, and prayerful words that he may be spared through all his life from any consequences of her rash act."[27]

At six o'clock in the morning on March 30, 1909, Mary Farmer and Reverend Hickey prayed together, and she received the last sacrament dressed in a plain black shirtwaist and skirt, her hair brushed back from her forehead and in two braids. Two or three locks were cut from her scalp so that the head electrodes might be properly adjusted, and the women attendants slit the left side of her skirt as far as the knee and cut the stocking.[28] Hickey was beside her for the march from Cell 7 to the chair, approximately ten steps. Three women witnesses—Dr. H. M. Westfall and Agnes Baird and Margaret T. Byrne, both nurses—also followed. After the usual test of the apparatus had been made, Warden Benham gave a signal, and Mrs. Farmer was led in.

The *Watertown Re-Union* of March 31, 1909, wrote, "The Farmer woman walked unfalteringly to the death chair. Her eyes were half-closed, and she saw nothing of the death chair and rows of witnesses. In her hands, she clasped a crucifix, and as she was being strapped into the chair, Father Hickey stood by her side and offered prayers for the dying."

The prison physician acknowledged that Farmer was dead with the first shock, but because her muscles continued to twitch, two more shocks were given, each with 1,840 volts. She was declared dead at six fifteen in the morning. Mary Farmer was put to death almost ten years to the day after the first woman ever executed in the electric chair, Martha M. Place. After Mary was pronounced dead, her body was removed for autopsy. During the postmortem, the physicians were shocked to find a photograph of her two-year-old son under her dress.

As promised, Reverend Hickey released Mary's statement to the press:

To Rev. JJ. Hickey:

My husband, James D. Farmer, never had any hand in Sarah Brennan's death, nor never knew anything about it till the trunk was opened. I never told him anything what had happened. I feel he has been terribly wronged.

James D. Farmer was not at home the day the affair happened, neither did James D. Farmer ever put a hand on Sarah Brennan after her death.

Again, I wish to say, as strongly as I can, that my husband, James D. Farmer, is entirely innocent of the death of Sarah Brennan; that he knowingly had no part in any plans that had led to it, and that he knew nothing whatever about it.

Signed

Mary H. Farmer

Mary was buried in the Saint Joseph Catholic Cemetery in Auburn, New York. Arrangements had been made for her burial by her husband through Reverend Hickey. The photograph of her son was placed in her clasped hands. Just before Mary's death, Madeline Z. Doty, one of the first women lawyers in the state, wrote a letter to the *New York Times* arguing that

Farmer's life should be spared. It was poverty and concern for her child that led to the crime, she wrote:

> She had little pleasure in her life, and when she grew to be a woman and had a baby of her own, she resolved it should have what she lacked. Can you imagine a woman, a mother nursing a small baby, deliberately taking an ax and hacking up a human body unless she had a red twist in her brain? She is not to blame for that red twist . . . for no woman whose whole environment was good would murder another human being in cold blood for the sake of a few dollars, unless that woman were an atavist or insane."

She was not asking that Mrs. Farmer be set free, but that her sentence be commuted to life in prison.[29]

James Farmer would not share the same fate as his wife. On October 19, 1909, Farmer's murder conviction was struck down, but he was still not in the clear. District Attorney Pitcher went before a judge asking that the indictment against James for first-degree murder be thrown out. Instead, Pitcher wanted a new indictment charging Farmer with being an accessory to murder as well as forgery, and his case was remanded for trial.

James Farmer's second trial began on February 22, 1910. The same witnesses who had been called for Mary Farmer's trial and his first trial were called again. And the same attorneys who had represented him at his first trial represented him at the second, along with E. Robert Wilcox, who had defended Mary. District Attorney Pitcher, assisted once again by Floyd S. Carlisle, tried the case for the People. According to the *Herald,* "The evidence was about the same as his first trial. The prosecution tried to show his presence in the house at the time the killing took place and tried to show that he knew of it then or immediately afterwards. The defense offered evidence to show that he was not at the house at the time, and that his actions afterwards showed a man free from any guilty knowledge."

After four hours of deliberation, James Farmer was found not guilty. *Watertown Daily Times* reported,

Thereupon began such a demonstration from the hundred people gathered in the room as the old courthouse has seldom seen. Men and women stood up to cheer, the hand clapping drowning the whacking of gavels in the hands of the court and the clerk. Deputies called out for order and as the din subsided the voice of the judge rang out. Instantly, the room was as quiet as a vacant house. "Officers, if you have seen anyone applaud, bring him before the court," Judge Emerson directed. "We will see if this demonstration can't be stopped."[30]

Realizing that he was unable to get a conviction for accessory after the fact, District Attorney Pitcher dropped the forgery charge. James Farmer was now a free man. He regained custody of his son Peter. They lived quietly, and little is known about the rest of his life. He died at the age of sixty-nine of a heart attack in 1934. He was buried in Glenwood Cemetery in Watertown. His obituary read, "Mr. Farmer was held in high esteem by residents of the Brownville section. They believed him innocent of the charge from the first, and it was his friends that enabled the case to be carried to the court of appeals."[31]

CELIA COONEY
(1904-1992)

THE BOBBED HAIRED BANDIT

All Celia Cooney wanted was for her child to have a better start in life than she'd had. After all, that is what mothers do, right? It was certainly more than her own mother had ever done for her. But how were she and Ed going to take care of a kid, in one crummy room? On only one income? Ed had insisted that she quit her job in the laundry when they found out she was pregnant. Not that she minded no longer having chapped hands. Ed had a good job at the garage, but it wasn't enough. Babies needed so much: food, diapers, clothes, and a crib.

It was love at first sight for Celia and Navy veteran Ed Cooney when they met at the Fulton Theatre in Brooklyn. While Ed was tall, blond, and blue-eyed, with a real nice smile, Celia was petite, just a tad over five feet tall, with black hair and black eyes. "They say that people fall in love with their opposites, and I expect it's true," Celia later said. Celia and Ed "kept company" for a few months before Ed bought her an engagement ring, a sweet little thing with a red stone. By May they were married and living together in a furnished room. Celia had a good job working at the Ostrander Company, earning twelve dollars a week, and Ed took home thirty dollars working in a garage. But they were not saving any money; they were spending it as fast as they made it. Both Ed and Celia liked the finer things in life, especially nice clothes. Ed insisted on buying her a real sealskin coat so that Celia would be warm during the winter.[1]

But now they had a baby to think about. Celia wanted a real home, a decent home, but how could they afford it? One night, Ed mentioned that

the "stick-up business," was an easy way to get money. On the night of January 5th, he borrowed one of his boss's motorcars, making sure to doctor up some phony license plates to mislead the police, and drove to pick up Celia.[2] Ed had purchased two guns for three dollars each, and a handful of bullets. The couple decided to hold up a store first, even staging a practice session in their apartment. "I put on my hat and coat and put the little automatic in my pocket. So we moved the table over, and Ed stood behind it like he was a clerk and I pretended to walk in and ask for a dozen eggs, and he pretended to give them to me and as he was handing them, I backed off and pulled the gun out of my pocket and said 'Stick 'em up quick!' Just like I'd read in a magazine."[3]

For Celia it was like something out of the detective magazines and cheap pulp novels she devoured. "I had been reading magazines and books about girl crooks and bandits and it began to seem like a game or play acting after Ed really came home with the guns. It was more exciting than anything I ever thought I'd ever do."[4]

Now the night they had been practicing for had come. Although her nerves almost got the better of her, Celia quickly calmed down when Ed returned with the motorcar. Celia thought she "looked pretty nice—seal coat, beaded grey dress, black shoes and stockings and a cunning tam. I had dolled up like I was going to a party in everything I had."[5] It was nine-thirty, dark, and freezing; the cold kept people off the streets. Celia and Ed figured there would be a lot of money on a Saturday night, and they waited patiently until there were only a few customers in the store. There on the corner of Seventh Street and Seventh Avenue in Park Slope, Ed and Celia found their target—a Thomas Roulston grocery store, part of the new grocery store chains that were putting neighborhood stores across the country out of business.

Ed eased up, leaving the motor running. There were no customers in the store, just the clerks in their white coats. Celia was to enter first and ask to buy something, while Ed kept a lookout. If things were clear, Ed would enter, and Celia would start the holdup.

At first Celia was unnerved when she saw six male clerks in the store, some of them as big as her husband. She walked up to the manager at the cash register and asked him for a dozen eggs. While the manager was wrapping up the eggs, Ed walked in, and Celia knew that her big moment had come. She took two steps backward and pulled a gun from her pocket. "Stick 'em up! Quick!"

Having exhausted her one line, Ed took over, telling the manager and the clerks to get in the back. While Celia held her gun on them, Ed rifled through the cash register, grabbing bills and coins and stuffing them in his pockets. He noticed an envelope sticking out of a little safe, so he grabbed it too; he hit the jackpot, as it was full of tens and twenties.

"Don't make a move! If you want your head blown off just try and follow us out," Ed yelled. Celia went out of the door first, while Ed covered the clerks. The sidewalk was clear, the engine still running. They hopped in the car and took off like a shot. Back at their room, Ed counted out the money. They had scored six hundred eighty dollars. It would be their biggest score in their short careers as bandits.[6]

The next morning there was a story in the *Brooklyn Eagle* about the robbery. "Woman with Gun Holds Up Six Men." Celia was described as a "richly dressed woman in a fur coat, good-looking, about five feet five inches in height, of dark complexion, with bobbed hair." Ed wasn't considered worthy of a physical description. For the newspapers, the big story was that the robbery involved not just a woman, but a woman with a gun. Even the manager of the Roulston grocery couldn't believe that a woman had done it.[7]

Celia Cooney was a movie villain come to life, a tough-talking, hard-boiled woman bandit. In the *Eagle's* version of the story, Celia boldly commands the clerks: "Get to the rear, you fellows. And move quick, you sons of guns. If you try any steer, I'll pump you full of lead." Celia as the boss made much better copy than yet another gun moll. Girlfriends often acted as lookouts or drove the getaway car. A bandit Queen who called the shots was a novelty that sold papers. A bossy woman with a gun tipped the balance of power.

Celia and Ed used their ill-gotten gains to rent the parlor floor and basement in a two-story frame house at 1099 Pacific Street. It was not far from his job and a block from his mother's house.[8] Then they went shopping for furniture, which came to more than a thousand dollars. Celia convinced Ed to do an installment plan, two hundred dollars now, and then fifty dollars a month. In less than a week all the money was gone. It turned out that it cost a lot of money to live like the people in the magazines. Celia was no longer working, and Ed's thirty dollars a week wasn't enough to pay the rent on their new place or the fifty-dollar installment plan.[9] To keep up their new lifestyle, they would have to keep stealing.

They spent the week in the basement practicing their shooting before heading out to rob an A&P in Brownsville. The robbery netted them less than a hundred dollars, so they decided to push their luck. They headed to the Bedford section of Brooklyn to another chain grocery store, this time an H. C. Bohack Company. The Bohack job turned out to be a little better moneywise, two hundred fifty dollars.[10] The money was great, but Celia wondered where the excitement of their first job was. After only three stick-ups, Celia was already lamenting that robbery had turned out to be just another job, just one that paid better.

The excitement that Celia was seeking turned out to be seeing her exploits splattered across the Sunday papers. "Bobbed Hair Girl Bandit Terrorizes Brooklyn," and "Pretty Girl Robber Raids Stores" were just some of the headlines. "Who'd ever thought that little Cecelia Cooney, working in a laundry at $12 a week, would be all over the front pages of the newspapers like that? Gee! I felt big! And I couldn't see why Ed sat so sore, still bent over the pages."[11]

After the robberies on January 12, Celia and Ed were no longer just another pair of bandits in Brooklyn. Their crimes caught the attention of the media across the city, who recognized a good story when they saw one. In 1924 New York City had eleven daily newspapers and Brooklyn had four; today the city has only three. Each paper scrambled to get the story and to get it first. If they didn't get it first, then they put their own spin on the story.

All of New York City was amused by the antics of the Bobbed Haired Bandit, a smartly dressed woman, armed with a "baby automatic." Dozens of column inches were penned on the "gun miss," while readers alternately sympathized, gushed, and raged in letter after letter to the papers. While the *New York Times* was read by the professional and upper-middle class, Hearst's *Journal* and *American*—and the new kid on the block, the tabloid *The Daily News*—catered to the lower-middle and working class of the city. The story of "the Bobbed Haired Bandit" was the perfect story for the cut-throat, competitive newspaper business, all looking for the next big scoop. A gun-toting female bandit that the police couldn't seem to catch had everything: drama, thrills, conflict, morality, and a role reversal that made the story leap off the pages. So, what if it wasn't actually true, and Ed actually did all the tough talking. That wasn't going to sell papers.

Celia seemed to some to epitomize all that was wrong with the twenties. Young women throwing off the shackles of Victorian morality to drink, have sex, and commit crimes. It was an exciting time but also an anxious one. The old ways were broken. Long hair was seen as feminine and virginal, while bobbed hair was a sign of youth gone wild and the decline of Western civilization.

All this publicity, while great for circulation, was bad news for both the police department and the mayor of New York, John F. Hylan. Newspaper editors who disliked Mayor Hylan used the story of the Bobbed Haired Bandit to attack his administration and his police commissioner, Richard Enright. Most of the tabloids sold the story as the wily female bandit vs. the Keystone Cops of the New York Police Department. With each false clue and every fruitless roundup, the press roasted the police, using the Bobbed

Haired Bandit as proof that Mayor Hylan was powerless to stop the lawlessness of the Prohibition era.

Richard Enright, the police commissioner, was the first in the history of New York to be selected from within the ranks of the New York Police Department. Traditionally the police commissioner had been selected more for his political connections than experience or effectiveness. A prominent example was Theodore Roosevelt, who had been an assemblyman in the New York State Legislature before he was tapped to serve as police commissioner from 1895 to 1897. Hylan promoted Enright from lieutenant to the top job only five years earlier in 1919. His rise from the ranks kept Enright loyal to the cops on the beat, but it meant that he had no power base outside of the force and his boss, Mayor Hylan.

Enright faced political pressure to appear in control of law and order in the city. Crime was up in the city. If the cops couldn't stop people from drinking, that meant they were either incompetent or corrupt. When they needed someone to blame for the frequent charges of favoritism, corruption, and incompetence, he bore the brunt. Making matters worse, the crime spree was taking place in his own turf; he lived on St. Mark's Avenue in Brooklyn. But he still had the support of the mayor, who believed the press was the real problem.

The police were flummoxed, anxious to make an arrest. Faced with ridicule from the press, they set up a massive hunt for the Bobbed Haired Bandit, placing roadblocks and arresting and stopping all bobbed haired women who looked suspicious. F. Scott Fitzgerald claimed that even his wife Zelda, who sported the popular hairstyle and drove a car, was stopped on the Queensboro Bridge in Queens and accused of being the infamous bandit.

On January 14th, Enright announced that he had caught the bandit, a twenty-three-year-old actress named Helen Quigley, but he had the wrong dame.[12] Helen's only crime was her bad taste in men. A teenager named Vincent "Apples" Kovaleski confessed, after a little light coercion from the police, that he had committed the three robberies that Ed and Celia had committed and that Helen was his accomplice. Helen loudly proclaimed her innocence, admitting that she had agreed to go out on a date with Vincent but then she had stood him up. Clearly, he was sore and trying to get back at her. Unfortunately for Helen, three store clerks picked her out of a lineup.[13] She was formally charged with assault and robbery, along with Kovaleski, and held on ten thousand dollars bail each. While the cops were sure they had their man, or dame in this case, the newspapers weren't so sure that it was case closed.

Celia had an attack of conscience that this poor girl was taking the heat for a crime she did not commit. And there was also the little matter that she was getting all the headlines as well. Celia had started to get used to seeing their exploits in the paper, and she did not want to share. Since the cops were staking out all the chain stores and grocery stores, Ed and Celia decided to rob Weinstein's drugstore instead. They ended up with only a measly fifty dollars, but Celia left a note for the police that mocked the police's failed efforts. "You cops are a bunch of hokum. You're inefficient. The girl you've just arrested is the wrong one. Let the poor, innocent girl go. I'm the one that knows about the robbery. She knows absolutely nothing, as does the big boob locked up with her," the note read. The contents of the letter were reprinted in almost all the papers.[14]

Not only had the police arrested the wrong girl, but there was also a rash of copycat robberies. It seemed like every flapper and her boyfriend was getting in on the act. The same night that the Cooneys were holding up Weinstein's, another bobbed haired bandit acted as a lookout, while two men robbed a drugstore. This was a problem for the cops. Helen Quigley's arrest was supposed to be the end of the bobbed haired bandit. Now there were two of them out there. The press had a field day with the news. But it didn't help Helen Quigley, who had her bail doubled to twenty thousand dollars.[15] Soon any young woman with dark-bobbed hair and a sealskin coat was a potential suspect. The cops arrested Mary Cody, the mother of five children, and nineteen-year-old Rose Moore, on suspicion of being the bandit.[16]

Captain Carey had to explain why the police hadn't been able to apprehend the couple. "One reason we haven't caught her is that we have an insufficient number of uniformed policemen to patrol the streets of Brooklyn." He also pointed out how little they had to go on. No fingerprints were left behind, and the couple didn't stay long enough at the scene for the victims to get a good look at the perpetrators. Commissioner Enright held a special meeting of the detectives in the department and basically read them the riot act. Heads were gonna roll if the Bobbed Haired Bandit wasn't caught and brought to justice. Two hundred and fifty plainclothes detectives were ordered onto the streets of Brooklyn,[17] plus the regular force of patrolmen was beefed up with officers fresh out of the academy. They were given orders to shoot and kill on sight.[18] Eventually they created a special "Bob Squad" consisting of eight Brooklyn detectives.

Reporters speculated on who the Bobbed Haired Bandit could be.[19] A number of detectives interviewed insisted that she was a drug addict. What other reason could there be for such bold and brazen behavior from a young woman? The thing that troubled people the most was that she could be anyone, their daughter, their next-door neighbor, a co-worker, someone on a bus, or a female Jekyll and Hyde, hiding in plain sight. No theory was too bizarre. Maybe she was a man dressed like a woman to throw cops off the scent. The cops arrested two young men who were standing outside of a drugstore solely because they were dressed like flappers. Although they could not be picked out of a lineup, they were charged with the crime of robbing the Weinstein's drugstore. They were eventually released.

The Cooneys' crime spree came to an abrupt halt on April 1, 1924, at the National Biscuit Company's payroll office. It dawned on Ed and Celia that Brooklyn was getting too hot for them. Everyone was talking about the Bobbed Haired Bandit. The robberies that the couple were pulling off, while drawing a lot of media attention, often brought in just enough money for them to survive on. The baby was due in two months. What if she went into labor in the middle of a job? But they were broke, and getaways cost money. To secure their future, they needed one big score, and then they'd blow this town.

Celia was game. It meant saying adios to their families, but they felt that they had no other options. Ed had planned it all out; the payroll office at the National Biscuit Company was not far from their house. They would hold up the payroll office and then head for Jacksonville, Florida. Ed was sure that he could buy into a garage down there with the money, and Celia could give birth in a hospital.

The whole plan was ill-conceived from the beginning. While casing the joint, Ed noticed that there were an awful lot of people working in the office, more than they expected. The other problem was that Ed had grown up in the neighborhood. There was a very good chance that someone might recognize him. Their next mistake was hiring a chauffeur to drive to Brooklyn. Not only did they have to subdue him and throw him in the back of the car, but he too could identify them.

On the day of the robbery, the couple dressed as if they were going to a show. Ed wore a new overcoat and a fedora, and he carried a bandana to cover his face. Celia wore her gray beaded dress, her sealskin coat, and a turban, along with a heavy black veil. When they got inside the office, Celia noticed that there were twenty people inside. When the cashier, Nathan Mazo, tried to make a grab for Celia, who was eight months pregnant, she stumbled back and fell over a chair. Thinking she had been struck or cut, Ed fired two shots, injuring the cashier. It was the first and only time anyone had been hurt in one of their robberies. Thinking the cashier was dead, the pair fled in a panic, leaving behind eight thousand dollars in an open safe. Their final mistake was when Celia realized that she'd dropped a little notebook somewhere along the line.

Because it was a daylight robbery, the victims had gotten a good look at the couple, especially when Ed's mask slipped, revealing his face.[20] The cops finally had a solid description, but they still thought that Celia and Ed were holed up somewhere in the city. The cops had gotten a tip regarding the Cooneys from a neighbor, who saw them flashing money around, but they dismissed it. The cops in the neighborhood had known Ed since he was a kid. He'd never been in trouble with the law except for a minor scrape when he was a teenager. He was a big, friendly guy who always said hello, but as the investigation continued, one of the witnesses mentioned that the suspect worked in a nearby garage. The cops finally put two and two together and came up with Ed and Celia. Now that they had the right suspects, the Cooneys were charged with the crime, and police headquarters sent a circular with Celia and Ed's description to every city in the country. It requested that they be arrested on sight.[21]

Nathan Mazo's wounds were only superficial, but like several people connected to the case, he enjoyed his moment in the spotlight, casting himself in the role of hero. "Believe me if I'd got that gun, I would have saved the police a lot of trouble. I'd have killed them both," he told reporters as he lay in his hospital bed. Of course, the tabloids twisted the tale; the gun girl finally using her weapon made much better copy than Ed firing the almost-fatal shots. Celia was no longer just the Bobbed Haired Bandit, now she was outlaw "Jessica James."[22]

When the police reported that Celia was pregnant, the newspapers loved the new angle. Whereas Celia had been seen as a dope fiend, or a good-time girl, now she was just a young mother trying to do right by her child. Celia later wrote, "When I went into that first store and said 'Stick 'em up' I wasn't seeing diamonds, gin and jazz—I was thinking of little pink baby shoes, and that maybe the baby coming wouldn't have the rough time I had."[23] Many papers erroneously reported that Ed had lost his job, forcing them into a life of crime. Some papers resisted the Madonna-like makeover, insisting that having a baby was not a good enough reason to commit robbery. The *New York Times* insisted on treated Celia Cooney as a hardened criminal.[24]

The Cooneys fled New York on a Clyde Line steamer to Florida. On April 3rd, they arrived in Jacksonville, Florida, with only fifty dollars to their name and no hope of Ed getting a job. The papers were filled with not just the story of their holdup, but their names, aliases, and the news that Ed would likely be looking for a job in a garage.[25] They found the cheapest boarding house they could afford and holed up. They were now worse off than before they started. No job, no money, and the police breathing down their necks. On April 10th, Celia went into premature labor. Unable to stand seeing Celia in pain, Ed convinced her that they needed to find a doctor, despite their lack of funds. He found a local physician, Dr. Sisson, who insisted that Celia needed to be taken to the hospital immediately. After a difficult labor, Celia gave birth to a baby daughter.

With no money to pay for the bill, Celia and her baby had to leave the hospital immediately. The couple also had to move boarding houses, to one that did not require money upfront. But the baby, named Katherine[26] after Ed's mother, was sickly from the start. Two days after her birth, she died.

Although they were not able to have her baptized in time, the couple wanted to give their daughter a decent funeral. It was the undertaker who eventually led the police to the grieving couple.[27]

Ed and Celia were arrested early in the morning, when two New York cops, F. S. Gray and William G. Casey, knocked on the door at one in the morning at the rooming house where the couple were staying. Depressed after Katherine's death, Ed's thoughts had turned to death. He would shoot Celia, he said, and then turn the gun on himself. They were arguing about it when someone knocked on the door. At first neither of them said anything. Celia called out, "Just a minute, wait till I get my clothes on." Celia held an automatic while Ed held two revolvers in his hands. She opened the door, gun pointed at the floor, smiling suddenly at the startled policeman. "I won't shoot if you won't," she said and threw down her weapon.[28]

The capture of the Bobbed Haired Bandit made the front page of every major New York City newspaper, as well as the *Washington Post, Chicago Tribune, San Francisco Chronicle, Boston Globe,* and *Los Angeles Times.* The *Daily News* reported, "The spectacular career of the most-advertised desperado and her tall, male companion was ended—they are through." As she was brought up to New York City after her arrest, thousands of people turned out to see her as her train passed by. Celia couldn't help obliging them. This must be what it felt like to be a movie star.

The morning newspapers had published the time of her arrival. When she arrived in Manhattan, a large crowd greeted her. Coincidentally, President Coolidge and his wife were also at Penn Station on their way back to Washington, D.C. The *Brooklyn Eagle* estimated that ten thousand people were there to see her, and fewer than five hundred "view[ed] the departing Chief Executive of the nation." Coolidge, Schmoolidge! Celia Cooney was a hometown-girl-turned-celebrity. Silent Cal couldn't hope to compete with the petite gun moll from Brooklyn. The *New York World* described the crowd: "Neither Presidents nor Jack Dempsey had attracted such a throng to Pennsylvania Station as Celia Cooney, Brooklyn's Bobbed Haired Bandit and her husband Edward did when they reached this city at 3:30."

Women outnumbered men in the crowd. "They hung from every stairway and rail landing from the train level." Ring Lardner wrote that Penn

Station was "so crowded, with photographers and hero worshippers that the detectives can hardly get the couple out. Everywhere the little gal is greeted with smiles and the only wonder is that some of her admirers did not rush up and kiss her." It took ten minutes for the police to clear a path so that they could open the door to the train car where Ed and Celia were riding.

The chief of detectives, John S. Coughlin, and Detective Captain Daniel Carey, who ran the day-to-day operations in Brooklyn, were part of the group waiting to take the Cooneys into custody. No one had expected the crush of people who turned up at the station. There weren't enough officers to deal with the mob. After all the passengers had left the train, it was then decided to move the prisoners. Ed was taken out on the other side of the car and whisked up a back staircase. With four men guarding her, Celia faced a battery of flashbulbs going off like fireworks as she exited the train.[29]

An attorney, Sam Leibowitz, arrived with a writ of habeas corpus. A criminal defense attorney, he had been retained by one of Ed's brothers. Within a year, Leibowitz would be known as the man who successfully defended Al Capone. He saw the Bobbed Haired Bandit as his way of making a name for himself. Leibowitz had argued before a state supreme court judge that the Cooneys had been arrested without a warrant, which meant that they were being detained illegally. His plan was to prevent them from talking to the police further without counsel. Jail was a far safer place for them to be until the trial.

The cops were ticked off at Leibowitz's arrival. They thought it was an open-and-shut case. The Cooneys hadn't asked for a lawyer. And anyway, how could they pay for one? Inspector Coughlin also was annoyed. The plan was to rush the Cooneys downtown for questioning, then head over to Brooklyn to the district attorney's office for more questioning. They were to be arraigned that day and then indicted by the grand jury. But Sam Leibowitz was screwing up the speedy resolution to the case.

Instead of going to police headquarters, they headed straight to the supreme court on Chambers Street. Assistant District Attorney Walsh from Brooklyn and Assistant District Attorney Driscoll wanted Leibowitz away from the case. Judge Giegerich asked the couple if they wanted Leibowitz as their lawyer. Ed informed the judge that his brother did not have the authority to hire counsel. But after reading his brother's letter, Ed didn't know what to think. When Celia took the stand, she decisively waived right to counsel. Leibowitz was stunned that the Cooneys were throwing away their chance at a decent defense, but there was nothing he could do about it. Celia and Ed were surrendered to the police.[30]

The couple were then taken to the Brooklyn district attorney's office. Although the office tried to pin crimes on the couple that they hadn't committed, Celia and Ed admitted to committing ten robberies from their first on January 6th to the botched National Biscuit Company job on April 1st. The district attorney's office prepared ten separate charges of assault and robbery. Celia and Ed each tried to take the blame for their crime spree, in particular the shooting of Nathan Mazo. While Celia claimed that she fired the shot that hit Mazo, Ed refuted that, telling the cops that he only pulled the trigger after Mazo pushed Celia to the ground. "My wife didn't do that shooting," he insisted. "I shot the cashier."[31] Celia also took pains to point out that they never took money from their victims, only from the cash registers and stamp drawers. She also told the assistant district attorney that she had hoped that their final job would give them enough money so that they could get a fresh start in Florida.

Hughes was delighted that the Cooneys had confessed, and he seemed to like the couple. "They are much in love with each other, and each desire to shoulder most of the blame." The Cooneys were then escorted to the jail at Brooklyn police headquarters on Poplar Street. It was midnight by the time the couple finally arrived, and both were exhausted. Once in her cell, Celia made herself comfortable and went to sleep. Ed, on the other hand, was restless, pacing up and down, smoking cigarette after cigarette.

After a quick cup of coffee, and a dab of lipstick for Celia, it was time for the lineup, where the victims and witnesses were brought in one at a time. In every newspaper report, the couple alternately teased and taunted their victims.[32] On a serious note, Helen Foggerty, an employee at the National Biscuit Company, fainted after identifying the couple. When Nathan Mazo identified the pair, Celia told him that she was sorry that he got shot.[33]

The newspapers still did not know what to make of Celia. Was she a brazen criminal who enjoyed the limelight? Or a bereaved mother, remorseful about living a life of crime? Was she ready and willing to face the music? How repentant was she? And was it really just for the baby?[34] The *New York Times* pointed out that Celia easily could have had her baby for free in several charitable hospitals. Celia was deemed insufficiently distraught at the loss of her child. It would have never occurred to the mostly male reporters that Celia's grief was too deep for her to cry on cue. The press flip-flopped between these two narratives daily.

Of all the indictments handed down by the grand jury, District Attorney Dodd chose to press charges against them for their very first job, because of the large sum they allegedly stole, two hundred and fifty dollars, although Celia and Ed claimed that they came away with only sixty dollars. Warrants for the rest would be held with the respective prison authorities holding out the threat that they could face those indictments after finishing their sentences.

Samuel Leibowitz was not ready to give up just yet. He showed up at the courthouse, along with his partner, Jacob Sheintag, when Celia and Ed were about to be arraigned. Sheintag stepped up beside the couple, "Your honor, we represent these two. They desire to enter into a plea 'not guilty.'" Once again, after consulting with her husband, Celia spoke for them both, telling the judge, "We have no lawyers, don't want any, judge." They both pleaded guilty to the charges.[35]

Crowds turned up wherever the couple happened to be—at the courthouse or the jail.[36] The press was just as eager to be the ones to get Celia's exclusive story. At first, she played hard to get, but she soon realized that she could make some dough from the situation. William Randolph Heart's *New York American* got the scoop, paying a thousand dollars to tell her story,[37] serializing the "Bobbed-Hair Bandit's Own Story: The strangest, weirdest, most dramatic, human interest story ever written," in twelve installments over the course of two weeks. Hearst's King Features Syndicate distributed the story to papers across the nation. Each installment featured a staged photograph of Celia taken at the jail, along with her signature. The story was written with the assistance of reporter William Seabrook. An avid reader of the tabloids and pulp magazines, Celia understood how to shape her story for readers like her.

Celia and Ed were reunited on April 25. The couple, holding hands, were able to spend half an hour together. After their meeting Celia managed to get a message to Samuel Leibowitz to set up a meeting. Leibowitz, hoping that the third time would be the charm, went to the jail to chat with the couple. Celia had decided to fight after all, which made the press ecstatic. Leibowitz told the press that Celia "was rushed off her feet and did not know what she was doing," and now that she'd been given the time to think, she realized that "we ought not to have pleaded guilty." He explained to the *Sun*, "There are two main angles of defense in Mrs. Cooney's case. First there is high medical authority that she was mentally irresponsible throughout the period during which acts charged against her were committed. The truth of this will be demonstrated by calling prominent physicians to the stand."

Celia only agreed to the plan after Ed pleaded with her for an hour. Celia also wanted her husband to plead not guilty, but Ed refused, insisting that he take the blame for their string of robberies.[38] After months of the press treating him as less than a real man, Ed was stepping up to the plate and taking responsibility for leading Celia astray.

Judge Martin was not pleased at this turn of events. He decided to appoint his own "lunacy board" of four alienists: two to study Ed and two to study Celia, to determine their sanity. The couple's sentencing was put off until after the alienists could make their report. Leibowitz could have had Dr. Sissons take the stand to testify about Celia's mental state, that the pregnancy hormones could have led to her taking up banditry.[39] As for Ed, his mother and brother had revealed to Judge Martin that his father had died in an asylum, and they were concerned that Ed might have inherited his father's mental instability. There were some questions in the press, given Ed's sullen demeanor, that he might be mentally handicapped. In the twenties, it was believed that criminal behavior was some sort of mental defect, that criminals were less intelligent on average.[40] As for Celia, no normal woman could ever be a violent criminal, therefore she was not normal.

Celia and Ed were scheduled for a hearing at the county court, a hearing to schedule another hearing. The Cooneys were delighted to get the chance to be together, embracing in the back of the van, despite the two other prisoners. "How are you feeling, Eddie?" Celia asked. Ed smiled and answered that he felt "as well as could be expected under the circumstances." Escorted into the courthouse, Celia waved a handkerchief at her fans. Once inside they had to wait half an hour in the detention room. They were not accompanied by Samuel Leibowitz, who had no idea about the meeting. Judge Martin called the couple into his chambers. The proceedings in the judge's chambers were not disclosed.[41] After the meeting, Celia announced that she no longer planned to mount a defense, she was sticking to her original plea.[42] Judge Martin had convinced the couple to give up the fight. Poor Samuel Leibowitz had been outmaneuvered.

During the week before their sentencing, Warden Honeck allowed the couple to meet periodically. Otherwise, Celia spent her time reading magazines, while Ed found it difficult to pass the time. A few days before they were due back in court, Celia wrote to Judge Martin, asking that the couple be sent to the same prison. There was one last chance for Celia and Ed. The lunacy board still had to make its investigation and submit their report before sentencing. After being subjected to four different mental exams, interviewing her relatives, former employers, and landladies, the board concurred that Celia was sane. The official report on Ed was that while he was moody, he certainly was not insane.[43]

A report by Mrs. Marie Mahon, a probation officer, was submitted to Judge Martin just before Celia was sent to prison. It laid bare her horrific childhood, from her birth in a basement, to an alcoholic father who never seemed to hold a job for long, to an illiterate mother who stole Celia's clothes and deserted her in a room for three days. From early childhood Celia was sent out into the streets to beg. At night she slept on a coal heap. At the age of four, she was taken in charge by the Children's Society of New York but released into her mother's custody after less than a year. For a while Celia knew a measure of stability when she lived with an aunt in Brooklyn. She attended parochial school until she was fourteen, when she and her mother went to live with her sisters. But the mother deserted the family, returning to Celia's father. Until she was arrested, Celia hadn't seen either of her parents in six years.[44]

On May 6th, Celia and Ed arrived at court; she wore a new blue tailored suit for the occasion. Crowds lined the streets to get their final glimpse of the Bobbed Haired Bandit before she was sent up the river to the joint. The couple were sentenced to a maximum of ten to twenty years in prison, and, as Celia feared, they were set to serve out their sentences in different prisons, Celia at Auburn and Ed at Sing Sing. Spying her sister, who was there with their parents, she whispered, "Take care of my seal-skin coat."

Back at the Raymond Street jail, at first Celia seemed fine. About Judge Martin, she said, "He was a nice Judge. I expected the limit and I got it. I was not disappointed. I thought the Judge would give me a lecture, but he didn't. I deserved what I got."[45] In her cell Celia finally broke down and wept.[46] When Celia's mother, Mrs. Roth, came to say good-bye, Celia relented. When the warden returned, he found Mrs. Roth sitting on the bunk, with Celia's head in her lap, stroking her hair with knobby fingers.

When Ed was brought in, the officers turned away, as the couple embraced. "It'll be a long, long time; a long time," Ed moaned. "We've got to make the best of it."

"We got to, Ed," Celia agreed. "And the time ain't so long. We'll be together again, sometime, anyway." For a few minutes they talked in whispers until Warden Honeck said at last, "All right, Ed. Time to go."[47]

Celia arrived at Auburn in the custody of Mr. and Mrs. Marlow, the keeper and matron of the prison. She spent her first three years in prison working in the prison laundry. Then she learned typing and shorthand, and soon she was working in the office of the warden. By the end of her time in prison, Celia was teaching typing and shorthand to the other prisoners.[48] Ed wasn't so lucky. He had his fingers smashed in a machine in the prison auto shop, his left hand mangled so badly that it had to be amputated below the wrist.[49] He also contracted tuberculosis in prison and was sent to the TB hospital at Clinton Prison in Dannemora for the next five years. The couple wrote faithfully to each other each week.

After seven years the couple were released from prison. Ed was released first, in October 1931; Celia was released a few weeks later, on November 6.[50] She arrived in New York, wearing a new outfit, with forty-five dollars of state funds in her purse. As a condition of her parole, Celia was not allowed to act in a movie or write her life story. She was to avoid publicity at all costs or risk being sent back to prison. To comply, the couple refused to see any reporters. After his release from prison, Ed filed a one-hundred-thousand-dollar case against New York State for the loss of his arm. His lawyers, Samuel S. Leibowitz and Jacob Sheintag, won the case, which granted a settlement of twelve thousand dollars.[51]

The couple took the money and bought a small house on Long Island, but Ed never completely recovered from tuberculosis. He went to work for the Works Project Administration until he couldn't work anymore, and the family went on relief. The couple went on to have two children, Patrick and Edward Jr. but Ed didn't get to enjoy his freedom for very long. Two months after the birth of their second son, he died at the age of thirty-seven.

Celia spent the rest of her life in relative obscurity. She started using her maiden name, Roth, after Ed's death. Times were tough for the widow and her two boys. Celia had to sell the house on Long Island. The family moved around for a time before finally settling in Queens. Once the boys were older, Celia found steady work in a department store. She later worked as a typist and later still at Sperry Gyroscope. She remarried in 1943, but the marriage did not last long, and she kept her second husband's last name. By all accounts, including her sons', Celia was a dutiful and selfless mother, working to support her boys, one of whom became a deacon in the Roman Catholic Church.

After moving to Florida with her youngest son, Celia passed away in 1992. Neither of her children knew of her bandit past until after her death. They were shocked to find out that their mother had done time. "It was a terrible, terrible shock," her son Ed said. "I mean I just never *dreamed* that any of this had taken place."[52]

For a brief moment in time, Celia Cooney was somebody. She wasn't just a working-class girl who'd committed a string of petty crimes. She had transformed into the girl they called "the Bobbed Haired Bandit." To traditionalists, she was a symbol of the permissive society that gave too much freedom to women; to the writers of pulp fiction, she was the sassy antiheroine come to life; and to the mayor and the police commissioner, she was a petty criminal who made them look like fools.

RUTH SNYDER
(1895-1928)

THE DOUBLE INDEMNITY MURDER

Queens Village, just across the East River from Manhattan, was a picture-perfect suburb filled with Dutch Colonial and Tudor homes. It was a place where middle-class parents could raise a family, living peaceful lives far from the noise and pollution of the "city." Where children played stickball in the streets. Murders simply did not happen in bucolic Queens Village.

On Sunday morning, March 20, 1927, Mrs. Harriet Mulhauser was woken up by a phone call from nine-year-old Lorraine Synder. "Come over to the house quick," she pleaded, "Mama is very sick." Mrs. Mulhauser entered the front door and heard moans coming from upstairs. Dashing up the stairs, she found Ruth Synder lying on the floor in her nightgown. Her feet were bound loosely by a clothesline, but her hands were untied. Lying next to her was a second length of rope and a gag.[1] Ruth babbled hysterically, something about two Italian thugs who had whacked her on the head, and that her husband Albert had been attacked. Mrs. Mulhauser telephoned her husband and told Lorraine to go over to her house.

When her husband arrived, he loosened the ropes that bound Ruth's hands and feet. "They hit me over the head and tied me up," she said. "I'm afraid for Albert!" Mr. Mulhauser found Albert Snyder lying face down on one of the twin beds in the bedroom, his hands tied behind his back with a towel and his ankles bound with a red and yellow necktie. Looped around

his neck was a length of picture wire and lying on the floor next to the bed was a revolver. Visibly shaken, Mulhauser pulled a sheet over the body.

Mr. Mulhauser called to another neighbor, and the two carried Mrs. Snyder to her bed. Mulhauser then called for an ambulance and then the police. A doctor who lived nearby, Dr. Harry Hansen, was summoned. When Dr. Hansen examined Ruth, he found no evidence that she had been hit on the head as she had claimed. He told her that the headache that she complained of did not appear to be the result of a blow to the head. Ruth then claimed that it must have been from lying on the cold floor for so long.

At ten o'clock that morning, detectives showed up, along with Dr. Howard Neail, the highest-ranking forensic pathologist in Queens County. Examining Albert's body, he found a gash an inch long and a quarter inch wide on the right side of the head near the forehead, which was superficial but looked worse than it was. Just below it was a slight abrasion, and there was another directly on the back of the skull. There were also assorted minor cuts and scrapes. When Neail turned the body over, Albert's face was swollen and blue from strangulation. A cotton rag protruded from his mouth, and strips of cotton hung like worms from his nostrils. A cloth pad—wrapped in a blue, white-dotted bandana handkerchief with a border of anchors—was found lying on his pillow and reeking of chloroform.

A .38-caliber pistol was found on the bed. It was loaded with three rounds, and three loose cartridges were on the floor. A leather holster was found under the dead man's pillow. Underneath his body they found a second length of picture wire with a gold pencil clipped to it. Neail also examined Ruth. He noticed there were no signs on her wrists of her having struggled free or any bruises from lying on the ground for five hours. "Five hours! Five minutes would be more like it!" he said when he was told that she claimed to have been unconscious for five hours. Only after she was finally told that her husband was dead did Ruth manage to squeeze out a few tears.

Ruth told the detectives a confused account of the events of the night before. She and Albert had gone out to a bridge party. The couple, along with Lorraine, didn't return home until almost two in the morning. Her mother, Ruth explained, was away on a nursing job, so they had had to take Lorraine with them. Her husband dropped them off at the front door and put the car in the garage. For about five minutes, while she and Lorraine went upstairs, the front door was open.

Ruth informed the detectives that she and Albert slept in separate rooms. Sometime after she went to bed, she thought she heard Lorraine in the hallway, and she got up to check on her. That is when she was grabbed by a large man. He dragged her into her mother's room, and she heard someone call out to him. She claimed that her assailant was swarthy with a mustache and that he looked Italian. He knocked her on the head, and she was unconscious for five hours. "It was about eight o'clock when I awoke. I was still and strained, bound and gagged. I had a hard time taking the ropes off my hands. Then I took the gag out of my mouth and tried to scream."[2]

The initial theory was that it was a burglary gone wrong. The house had clearly been ransacked. Even the sofa cushions and the pots and pans in the kitchen were tossed about. The contents of the dresser drawers in the Snyders' bedroom, as well as Ruth's mother's bedroom, were jumbled on the floor. Snyder's wallet containing $110 was missing, along with a coat, and Ruth reported missing jewelry worth $200. A search revealed the alleged jewelry wrapped in a rag and tucked underneath Ruth's bed. Ruth said her memory failed her and that she'd forgotten she'd hidden the jewelry there. A coat that she claimed was missing was found in the coat closet, along with a valuable leopard-skin coat.[3]

If burglary were the motive, it appeared that only Snyder's wallet was missing. The couple had nothing of value—no paintings, no objets d'art, no expensive jewelry. If money was all they were after, why not jump Albert when he was putting the car in the garage? Most robbers spend time casing a place they are about to rob. Why didn't they take the one obviously valuable item, Albert's watch, and chain? Also of note was the thoroughness with which the house was searched. Why was the kitchen, of all places, ransacked? Detectives estimated it took the burglars two hours to search. Burglary is time-sensitive, get in and get out. Things just did not add up. It looked like the house had been deliberately turned upside down to throw the police off the trail. If Ruth knew that her husband slept with a gun under his pillow, why didn't she cry out for him when she was grabbed by the assailant? There was also no sign of forced entry.

The police found a small book that contained several names and addresses. When Ruth was questioned about them, the police noticed that she got flustered when they came to an entry for an "H." Judd Gray at 37 Wayne Avenue in East Orange, New Jersey. They found this especially curious when a pin bearing the initials "J. G." was found on the floor of the master bedroom, and they also found several canceled checks made out to him. At first Ruth denied knowing him. She then recalled him hazily. Every question after that was about Judd Gray. When had she last seen Judd Gray? How often had she been seen with him? Ruth wept and refused to answer. When she was told they were taking her to the police station, she claimed that she was sick and demanded a lawyer. When a doctor confirmed there was nothing wrong with her, Ruth jumped out of bed in her negligee and proceeded to dress in front of the police.

At the police station members of the bridge party were also being questioned. The police worked all day long at the Snyder house and throughout the neighborhood, gathering details about the Snyders' home life. The police learned from other guests at the bridge party that while Ruth encouraged her husband to drink freely, she herself drank practically nothing, which was unusual given her previous behavior. Guests remembered that Albert and a man named George Hough had gotten into a pretty heated argument. However, Hough was able to prove that he had gone back to his hotel and hadn't left since.

Little Lorraine proved to be helpful, telling the cops that her mommy and daddy fought all the time because Mommy liked to stay out all night long. A neighbor claimed that Ruth often came home late at night via taxi. On one occasion, Albert came out and met her on the sidewalk, where they loudly argued in full view of the neighbors. When she was questioned about her late nights, Ruth snapped that it was none of their business! When Detective Carey from Manhattan told her that the crime scene did not look like a real burglary, flustered she asked him, "What do you mean? How could you tell?"

At the police station Ruth repeated the robbery story but was only able to give a very sketchy description of the murderers. One was described as a man with a black moustache, who spoke broken English. After fourteen hours of grilling, with detectives questioning her left and right while her requests to sleep were denied, Ruth finally broke down. She confessed that Judd Gray had murdered her husband. He had concealed himself in the room usually occupied by her mother.

Albert was deaf in one ear, so that night Ruth had made sure that he was lying on his "good ear," making sure that they would not be interrupted during the murder. The couple had gone downstairs, where they drank and Gray allegedly told her, "I can't live without you."[4] The murder was committed between three-thirty and four o'clock in the morning.[5] After they ransacked the house, Judd tied her wrists and ankles.

Things unraveled swiftly after that. Between tears and laughter, Ruth told them that Judd was in Syracuse, New York, at the Onondaga Hotel. By two-thirty in the morning, they were knocking on his door. The man who opened the door was nobody's idea of a stone-cold killer. Judd Gray was a slight, owl-faced man with a deeply cleft chin who wore thick-rimmed spectacles. He was fully dressed because he had just come in from having dinner with a friend. At first Judd shrugged his shoulders when he saw the police. He denied any knowledge of the crime. He told the police that he had been in Syracuse since Friday. A friend, Haddon Gray, no relation, told police that he had had lunch with Judd on Saturday. He admitted that he and Ruth were lovers, that they were in love, but he had never met her husband.[6]

But Judd had made several mistakes. When detectives searched his room, they found an iron pinch bar and a pair of rubber gloves. One of them found the L.I. Railroad train schedule and a ticket in the garbage can in his room. When the police discovered it, they had him dead to rights. He was handcuffed and brought back to New York City.[7] Initially Judd stuck to his story, but he wilted quickly. In a short time, he made a full confession. There was one difference between his confession and Ruth's. He claimed that while he struck the first blow with the sash weight, Ruth delivered another blow herself. And then the two of them wrapped the picture wire around Snyder's neck, thinking this would make the police think the crime had been committed by professional burglars.[8]

There was nothing about Ruth Snyder that suggested that she would be anything more than an ordinary woman. Born Ruth Brown on March 27, 1895, she was the daughter of a working-class Scandinavian family. She dropped out of school after eighth grade and became a telephone switchboard operator while attending business school at night, taking typing and shorthand. She was a hard worker and determined to get ahead, but like most women at the time, she thought more of marriage than having a career. Bright, pretty, and vivacious with bobbed blonde hair, she loved to laugh and have a good time. She was only nineteen when she met thirty-two-year-old magazine editor Albert Snyder, who took an interest in her.[9]

Although she was not in love with him, Ruth liked that Albert was older, well read, and more established than boys her own age. She also liked being wined and dined. A few months later, on her birthday, he proposed with a huge diamond ring. As Ruth told her friends later, she couldn't turn down that ring! But the cracks soon began to show in the marriage. Albert turned out to be staid and conservative, and he possessed a hair-trigger temper. The man who courted her with restaurants and flowers disappeared. While Ruth liked people and parties, Albert liked to go fishing, spending weekends on his boat. Albert didn't want to have children, whereas Ruth had dreamed of having a family since she was a little girl. When their daughter Lorraine was born, he was disappointed that she wasn't a boy.[10]

After first living in Brooklyn and the Bronx, they soon moved to Queens Village. For Albert, moving to Queens was a sign of success, but Ruth felt lonely and isolated away in the suburbs. There was also a shadow hanging over the marriage—the ghost of Albert's late fiancée, Jessie Guischard, who had died before the wedding. No matter what Ruth did, it was not good enough compared to the saintly Jessie. It was a pity, he would often tell her, that Ruth couldn't be more like her. To make matters worse, a portrait of Jessie graced their bedroom wall in a formal photograph, which followed them wherever they lived. Every time they had an argument, Albert would bring up Saint Jessie.[11]

Divorce was out of the question. In New York State in 1927, Ruth would have to prove either adultery or depraved mental cruelty. While Albert might have occasionally slapped Ruth, he wasn't physically abusive. Although she suspected that he was unfaithful, she couldn't prove it, not unless she hired a private detective or framed him for adultery. After ten years of marriage, Ruth was at the end of her rope. And she found a lover.

Sometime in June 1925 Ruth met the man who would become her downfall, corset salesman Judd Gray. They met when Ruth was having lunch with two friends. In walked an old friend of one of them, Harry Folsom with

Judd Gray. Like Ruth, he was unhappily married and had a child, a daughter named Jane.[12] He was tired of his domestic troubles and ripe to meet a woman who put him first. Accounts differ as to who made the first move, but it was soon after Judd returned from one of his sales trips that he invited Ruth to his office to pick up a corset. The couple consummated their relationship, and from that moment on, the two were inseparable.

Judd was in thrall to Ruth. When they were apart, he wrote letters to her calling her "Momsie" or "Mommy."[13] He had been dominated by women all his life, and Ruth was just another woman who used his weaknesses. She became his obsession. They would talk on the phone when Albert was at work, or they would meet for lunch if Ruth could get her mother to baby-sit Lorraine. Sometimes they took Lorraine with them; while Ruth and Judd were upstairs at a hotel, Lorraine would either sit in the lobby reading a book or ride the elevators up and down. Soon all the hotel employees knew the little girl. Judd would sometimes come for lunch at the house,[14] meeting Ruth's mother, who while she did not condone adultery, was happy that her daughter had someone who sincerely loved and took care of her. Judd would shower Lorraine and Ruth with presents.

Eventually Ruth decided that Albert did not have enough life insurance; he had taken out only a measly thousand dollars. Ruth managed to convince the Prudential salesman to sell Albert an additional forty thousand dollars in insurance. Ruth cleverly placed the policies in such a way that Albert thought he was signing just one policy but in triplicate.[15] She even managed to make sure that one of the policies paid out even if Albert met with an accident or grievous bodily harm. In other words, even if he were murdered, Ruth would be a rich woman.

After a while Ruth started talking about killing Albert, claiming that her husband was threatening to murder her, and that she needed to kill him first. Judd was reluctant to be a part of her scheme, but Ruth kept working on him, until he eventually caved and agreed to the plan. They both chickened out of their first attempt. It wasn't until a week later that they both plucked up the courage to go through with their plan.

After he was arrested, Judd quickly turned on Ruth. He claimed that he had never wanted to hurt Snyder but that she had hypnotized him into committing murder.[16] Judd never denied killing Albert, but he was simply Ruth's victim just like Albert. She was Eve in the Garden of Eden, luring Adam to eat the apple. He told the *Daily News,* "She would place her face an inch from mine and look deeply into my eyes until I was hers completely. While she hypnotized my mind with her eyes, she would gain control over my body by slapping my cheeks with the palms of her hand."[17]

Edgar F. Hazelton and Dana Wallace, a former district attorney of Queens County, were both retained for Ruth shortly before the arraignment. Both were well-known in Queens for their record of eleven straight acquittals in murder trials; their trademarks were pugnacity and enthusiasm. "We plead not guilty," Hazelton said, speaking for both defendants. The lovers were held without bail. Acting for the State was Richard S. Newcombe, district attorney of Queens County. He announced that he would go before the grand jury and that he expected indictments for first-degree murder. He would then move for a speedy trial for the defendants.

The scandal of the murder and its seamy details shocked polite New York society. The city's newspapers went into a collective frenzy over the story. From March 21, 1927 until their executions on January 12, 1928, New York's tabloids reported on the case in exhaustive detail, with the *Daily News* and the *Daily Mirror* running as many as eight articles a day.[18] Most of the 130 reporters who covered the trial were employed by the tabloid papers. Tabloid newspapers not only reported on the case, but they also molded public opinion of the murder, the trial, and, most important, Ruth and Judd themselves.

The mad dash for the sensational was the pinnacle in what became known as "the war of the tabs." That is, the city's three tabloid newspapers— the *Daily Mirror,* the *Daily News,*[19] and the *Evening Graphic,*[20]—vied for whose coverage could be most sensational or scandalous. The more respectable daily newspapers, like the *Herald Tribune* and the *Times,* saw the murder as a harbinger of civilization's end, the predictable result of Jazz Age hedonism. The *Herald Tribune* attributed the murder to "psychopathic suburbia" and said it heralded a "pale yellow dawn of a new decadence."

The couple's very ordinariness meant that the tabloids could mold them to fit any narrative that they chose, or to shape their agenda. Ruth Snyder led a life that was no different than any of the female tabloid readers. She had worked for a living before she married and became a mother. She had been married for twelve years, was a housewife and a mother. But within the pages of the tabloids, she was a "synthetic blonde murderess," a "vampire wife," and "Ruthless Ruth, the Viking Ice Matron of Queens Village."

She was simultaneously portrayed as a modern woman by the tabloids and a devoted wife and mother by her lawyer. It was the contradiction that people had problems with: the idea that Ruth could be both a modern woman and a devoted mother. Ruth was either a Madonna or a whore; she couldn't be both. Ruth was accused of being a bad mother who dragged her young child along while she trysted illicitly with her lover upstairs at a hotel. One newspaper described her as "a fattish, discontented Queen's housewife who never learned to say 'no.'"

In contrast to Ruth, Judd's wife Isabel was described as "a shabby little wife. She wore a beaver coat of inferior quality, and there was a long rent on the right shoulder. Her blue felt hat was not smart. Her black oxfords were a far cry from the nifty cream slippers that Mrs. Snyder wore in court."[21] She was the dutiful wife, the redeemer saint, who at first refused to believe that her husband could not only be unfaithful but commit murder.[22] She arrived at the jail to see Judd, as did Samuel L. Miller, who would be assisting in his defense. "The murderer ran to her and their arms locked in a long embrace. There was a long kiss too, and both wept like children, but neither spoke a word."[23]

It was a touching scene, with about forty newsmen eavesdropping, taking down every detail. "This miracle of love known as wifely loyalty," had journeyed all the way from East Orange, New Jersey, to present a united front for the press. But it would be the last time that Isabel Gray would visit her husband before the trial. And she was conspicuously absent from the courtroom during his trial. It was too painful and too public.

On the other hand, Judd Gray was seen as an awfully nice fellow, married to his childhood sweetheart, who taught Sunday school at the First Methodist Church. Even the detective who arrested him commented, "He's as nice appearing a gentleman as you'd want to meet." And his mother said that "he seemed normal in every respect."[24] But he was also a murderer.

How could that be explained? He must be insane! Judd's lawyers decided to go for the insanity defense. Four psychiatrists, two hired by the defense, and two by the prosecution, tapped his spinal fluid, X-rayed his head, and interviewed him for days, but they could not find him insane. Even the psychiatrists liked him. "Gray seemed more than ever a fine, cultured fellow," said Dr. Lahey.[25]

If he was not insane, then he must be a weak, feeble, feminine man who didn't have the moral fiber to stand up to Ruth's wiles. He was a "mama's boy," less than a man. If he were more of a man, he would have taken the rap for the crime, exonerating his lover. At five feet five inches, weighing no more than 130 pounds, and terribly nearsighted, Gray suited the idea of a weakling. He was no one's idea of a passionate lover. Some reporters changed their tune when they heard Judd testify in court. They were surprised to find that he had a rather deep voice, a prominent chin, and big jaw.[26]

While Judd's lawyer Samuel Miller tried to prove he was insane, Ruth's lawyers insisted that she was very much sane but had nothing to do with the crime and her confession was made under duress and was false.[27] Edgar F. Hazelton, one of her attorneys, stated that they would not only prove that she had been victimized by Gray, but also that he had pursued and persecuted many other women. Hazelton attacked Gray, saying that he was a coward, and "he not only committed this murder, but he tried to blame it on Mrs. Snyder, and he tried to entangle his friends in his crime."[28]

Her lawyers asked the court that Ruth and Judd be tried separately and not together. This decision could be given only by the trial judge. Joint trials gave the prosecution an advantage; it was almost inevitable that the case presented against one would incriminate the other as well. For defense lawyers, joint trials meant that the defendants were open to being cross-examined by the other defendants' lawyers. Both Ruth and Judd would be better served if they could be tried separately. Justice Scudder denied the motion. The two former-lovers-turned-murderers would be tried together.

If Ruth deserved the benefit of the doubt, so did Judd. On the other hand, Judd looked good in a joint appearance, and Ruth came off worse. A large part of this was her own fault. Her typical court outfit consisted of a tight-fitting, short, black crepe dress; a black velvet turban; black silk stockings; black kid gloves; and no makeup. The turban emphasized her square jaw, giving her a grim, determined look instead of that of a grieving widow. There was speculation that her clothes came from Paris, expressly for the occasion.[29] Her behavior helped her even less. She bantered with reporters and photographers, yawned openly, joked with the prison matrons, and allowed herself to be photographed reading various tabloids for publicity shots. She struck poses even when there were no cameras around, placing her elbow on the table and resting her chin in her hand.[30]

Ruth wasn't above trying to use the tabloids to portray herself as an innocent victim. Just before the trial she addressed a personal appeal for sympathy to all wives and mothers. The document, written in her own hand on three pieces of paper and passed out between the bars of her jail cell, contained a denial of the charge of murder and scorn for her former lover, whom she referred to as a "sneaking jackal who was trying to hide behind my skirts and who is trying to drag me down into the pit that he dug for himself and to brand me as a woman who killed her husband." She asked that the public withhold judgment of her and a plea that "mothers and wives abide with me in thought during this stifling ordeal."[31]

All discussions of her situation had to include how unjust it was. She refused to believe that she might receive a long prison sentence, let alone the possibility of the death penalty. Nothing short of a full acquittal would do. "I have no fear of the outcome because I know I am innocent," Ruth said "They can't send an innocent woman away for a crime which she did not commit. Not in this country."[32] Legally speaking, the only way for a full acquittal was if her lawyers could prove that Albert's murder was done without her knowledge or if she had been coerced into it by Judd by force. Everything depended on her description of what happened that night in March.

The trial of The People vs. Snyder and Gray opened a blaze of publicity at the Supreme County Seat, Long Island City. The presiding judge, Justice Townsend Scudder, hated criminal trials so much that when one came up on the docket, he would try and trade with another judge. When the Snyder/Gray trial came up, he was unable to find a way out. He announced that he would not tolerate an entertainment atmosphere; he barred photographers from the courtroom and the corridors during the trial. He also insisted that there would be no standing in the courtroom, nor would minors be allowed—and absolutely no picnic baskets either.[33]

Space was reserved for 127 newspaper writers, along with 110 spectators. Many of the seats were reserved for members of the bench and the bar. Special telegraph wires and facilities for rapid transmission of news had been installed, and in the press room, telephone booths with direct telephone wires.[34] Because the acoustics in the courtroom were bad, loudspeakers were set up so that everyone could hear. One seat was set aside for playwright, actor, and producer David Belasco, who requested permission to attend. D. W. Griffith was a regular attendee, studying faces and taking notes. British aristocracy was represented by the Marquess and Marchioness of Queensbury.[35]

The trial lasted eighteen days. The prosecution planned on calling between sixty and seventy witnesses. The central issue at stake was whether both defendants were guilty of the premeditated murder of Albert Snyder. For the prosecution, this was fairly simple. Both defendants had been at the house on the night of the murder and had played some part in the crime. Confessions had been obtained from both Snyder and Gray, and there were any number of witnesses to testify to matters such as the nature of their relationship, Ruth's unhappy marriage, and the taking out of the insurance policies.

For the defense, however, there was a major complication: Ruth, retracting part of her original confession, now denied participating in the murder, laying the blame for the planning and execution of the crime solely on Judd. Judd continued to maintain that Ruth had planned the murder, seducing him into being her accomplice. Throughout the trial, Justice Scudder went out of his way to instruct the jury that statements made on behalf of one defendant were not to be considered binding on the other. The trial inevitably became not so much one of the State vs. Snyder and Gray as one of Ruth vs. Judd, an opinion that was seized upon delightedly by the press.

Richard Newcombe opened the case for the prosecution, explaining how Ruth and Judd had planned and executed the crime. Most of his opening statement focused on Ruth, her face alternating fear and anger. For four days the State presented damning evidence to prove its case with a series of equally damning witnesses. They included Albert's brother Warren; Leroy Ashfield, whose testimony proved that Ruth had duped her husband into taking out the additional insurance policies; the office manager of the Waldorf Astoria; Dr. Neail, who presented the medical findings; and Judd's friend, Haddon Gray, who had initially provided an alibi for him.[36]

Edgar Hazelton began his defense of Ruth Snyder, claiming that Ruth had been a good wife and mother, much maligned by the press. She wasn't much of a drinker or dancer but a homebody, a woman who had loved her husband but been ill-treated and neglected by him. "In that home of no love," Hazelton exclaimed, "Judd Gray found a willing victim for his nefarious purpose and design." Admitting that Ruth had indeed committed adultery, he pointed out that this was not what she was on trial for and went on to state that the defense would prove that it was Judd's idea to murder Snyder for the insurance money. Judd's intention was to extort the insurance money from her.

Samuel L. Miller, in his opening statement for the defense for Judd Gray, did not deny his client's guilt, but aimed for the jury's sympathy by painting Ruth as a "designing, deadly, conscienceless, abnormal woman, a human serpent, a human fiend in the guise of a woman," who controlled Judd with a force he was unable to resist. Judd had been "dominated by a cold, heartless, calculating mastermind and master will." The defendant, he stated, "will present the most heart-rending, the most woeful and the most tear-stained drama of human helplessness, human dominion and human fallacy."

During the trial, the jury heard former police commissioner McLaughlin testify that Judd had told the police that Ruth had tried several times to kill her husband, including slipping him sleeping tablets and then disconnecting a gas jet in his room.[37]

The courtroom was packed the day that Ruth Snyder took the stand dressed in black, with a rosary and crucifix around her neck. Men and women fought and clawed for entrance to the courtroom, and once inside, they raced and pushed each other out of the way for seats. Ruth had already told two separate versions of what had happened that fatal night, and now she told a third story in court. She testified for two hours in a modulated voice that made her answers come across as pat and rehearsed. Renouncing her signed, sworn statement, she now claimed to have fought with Judd to prevent him from committing the murder. In this version, she left the doors open, not so that Judd could sneak in and murder Albert, but so that she could persuade him not to do the deed; she wanted to end their love affair.

During their conversation, she said, she left to go to the bathroom. While she was gone, Judd murdered Albert. When Ruth came out, she heard the blow, rushed into the room, and struggled with Judd, trying to save her husband, and then fainting. When she was unconscious, Gray finished murdering Albert. When she came to, Gray told her that she was in as deep as he was. "I was mortally afraid of him. I saw what a terrible man he was. I couldn't see any other way than to do what he asked me to do." This fear, along with police duress, led her to lie to them about what had happened and to keep on lying. Judd's motive was the insurance money; he planned on extorting it from her after the claim had been filed.[38]

She failed to impress the jury, however, and under skillful cross-examination by the prosecution and Judd Gray's lawyers, she came across as cold, glib, and self-possessed, repeatedly replying to leading questions with a calm "I wouldn't say that." At one point she was asked, "And in that letter Judd also told you he was going to finish off the governor (Albert)?" "Yes," she answered. Minutes later, when asked, "And all this time you knew that he was going to kill the governor?" she responded, "I did not know." The courtroom jeered at her contradictions and inconsistencies, and Ruth appeared to make several admissions of guilt.[39]

When Judd Gray took the stand, he offered no defense. As if he desperately needed to absolve himself by making a public confession, he told of Ruth's repeated attempts to kill Snyder, of how she constantly hounded him to commit the murder. Ruth had kept him intoxicated for weeks with alcohol and her charms. He went through the act of committing the murder in detail, "I struck him on the head as nearly I could see, one blow." He revealed that his shirt and Ruth's nightgown were covered in blood. After removing the bloodied shirt, Ruth handed him one of her husband's to wear.

For more than four hours, he spoke in short phrases uttered in a monotone, his eyes closed through most of the confession. The jury hunched forward, awaiting each word. Ruth sobbed uncontrollably during his testimony, wailing and falling across her folded arms. Under cross-examination by Ruth's attorney's, he remained unshaken, his testimony consistent with the facts of the case.[40]

Both Ruth and Judd announced from their cells that they were ready to face the verdict. Judd was resigned to what he considered to be an inevitable fate. "I'm not afraid of death. I suppose it is the chair for me. I told the truth and I feel better. I hope for the best, but I'm not afraid of the worst." Ruth, on the other hand, expressed her faith in the jury. "They won't send a woman to the chair," she was reported to have said. "I know the jury believes my story."[41]

On May 9, the prosecution and the defense made their closing arguments. Justice Scudder made his summation to the jury. He explained to them the different verdicts they could find and outlined the main facts of the case. The charge was first-degree murder. This was nothing more than the deliberate and premeditated killing of another human being. A lesser verdict might be murder in the second degree (if the intention were to kill, but there was no premeditation involved) or manslaughter (if there had been no intention to kill).

The jury was not obligated to bring the same verdicts against both defendants, the judge emphasized, adding, "The only question for you to decide is did they both, or did either of them, commit that crime? Are they both, or is either of them, guilty? Or are they innocent?" At five twenty in the early evening the jury went out. Less than two hours later they returned. When asked for their verdict, the foreman replied, "The jury find the defendants, Mrs. Ruth Snyder, and Henry Judd Gray, guilty of murder in the first degree." Following a motion requesting postponement of the sentence, they were remanded for sentence on May 13. Upon hearing the verdict, Ruth swayed for a moment, before dropping back down into her seat, covering her face with her hands. Judd stood still, looking aghast at the jury. A deputy touched his arm, and he sat down like an automaton. The guards led both prisoners back to their cells.[42]

Ruth spent her remaining days in the Queens County jail pleasantly, stringing beads for a handbag and reading the ten or twenty letters she received each day, only answering the ones that enclosed stamps. "If I had a life sentence to do," she remarked to one of the jail attendants, "I'd like to do it in Queens." Ruth was cheered that many of the celebrities who had attended the trial expressed their opposition to capital punishment. Maybe this would influence public opinion. She was also buoyed by the fact that Judge Scudder had openly expressed his aversion to the death penalty.

Although the courtroom was jammed as usual with spectators, there was a different feel on that Friday the 13th. All the celebrities had vanished after the verdict. The tables that had been set up for the press had been taken down, so the reporters milled around the room. As the defendants and their counsel waited, Ruth was in high spirits, giggling like a schoolgirl. Spectators would never have known that she was about to find out whether the State was going to put her to death. Hazelton lost his temper with her, warning her to stop laughing, that she was about to be sentenced to death.

At ten a.m. Justice Scudder took the bench, and the defendants were led before him. Ruth came first and stood to the left of the bench; Judd followed and stood about five feet away from her. For once the pair were not separated by their lawyers, only by an officer of the court. Ruth wore the same black dress that she had worn throughout the trial. No longer needing to impress the jury, she also wore lipstick and a bit of rouge, her blonde hair tightly marcelled underneath a black hat. Judd stood ramrod straight, clutching his daughter's copy of *A Child's Book of Prayer*. No relatives for the pair appeared in court as sentence was pronounced.

To the frustration of the spectators in the courtroom, the proceedings were conducted without the benefit of loudspeakers. People stood on radiators to get a better view until the bailiffs pulled them down none too gently from their perches. Justice Scudder asked if there were any legal reasons why the death sentence should not be pronounced. Hazelton read a lengthy statement on behalf of Ruth, but Scudder overruled him. The court clerk then repeated the question of whether there were any reasons why the sentence of death should not be pronounced. For a moment it looked like Ruth might say something, but Hazelton quickly responded to the clerk that there was none.

In identical words Justice Scudder sentenced Judd to die at the same time. Judd stood perfectly still, his hands clasped behind his back, his eyes studying the floor. Outwardly he looked composed and resigned, but underneath nausea, fear, and horror overwhelmed him. In ten minutes, it was all over. After sentencing, Judd released a statement to the press: "I am one of the best examples of what whiskey, lust and will ultimately lead one into. I have seen many pitiful cases here as an inmate of this jail, as to what liquor and improper relations will exact in retaliation that it makes me more than anxious to urge my fellow men to see the light of God as our only true salvation."[43]

After returning to her cell, Ruth cried, "God, oh God! I never thought it would come to this. Judd Gray is to blame for it all." She began to cry, her sobs rapidly becoming hysterical shrieks and moans as she fainted on her cot. She was tended by prison officials and several doctors from St. John's Hospital. She claimed that she suffered from epilepsy, the same illness that afflicted her father, but doctors found no evidence of it. Instead, they believed that she was simply suffering from hysteria, a perfectly natural nervous reaction to the outcome of the trial. Her nerves simply snapped. She was given sedatives and fell into a deep sleep.[44]

Ruth also conferred with Father Murphy and announced her intention of converting to Catholicism. Murphy commented to reporters: "I think she has a very deep and profound sense of repentance. That, I believe, is the fundamental of real religion." To minimize publicity, he told them that the conversion would take place at a later date, but he performed it practically on the spot.[45]

Thousands of spectators thronged the streets around the courthouse hoping to observe the notorious pair as they left, but they waited in vain. At the request of their attorneys, the prisoners were allowed one last weekend in Queens County Jail to settle their personal matters. Judd Gray transferred all his liquid assets to his wife. Meanwhile, Ruth signed documents giving temporary custody of Lorraine to her mother, as well as requesting that she be made Lorraine's legal parent. She also gave her mother the platinum wedding band she had worn prominently during the trial, as she would no longer be allowed to wear it on death row.

On Monday, May 16, accompanied by six motorcycles, two of them equipped with armored sidecars carrying police riflemen, Ruth and Judd were removed from Queens County Jail and driven, handcuffed and in separate vehicles, to Sing Sing Prison in upstate New York. Although the crowds were half the size they had been on Friday, there were still plenty of people waiting outside the Queens County Jail; some had started lining up as early as six that morning, and by nine, the sidewalks were packed with people. Throngs of people lined the route, many of them women, hurling insults at Ruth. A heavy police escort was necessary to prevent the angry crowds from swarming over the cars.[46] Ruth could be overheard asking the attendants if stops were permitted on the way to Sing Sing. "There is a good roadhouse I know up there," she said. "I'd like to stop for a lobster dinner!"

At Sing Sing both prisoners were weighed, showered, and examined by the chief physician, Charles Sweet, then photographed and given prison clothes. Ruth's consisted of prison-manufactured underwear, cotton stockings, a blue and white spotted cotton housedress, and felt slippers. Judd was given blue jeans and a plaid work shirt to wear. The two were lodged in identical cells, ten feet wide by twelve feet long, containing a washbasin, toilet, and bolted-down cot. Warden Lawes gave a press conference at which he emphasized that there would be no communication allowed between the two prisoners.[47]

Immediately after the verdict, the lawyers for both Ruth and Judd began their appeals. In an attempt to prove Ruth's insanity, Hazelton and Wallace called in a psychiatrist to examine her, but she was declared sane. Her lawyers also employed the services of Joseph Lonardo, one of the first lawyers in the country to specialize in handling appeals. Between them they drew up a series of arguments that, in their opinion, refuted Ruth's participation in the crime. Among these was the fact that her original confession had been obtained "by undue police methods" and that the testimony she had given on the stand was true, and Judd Gray's false. They also argued that the joint trial, and the extensive publicity surrounding the case, had proven detrimental to their client.[48]

Judd's lawyers were also working on an appeal. Like Ruth's, his appeal concentrated on the harmful effects of the joint trial. Miller and Millard also argued that the amount of alcohol consumed by Judd and his emotional state at the time of the murder precluded the element of premeditation necessary for a conviction of first-degree murder. The crime was therefore manslaughter rather than murder.

In the meantime, time moved on for the two prisoners. Judd's wife Isobel visited him briefly in June; they discussed his appeal during the hour and a half visit. It was the first time that she had seen him since March. The guard in attendance said that no words of affection passed between them, and that of the two, Judd appeared more elated over the visit.[49] Judd's only previous visitors had been his mother, his sister, and his lawyer, Samuel Miller.

Ruth was eventually allowed to have several plain house dresses from her own wardrobe brought to jail. Because she proved to be an easygoing prisoner, her mother was given permission to bring several of Ruth's more fashionable dresses to the prison, too. She was not allowed to wear them, but she could sit with them in the cell next door during the day. Just being in the same cell with them helped Ruth's morale. Rules also were bent to let her use face powder and cold cream, although she was not allowed to keep the box of face powder in her cell. Reading material was available as well, but the staples were taken out of the magazines. Ruth's mother managed the long drive every Friday to visit her daughter.

Ruth's appeal went before the Court on May 27,[50] Judd's on June 10. While Judd was resigned to his fate, indeed longed for it, Ruth was more optimistic that she would either be granted a new trial or have her sentence commuted to life in prison. Even in prison Ruth tried to keep up appearances, letting her hair grow long. She also asked for a tennis ball to bounce in the exercise yard to lose weight.[51] She continued to enjoy visits from her mother and her brother, and at times she even found humor in her situation.

On Thanksgiving, Ruth and Judd found out that their appeals were rejected, and Judge Scudder's original ruling upheld. There would be no new trial. While Judd was calm and resigned, when Ruth heard the news, she sobbed hysterically for more than five hours.[52] After the appeal was denied, Ruth's knitting needles and sewing materials were taken away from her, lest she do herself harm. When she recovered, she began to hope that maybe, just maybe, there would be clemency from Governor Al Smith.

All the newspapers started polls. "What would you do if you were Governor?" asked the *Daily News*.[53] The *Daily Mirror* offered to pay twenty-five dollars for the best letter against Ruth and twenty-five dollars for the best letter in her favor. The letters were published in the paper along with the writers' photographs and short biographies. The response from the public was enormous. Public opinion was firmly against Ruth, especially among women. The *New York Daily News* polled readers on their view of clemency for Ruth and Judd and ran a daily tally under a headline counting down their days to live. The paper's final count showed 12,659 votes for the electric chair and 14,948 votes for clemency; 57% of the women voting and 51% of the men favored clemency.[54]

The prisoners still had to undergo the required official sanity examination at the hands of the New York State Lunacy Commission. On the same day, Ruth's mother, dressed in black mourning and escorted by a *Daily Mirror* reporter, arrived at the state house, where she finagled her way to the governor's chambers, bursting in on him unannounced while he was in a meeting, to plead for her daughter's life. The governor assured the distraught woman that Ruth would receive every consideration during the clemency hearing.[55] Three days before Christmas, Ruth and Judd were found to be sane by the New York State Lunacy Commission. The decision was unanimous.[56] The report was delivered to Governor Smith. Ruth and Judd's fates were now in his hands.

While she waited for the governor to make his decision, Ruth turned to direct emotional appeals to the public, dictating an autobiography, *My Last Story* to a reporter named Jack Lait for the *Daily Mirror*. Lait would smuggle the manuscript into the prison via Ruth's mother, who would hide the pages behind the toilet. Ruth would then copy the material in her own hand and return the pages to their hiding place. On January 5, the *Daily Mirror* kicked off the one-week-to-live countdown by publishing *My Last Story* on the front page. Ruth continued to deny that she was guilty, continuing to lay the blame solely on Judd. The circulation of the *Daily Mirror* was boosted by more than one hundred thousand copies. It was later sold as a pamphlet entitled "Ruth Snyder's Own True Story," on newsstands for twenty-five cents through the King Features Syndicate.

Judd Gray, in contrast, was utterly composed, totally uninterested in his lawyer's efforts to save him from the electric chair. He had wanted to be found guilty, and he now welcomed the approach to death because it was the only possible atonement for his crime. He spent his days writing to his wife Isabel and to his mother, and he also wrote dozens of letters to his daughter Jane, instructing that each one be opened on successive birthdays. When not writing letters, he was frequently found reading the Bible or in deep discussion with Sing Sing's chaplain.

Judd too had the urge to have his final say. Famous Features Syndicate offered him five thousand dollars for his life story. Judd read the manuscript to his sister during her visits, and she relayed the story to a ghost writer. The byline would read, "Henry Judd Gray, as told to his sister Margaret" and ran in forty dailies around the country. In the end Judd was paid three thousand dollars for his trouble. Aside from a few minor details, it adhered to Judd's testimony on the witness stand. It was full of remorse and religion, but Judd wrote candidly about his failing marriage.

The execution was set for the night of January 12th, 1928. Twenty-four witnesses, twenty of them journalists and four doctors, were selected from the thousands who had besieged Warden Lawes with requests to attend. Ruth and Judd made out their wills; Judd left his wife any property that he hadn't already transferred to her, with his mother as his executrix. Ruth left everything equally to her mother and her daughter Lorraine. Judd's wife Isabel made one final trip to Sing Sing to see her husband.

On January 10, two days before the execution, Governor Smith made a statement, denying clemency. Nevertheless, in hopes of a last-minute reprieve, a direct telephone link was set up between his suite at the Biltmore Hotel and the office of Warden Lawes, who was a noted opponent of capital punishment. Preparations were carried out, as the prisoners said good-bye to their families. Ruth was moved to her death cell thirty feet away from the execution chamber at seven twenty that night. Judd was moved to his, a hundred feet away, at eight thirty.

Shortly after Ruth's final meal, her lawyers visited her for the last time. Hazelton later recalled, "She was too far gone to know what she was doing. I never saw anything more terrible. I cannot describe her agony, her misery, her terror. I died a thousand times in the fifteen minutes we were with her. It was awful. When I asked, 'Have you asked God to forgive you?' she replied, 'Yes, I have, and He has forgiven me. I hope the world will.'"

Joseph Lonardo, who led her appeal and saw her last at nine fifteen that night, said, "She is composed and prepared for the end. I asked her if she had any last message for the world. She was quiet for a time. Then she pointed at a clock before her, which showed it to be 9:05. 'I have an hour and fifty-five minutes to live,' she said. 'I am very, very sorry. I have sinned and I am paying dearly for it. I have only hope that my life, that I am giving up now, will serve as a lesson to the world.'" Ruth had asked for and received permission to send a brief note of farewell to Judd. It contained only a few lines, but it cheered him up. He immediately requested a pencil to write back. "I am very glad," he said. "I had hoped you would forgive me. I hope God will forgive us both."

Judd was visited by his lawyer, Samuel Miller, who stayed with him until some minutes after nine. "He is absolutely resigned and courageous," Miller said. "He indulges in no self-pity. He realizes the enormity of his act." When asked about Ruth, Judd said, "We both sinned. I have nothing to say against her." Warden Lawes also expressed admiration for Gray's composure. "I have never seen a man more resigned. When I told him there was no more chance for him, he said, 'If it is God's will, then I am ready.'"

After his last meal, Judd was visited by the prison barber, who shaved Judd's head for the electric chair. Ruth's hair was cut away for the same purpose by one of the female prison guards. She was garbed in a shapeless dark green gingham dress and a cheap brown smock, her body reeling between the supporting clutches of the matrons. In her hands she clutched a large yellow crucifix. A few minutes before the execution, twenty-four witnesses, twenty of them reporters, were led into the death chamber and took their seats facing the electric chair. Among them was Thomas Howard, a young photographer working for the *New York Daily News* who had a seat in the front row. Although cameras were forbidden, Howard had managed to smuggle in a tiny ankle camera hidden by his trousers.

By eleven o'clock there had been no word from Governor Smith, so Ruth was led from her cell into the death chamber by two female guards. As they strapped her body and arms to the chair, she wept, saying, "Father, forgive them, for they know not what they do," repeatedly. When the warden gave the signal, the state executioner switched on the current. At the end of three minutes, the current was turned off and the prison physician, Dr. Sweet, examined her. The current was turned back on and another charge of electricity was sent through her body. At six minutes after eleven, Dr. Sweet turned to the witnesses and said, "I pronounced this woman dead." A minute later Ruth's body was wheeled into the nearby autopsy room. Afterward, her mother was allowed to remove the remains and bury them privately.

As the electricity shot through Ruth's body, Thomas Howard clicked the shutter, thus recording the execution on film for posterity and earning himself a place in the history books. After Ruth's electrocution, newspaper reporters covering executions at Sing Sing were handpicked by the warden and thoroughly searched and the lighting in the death chamber was dimmed so that cameras could not pick up any images.

At ten minutes after eleven, it was Judd Gray's turn to enter the execution chamber, totally composed between two prison attendants. A priest followed them, Judd and the clergyman both repeating words from the Beatitudes in the Scriptures. Even after the mask had been adjusted, he kept his eyes on the clergyman and began to intone the Twenty-Third psalm. Four minutes later Judd was dead.[57]

After the mandatory autopsies were performed, their bodies were released to their families to be buried. A detail of a dozen patrolmen was assigned to keep order outside the funeral parlor to keep spectators at bay. Judd Gray's body was escorted by six police motorcycles as the car made its way to Trinity Presbyterian Church in South Orange, New Jersey, for the funeral. Three hundred people had entered the grounds of Rosedale Cemetery during the morning, undeterred by the rain. Rope barriers were set up to keep spectators away from the canvas tent that had been erected to hide the newly dug grave. As the cars passed through the cemetery gates after the burial, the skies suddenly cleared, and a brilliant rainbow appeared in the sky. Judd's widow, Isabel, arrived to pay her last respects to the man who had betrayed her, along with his mother and Judd's sister.

Ruth's body left Sing Sing an hour after Judd Gray's. She received no police escort to the Grand Concourse Funeral Home in the Bronx, although a large crowd gathered hoping to catch a glimpse of the face of the blonde murderess who led Judd Gray to his doom. Her final journey was a far more peaceful affair after the months of screaming tabloid headlines. Her body was embalmed and dressed in a white dress. Then it was transported to Woodlawn Cemetery, where her headstone simply reads May R. Brown.[58]

Josephine Brown, Ruth Snyder's mother, received custody of Lorraine, having taken care of her granddaughter since the murder. The insurance policy itself paid thirty thousand dollars,[59] but the rest of the policies, worth forty-five thousand and five thousand dollars, were voided after the insurance companies filed suit. Since they were filed fraudulently, the court ruled in November 1928 that the policies could not be collected. However, four thousand dollars was awarded for the maintenance of Lorraine.[60] Other legal battles would take place between the Snyder family, who would not be able to sell the house given the notoriety of the case, and insurance companies. Lorraine would know that her parents had passed, but not know the reason, almost a year after the execution. Jane Gray, and her mother Isabel, lived with relatives in East Orange, New Jersey, after her father's execution. Like Lorraine, she wasn't told exactly how or why her father died.[61] Both girls faded out of the public eye, living private lives.

STEPHANIE ST. CLAIR (1897-1969)

THE NUMBERS QUEEN OF HARLEM

In 1920s Harlem, everyone knew Stephanie St. Clair. In 1923, with ten thousand dollars in seed money, she launched and ran a highly lucrative policy bank in Harlem that netted a quarter of a million dollars a year.[1] To this day she remains the only Black female gangster to run a numbers racket of this size. During her years as the Numbers Queen of Harlem, her charisma, dazzling lifestyle, and her reputation as shrewd, dangerous but still lady-like figure made headlines. She defied expectations of what a Black woman could and should do. Despite Stephanie's national prominence, her story is not as well-known today. It was as if Stephanie St. Clair came out of nowhere and disappeared just as mysteriously seventeen years later. She carved out a piece of the New York rackets, battling mobsters such as Dutch Schultz and Lucky Luciano, as well as corrupt and honest police, for control of gambling in Harlem.

The details of Stephanie's early life are sketchy, but according to biographer Shirley Stewart, who has written the definitive history of St. Clair, she was born on December 24th, 1897, on the French Caribbean island of Guadeloupe, fifty years after the emancipation of slavery in the French colony. She was one of four children born to Amedia St. Clair and Ancelin Martraux. She grew up in Le Moule, located on the northeast side of the island of Grand-Terre, one of the five islands of Guadeloupe. After her father's death, it was decided that Stephanie should leave Guadeloupe. With no dowry, and a loss of social stature, her marriage prospects were limited. In the United States or Canada, she would have a greater chance at economic and personal freedom.

On July 22, 1911, at the age of thirteen, Stephanie traveled to the United States on a steamer.[2] It was a long, arduous journey. Stephanie and the other young women traveled in steerage, spending the nine-day journey sitting on deck with only blankets to protect them from the elements. Other biographies echo the manifest of the S.S. *Guiana,* aboard which Stephanie traveled, but they put her age at "about" twenty-three when she arrived in New York, with an 1887 birthday—a full decade earlier. It is possible that Stephanie's age was given as older to get around the fact that she was traveling by herself without her parents or any family.

Stewart also says Stephanie, after arriving in New York, went on to Canada as a domestic servant for a family in Terrebonne, Quebec, a suburb in Montreal, before returning to New York five years later.[3] Stephanie was probably part of the 1910 to 1911 Caribbean Domestic Scheme, a program that recruited one hundred Guadeloupe Black women to labor as domestic workers for families in Quebec. These women had been recruited by a former American consul in Guadeloupe. Canadian employers paid the eighty-dollar passage from Guadeloupe to Canada, and in return the employees were expected to labor for up to two years at a monthly wage of five dollars, less than half of what white domestic workers made.[4] It was a new form of indentured servitude.

It must have been a shock for a teenage Stephanie, coming from a country where Blacks were the majority to a country where she was all of a sudden not only a minority but also indebted to the white family who employed her and with limited options. It is no wonder that she left for the United States as soon as she possibly could. Also, given Stephanie's temperament, it is no surprise that she decided to strike out on her own. Her background in the French Caribbean gave her an education that allowed her to read and write in both French and English, a significant professional advantage at the time.

Stephanie arrived in Harlem at a time of great change. Prior to 1910, few African Americans lived in Harlem; the neighborhood was made up of diverse ethnic groups, mainly from Europe, including the Dutch, Germans, Italians, Jews, and Irish and a small enclave of Bengalis from India. Real

estate speculation in Harlem had led to a major development boon, but the expected white tenants did not materialize, and many of the newly constructed buildings remained unoccupied.

Philip Payton Jr., an enterprising Black Harlem realtor, saw how he could turn an economic bust into a money-making venture, and he convinced white landlords to rent their long-vacant buildings to African Americans. Still the migration of African Americans to Harlem was a trickle. Whites resisted this migration, but then gave up the fight, sold their property, and left Harlem.[5] Soon Blacks moved uptown from the crowded Tenderloin and San Juan Hill neighborhoods. They were joined by Blacks fleeing the poor economic conditions as well as the racial discrimination and segregation in the South. African Americans eventually owned approximately sixty million dollars' worth of Harlem real estate.

By the time Stephanie St. Clair arrived, Harlem was emerging as the Black metropolis. A few years later, when the advent of Prohibition brought a national ban on the sale of alcohol, Harlem became a prime destination for the Mafia's bootleg booze, and Harlem boomed as a prime entertainment hotspot crammed with trendy clubs and cabarets, must-see venues for whites from other neighborhoods in Manhattan and visitors from around the globe.

Harlem had something for every kind of taste and social class. It was suddenly chic for white people to go to Harlem late at night. Throngs trekked to the neighborhood by taxi, limousine, and subway, hopping from one nightclub to another. Clubs like Connie's Inn, Small's Paradise, and the Cotton Club made Harlem world famous, as white patrons were able to watch "exotic" entertainment and imbibe booze without crossing the color line. While Blacks worked both in front of and behind the scenes, they were unable to enter as patrons with few exceptions.

White mobsters quickly realized that Prohibition offered them a chance to make big profits. The heaviest concentration of speakeasies was on "Swing Street." Located on 133rd Street between Lenox and 7th Avenue, these clubs were owned by African Americans. Not one was shut down until eight years after Prohibition started. Stephanie soon learned that in New York the line between legal and illegal was fluid.

In this environment, Stephanie found opportunity. Rejecting working as a domestic, Stephanie had bigger ambitions. But first, in 1915 she married George Gachette in a Catholic ceremony. Very little is known about her husband or their relationship. Did they have to get married because Stephanie was pregnant? Was it a love match? What is known is that by the time Stephanie started her career in the numbers game, George was no longer part of her life and they likely never divorced.

It is not clear how she did it, but somehow, Stephanie managed to accumulate ten thousand dollars by 1922. She never spoke about how she raised the capital, but she may have had some savings from her time as a domestic. An editorial in the *New York Amsterdam News* gave another theory of how she obtained the money. In 1923, she filed a lawsuit against her apartment building owner, Ada Howell, and a city marshal, claiming that she was illegally thrown out of her apartment on West 135th Street. In her lawsuit, "Mme Gachette claimed dispossess papers by the City Marshall were never served on her" and that her personal possessions were placed on the street and stolen by bystanders. Siding with Stephanie, the Seventh District Court awarded her a judgment of one thousand dollars.[6] Stephanie probably worked for a policy banker in some capacity to learn the business before going out on her own. Her detractors reminded people that her title was after all "Madam," but there are no records to indicate that she was ever involved with prostitution.

What is certain is that Stephanie used the money to launch a numbers operation. The numbers racket had a long history in the Black and Hispanic neighborhoods of Manhattan, as well as other major American cities such as Chicago and New Orleans. Traditionally the numbers game has been based on lottery policy numbers (twelve numbers drawn from a pool of seventy-eight), which were determined by a complex drawing requiring a structured organization to figure out the winning numbers.

But during the 1920s, at the time Stephanie was getting into the racket, the rules of the game changed considerably. The betting scheme was simplified, and the winning numbers selected became based on the daily closing results of the New York Stock Exchange. The winning total paid at six hundred to one, and the beauty of the new system was that by having the numbers recorded daily in the newspaper, the game could not be fixed.

During the late 1920s and very early 1930s, huge sums of money kept rolling in from the numbers game. A numbers operation was headed by a banker; a group of collectors or runners took the gambling slips from customers at beauty parlors, barbershops, churches, candy stores, newsstands, and street corners. Others employed by the "bank" included clerks plying adding machines. Of course, he or she also needed a good lawyer and an accountant. A banker could employ anywhere from ten to fifty people. Even after making payoffs to the cops, court officials, and politicians, a banker could still pocket between two thousand and six thousand dollars a week.[7] The big-time operators or bankers in the game were known as the Numbers Kings. These years were so profitable that the Numbers Kings created a new position, that of the controller, or buffer between themselves and their collectors or runners. In 1931, Henry Miro, one of the most prominent Numbers Kings and the largest banker in Harlem at the time, testified in front of the Seabury Commission that he had six controllers, each looking after twenty or more runners. The controller was responsible to the banker for his runners, and in return he received a small percentage, usually ten percent of the turnover that he handled.

Although policy banking was illegal, it was a nonviolent venture that yielded enormous profits. As a Black woman, Stephanie's options were limited. She could work as a domestic, hairdresser, or laundress. She didn't have enough of an education to work as a teacher, nurse, or librarian. Policy banking was also a profession that wasn't limited solely to men. While most policy bankers were men of color, there were women who were policy bankers. In 1924, a Cuban woman named Marcellina Cardena was alleged to have been the biggest clearinghouse banker in Harlem, employing more than one hundred runners.[8]

The money stayed in the community. If a bettor "hit" a number, that money could go toward paying rent or putting a down payment on a house, buying food and clothing, purchasing household items, enjoying a night out, or putting an extra-large donation in the collection plate in church on

Sunday. Everybody played the numbers, whether they were poor or middle class. A person did not need a lot of money to play.

For a ten-cent bet, a player could make sixty dollars, a considerable amount in the Harlem of the 1920s. The numbers racket became a strong tradition in the neighborhood, and even though it was mainly a nickel-and-dime game, people from all economic backgrounds played. One observer described the game as "the most widespread form of breaking the law in Harlem."

Not all Black New Yorkers were thrilled by the numbers racket. A segment of Harlem's African American population frowned on games of chance and looked down their noses at the people who operated the business. Opposition to gambling was rooted in Victorian ideas of appropriate and inappropriate forms of labor and amusements. Reformers and moralists argued that leisure activities should be wholesome and decent, upholding Christian and middle-class values.

They also believed that gambling encouraged false hope for a quick profit, contributed to the demoralization of the African American community, and seduced poor Blacks into squandering their meager incomes instead of encouraging thrift, prudence, and stability. Furthermore, some unscrupulous bankers refused to pay out if someone hit big. Even some members of the Black working class refused to play the game, keeping their hard-earned money rather than supporting an illegal racket. They found it morally troublesome. Gambling was an addiction that ruined lives and destroyed families.

Gambling profits also made it possible for many Numbers Kings and Queens to give back to their communities. Turf Club owner and policy banker Casper Holstein made numerous donations to various religious, educational, social, and political institutions. He gave money to the Urban League and to the Katy Ferguson Home, a settlement house for unmarried women and children. Stephanie herself was one of the organizers of the French Legal Aid Society in Harlem, encouraging her fellow immigrants to become naturalized citizens and registered voters.

Stephanie entered the numbers racket at the right time; she thrived in the underworld environment, making a name for herself as a policy queen. Throughout most of the 1920s, she maintained a low profile while she established a successful numbers bank, though it was by no means one of the largest or most prominent. By the end of the decade, Stephanie had a personal fortune estimated at around five hundred thousand dollars in cash. She also owned several apartment houses,[9] employing ten controllers, forty to fifty runners, and several bodyguards and maids. She was earning an estimated two hundred thousand dollars annually, making her one of the richest Black women in America.

Stephanie's personality was as big as her pocketbook; she was known around Harlem as "Queenie." She was flamboyant, brazen, and generous, but she also could be as unpredictable as the weather. At 5 feet 8 inches, she was tall for a woman, made even taller by the turban she wore occasionally. Harlem residents from the time would recall she had an imperious presence with a taste for the finer things in life, which included clothes and the opera, although she wasn't averse to frequenting the speakeasies in Harlem. She always dressed to the nines, tastefully attired in silk dresses, preferably in a silvery gray, her favorite color. Although she was capable of swearing like a sailor when the occasion called for it.

Given Stephanie's fiery and restless nature, Harlemites also began to refer to her as the "Tiger from Marseilles." She would contribute to the mystery surrounding her birthplace. She adamantly claimed, "European France" as her place of birth, speaking flawless French, not the patois of the Caribbean. Woe to anyone who got on Stephanie St. Clair's bad side. Her French accent and her refusal to back down from anyone, Black or white, no matter what his or her position, marked Stephanie out and made her grist for the mill of the Black press. In 1931 she sued the *New York Inter-State Tattler* for libel, demanding twenty-five thousand dollars in damages for a series of articles it had run. The *Tattler* had published an article that not only alleged that Stephanie had tried to frame certain Black policemen, which caused them to lose their jobs, but the article also referred to Stephanie's "special (female) secretary, a lovely, brown-skinned sweetheart." Stephanie claimed that this was a poorly disguised accusation of "sex-perversion."[10]

Stephanie lived at 409 Edgecombe Avenue along with the creme de la creme of Harlem society. The E-shaped, thirteen-story apartment building, built in 1917, was situated high up on Sugar Hill, above the Harlem River and Hudson Valley, overlooking the Bronx and lower Manhattan. In the 1930s and 1940s, 409 Edgecombe was the home of such prominent African Americans as W. E. B. DuBois, the premier Black intellectual and for decades editor of the *Crisis;* Walter White of the NAACP; the painter Aaron Douglas; and Eunice Carter, the first African-American woman to work as a prosecutor in the New York District Attorney's office.[11] Stephanie would breeze through the lobby in a fur coat.

Stephanie did not hide her occupation, nor was she ashamed of her profession. Her neighbors knew who she was and how she earned her living. Former 409 Edgecombe resident Katherine Butler Jones describes "Madame Stephanie St. Clair breezing through the lobby with her fur coat dramatically flowing behind her. She had a mystical aura about her, and she wore exotic dresses with a colorful turban wrapped around her head."[12]

Stephanie soon learned how things worked in New York City. When a police officer from the New York Police Department's Sixth Division threatened to arrest her, she scoffed and told him that he had nothing to support the charge. The policeman suggested that they go to the 125th Street station and talk it over with his lieutenant. Stephanie agreed and met with the lieutenant, who explained how business was done in the Big Apple. With no other option, Stephanie fell in line, greasing the lieutenant's palm with a three-hundred-dollar payoff. From that day on, she began to send regular payments of one hundred to five hundred dollars to an anonymous cop, whom she believed to be the lieutenant she had met. The mysterious recipient would call her after each payment to thank her.[13]

Despite the payoffs, the police continued to harass her and other policy bankers, arresting her runners, even as she made the payments regularly. In November 1928, Stephanie's housekeeper, Sarah Scott, who used the alias "Sarah Willoughby," was arrested for "having in her possession five thousand policy slips, two adding machines, and two policy record books." She vehemently denied the charge, claiming that she was being framed, that it was a case of mistaken identity and that the police were looking for Stephanie. Scott was s illiterate, she said, so she couldn't possibly be a banker. Scott proved to be no stool pigeon, refusing to talk. Unfortunately for Scott, her loyalty ended up landing her a jail sentence.[14]

The police demanded more and more money. Stephanie St. Clair was a proud woman, and she took it personally. The last straw was when she suspected that a cop had broken into her home and stolen five hundred dollars. The intruder had cut his hand, leaving bloody fingerprints on the windowsill. Stephanie telephoned the corrupt lieutenant and demanded that the police arrest and punish the intruder. It should be an easy case to solve, she claimed, because he'd left his fingerprints behind.[15]

No one was ever arrested for the crime. She pestered the police, but they brushed her off. Stephanie was outraged and fed up. If the rats would not cooperate, she would sink the ship and expose them to the public. Between 1929 and 1930, she purchased thirteen full-page ads in the *New York Amsterdam News*. Her first advertisement title read, "Complains to Mayor about Harlem Police"[16] She didn't name names, but she attacked the police viciously. It was a bold move to openly admit her connection to the numbers game.

In a letter to Mayor Jimmy Walker, she wrote: "Sometimes, detectives find policy slips in their search, but if you pay them from five hundred to two thousand dollars, you are sure to come back home. If you pay them nothing, you are sure to get a sentence from sixty to ninety days in the workhouse."[17] Two weeks later, in an advertisement addressed to the "members of my race," Stephanie assured her readers that the mayor and police commissioner replied to her letters. She also advised them about their rights under the Fourth Amendment. She also assured them that she would continue to fight for them always.[18]

The advertisements created a sensation. Stephanie used the power of the media to get her case across. She also wrote on issues that she was passionate about: police brutality, the importance of voting and of immigrants becoming US citizens, and housing concerns. In a community battered and bruised by a corrupt white establishment, Stephanie became a folk hero, but it also put a target on her back.

On December 30, 1929, Stephanie left home at ten thirty in the morning and walked to the viaduct at 155th Street, where she caught a bus. Immediately she sensed that someone was following her. When she got off and entered 117 West 141st Street, three policemen of the Sixth Division rushed her and arrested her after allegedly finding policy slips in her possession.[19]

Stephanie placed an editorial in the *New York Amsterdam News* announcing her arrest, claiming police misconduct: "Yes, arrested and framed by three of the bravest and noblest cowards who were civilians." She vowed: "I will fight them legally to the finish . . . and I will never stop."[20]

Stephanie was convicted in March 1930 on a gambling charge. Her white attorney, M. F. Grove, a former judge, sought a jury trial, but Judge Levine denied the request. Stephanie quietly mounted the witness stand in her defense and admitted that she was a numbers banker but that she had quit because of the exorbitant demands of the police. She contended that she was a "marked woman" and had predicted months in advance that John E. Roberts, the plainclothes detective, would "frame" her. Mrs. Elam Berry, who lived on the third floor of the building, testified that Stephanie was meeting with her to discuss incorporating the French Legal Aid Society, of which Stephanie was a founder. Another witness testified that no banker would be seen with slips and records in a hallway and that the "banks" were closed long before Stephanie's arrest that day.

The *New York Amsterdam News* reported, "Waging a desperate three-hour battle in the courtroom where three busy justices ordinarily dispose of 125 cases in four hours, Mme. Stephanie St. Clair, thirty-one, 409 Edgecombe Avenue, lost her brilliant fight Friday afternoon. Mme St. Clair held the center of stage in the court drama while spectators and attendants gripped their seats and drank in the proceedings."[21] Stephanie spent eight months of a two-year sentence in the workhouse on Welfare Island. She was finally released in early December 1930.

Upon her release, Stephanie was on a mission to expose the New York Police Department's close ties to the numbers racket. But there was the risk that drawing attention to corruption within the police force and city hall might mean facing continued police retaliation or reprisal from any of the mobsters who had members of law enforcement in their pocket. Regardless of the risk, she appeared before the Samuel Seabury Commission in December 1930.

The Seabury Commission was formed to investigate the massive corruption in New York City's government. Named after Judge Samuel Seabury, a crusader against corruption in government and scion of a prominent New

York City family, the investigation lasted two years and probed the relationship between police, politicians, and gangsters. At private and public hearings, testimony was heard from over a thousand witnesses including judges, lawyers, police officers, criminal informants, and prostitutes.

Stephanie was one of the star witnesses. Dressed to the nines in a mink coat, chic hat, and ever-present jewels, she burst like a thunderbolt into the proceedings and split them wide open. She testified that she ran a numbers bank from 1923 to 1928 and ended up paying bribes totaling about sixty-six hundred dollars to members of the police department. She stated that she had sent payments of one hundred dollars and five hundred dollars through a confidential messenger known as "Mustache" Jones to a lieutenant of the Sixth Division. It was done, she said, to protect her workers from arrest. Her story was borne out in part by canceled checks.

She didn't tell all, but she told just enough. During her testimony, Stephanie accused a district attorney, two judges, and scores of police, bondsmen, and political fixers. She gave names, dates, and the amount paid out in graft. Her testimony helped get a police lieutenant and thirteen other police officers suspended from duty.[22] Prosecutor Kessel subpoenaed the bank accounts and brokerage records of over 150 policemen, their relatives, lawyers, and bondsmen.[23] But Stephanie still was not done; she had a warning for Tammany Hall: "Many more will be in the same predicament if they do not stop framing colored people." The revelations from the Seabury Commission were responsible for the wrecking of Mayor Jimmy Walker's political machine, leading to his resignation in November 1932.

Although St. Clair's high-profile public utterances drew the attention of the white power structure, it appears that the Harlem community largely supported her. After her Seabury testimony, Stephanie felt vindicated. Corruption in Tammany Hall was not the only topic of inquiry for the Seabury Commission. A number of major Harlem policy bankers were compelled to testify, and under close scrutiny their revelations cast further light on the lucrative Harlem numbers racket. The numbers rackets in Harlem were a fifty-million-dollar business, astounding in the middle of the Great Depression.

White mobsters could see that the numbers game in Harlem was highly profitable, even as the Great Depression destroyed the economy. People were still eager to use their nickels and dimes to play a number that might be their ticket to easy street. Given the money involved, it was only a matter of time before a powerful white gangster would sense the potential of moving into Harlem to take over the rackets.

Initially many white mobsters, especially those getting rich from Prohibition, were not interested in Harlem's numbers business. They viewed it as an unprofitable game consumed by poor Blacks. White mobsters perceived Black numbers bankers as nonthreatening. Crime syndicate lawyer–turned–numbers banker Richard "Dixie" Davis explained that Black "policy bankers were not gangsters. They were merely gamblers running an illegal business on a very peaceful, non-violent basis."[24] The Seabury Commission showed that all those pennies, nickels, and dimes could be turned into green. And the repeal of Prohibition in 1933 meant that mobsters were looking for a new racket since they could no longer make a profit from illegal booze.

A ruthless gangster who wore cheap suits and had a hair-trigger temper, Dutch Schultz had been keeping an eye on the Harlem rackets. Born Arthur Flegenheimer, he was the son of German-Jewish immigrants. He once told a reporter why he changed his name to Dutch Schultz. "It was short enough to fit the headlines. If I had kept the name of Flegenheimer, nobody would have heard of me."

Known as "the Beer Baron of the Bronx," Schultz's organization extended through Upper Manhattan and the Bronx and included bootlegging, gambling, nightclubs, speakeasies, and extortion. Harlem seemed like the next logical step. Schultz had James J. Hines, a Democratic politician who controlled West Harlem, in his pocket. Hines received a payout of five hundred to six hundred dollars weekly from Schultz to protect the gangster's bootleg operations.

Schultz employed the same strategy to take over the Harlem numbers racket that he had used to muscle into the other rackets he dominated. As individual operators without firepower or real political connections, the Black numbers kings were powerless to stop the white interloper from taking over their businesses. The typical meeting consisted of the banker sitting in a room with a couple of Schultz's lieutenants. Then the Dutchman would enter, flanked by two bodyguards. Schultz would take out his .45, place it on the table, and inform the banker he was now an employee of the Schultz organization. Schultz eliminated nearly all runners, collectors, and canvassers who formerly solicited bets from players.

Stephanie St. Clair was not about to just hand over her business to Dutch Schultz without a fight. Desperately outnumbered and outgunned, she used every conceivable stratagem at her disposal. She refused to kowtow to the Dutchman; instead, she tried to convince the other big bankers who hadn't already submitted to his control to band together and fight. It was a tough sell. How could they fight the mob and city hall at the same time? They were hand-in-hand. If the big bankers were too scared, Stephanie would simply work on the smaller bankers who operated outside of Schultz's influence.

Stephanie told reporters that if Shultz set foot in Harlem again, she would "blast him out." She continued, "He is a rat. The policy game is my game. He took it away from me and is swindling the colored people. There are no mobs out to get Shultz. I'm the only one that's after him."[25] St. Clair's defiance of Shultz was also a flaunting to the police.

She took her fight all the way to city hall. La Guardia, who was once Harlem's congressman, had a vested interest in dismantling the three-million-dollar-a-year numbers game. Stephanie volunteered information about the rackets. Interim mayor Joseph V. McKee told his police aide, Lieutenant James Harten, to see the visitor from Harlem. Stephanie informed Harten that Schultz planned to put her on the spot, and what did the city of New York propose to do about it? Lieutenant Harten informed her that he would alert the police in Harlem to see that no harm came to her at the hands of the Dutchman or any other gangster.

Seeing that the fat cats at city hall were a waste of time, Stephanie went back to Harlem and decided to use some intimidation tactics of her own on the neighborhood's white shop owners, warning them not to collaborate with Schultz's organization. By her actions, Stephanie wanted to ensure that Harlem residents placed their bets with her, or, with one of the other Black policy bankers. She hired Bumpy Johnson after his release from Auburn Prison in 1932 to be her bodyguard. He helped her to protect her interests in the game.

Outgunned and outmanned, Stephanie wasn't going to go down without fighting. She'd come too far to just let a white man take away everything she'd worked so hard for. Stephanie stormed into the white-owned and white-run stores on Seventh Avenue that wrote numbers, and one after another single-handedly smashed plate glass cases, snatched and destroyed policy slips, and ordered the operators to get out of Harlem.[26] She even informed the authorities that the operators were selling policy slips to minors and helped gather evidence to prove it. Despite the risk to her life, she leaked details of Schultz's operations to anyone who would listen, including the police, the newspapers, and the federal authorities, which resulted in the March 1933 police raid of Schultz's clearinghouse. Fourteen employees were arrested, and the police seized between five and ten million betting slips, which represented a day's play of two million dollars and over two thousand dollars in petty cash.[27]

Dutch Schultz was getting impatient with the troublemaking and put out a contract on Stephanie's life. One such contract was offered to Catherine Odlum. Stephanie told a reporter that she had a signed affidavit that Odlum was approached by an associate of Schultz and offered five hundred dollars. Odlum was supposed to lure Stephanie to her apartment to have her murdered. Once again, Stephanie was forced into hiding. "I'm not afraid of Dutch Schultz or any man living," she declared. "He'll never touch me." Schultz's men went looking for her; the intense manhunt at one point forced her to hide in a coal cellar, where she lay buried under a pile of coal.

In the end, it was a losing battle for Stephanie St. Clair and the rest of Harlem's Kings and Queens of the numbers racket. Schultz's fire power and mob muscle were too much, and he was able to get the numbers securely under his control. While Schultz had successfully organized the numbers racket, he had an even bigger problem looming in front of him. He was being hounded for tax evasion by prosecutor Thomas Dewey. The government had a great deal of evidence, but Schultz had even better lawyers.

But Schultz's empire was starting to crumble. The Harlem numbers racket had served as the cornerstone, but now Dewey planned to go after it. Dutch, being Dutch, decided to kill the prosecutor; it was the only way to get the man off his back. But it was not that easy. Over the years, the Mob had put a national council in place, and Schultz would have to convince the most powerful mobsters in New York, including Lucky Luciano, Meyer

Lansky, Vito Genovese, and Albert Anastasia. The council rejected Schultz's plan. Furious, Schultz stormed out of the meeting, but it was clear that he was not going to give up his plan to get rid of Dewey. His decision signed his own death warrant.

On December 3, 1935, two hit men—Charlie "the Bug" Workman and Emanuel "Mendy" Weiss—walked into the back of the Palace Chop House, a Newark, New Jersey, bar and restaurant where Dutch Schultz and two of his bodyguards were meeting with his accountant Otto Berman. The hitmen opened fire, killing Berman and one of the bodyguards, leaving the other one dying. Seeing that Schultz was not with the other three, Workman went into the men's room, where he saw movement at the urinal and opened fire. While Workman fled, Schultz staggered out of the bathroom, headed for the table, and slumped into a chair. An ambulance rushed him to the Newark City Hospital.

Schultz fell into a coma and died three days later. But Queenie had the last word. Before he died, the Dutchman received a telegram from Stephanie St. Clair that read, "Don't be yellow. As you sow, so shall you reap." Stephanie appears to have withdrawn from the numbers game not long after Schultz was killed. The remaining policy bankers either quietly left the business, like Casper Holstein who retired to St. Croix after spending a year in prison for racketeering, or they began working for the mobsters. Lucky Luciano took over the numbers racket, with Bumpy Johnson his man in Harlem.

In June 1936, Stephanie met Sufi Abdul Hamid, a Black rights activist, when he proposed that she invest in motion pictures, which she declined. She had probably become aware of Hamid during his involvement in the "Don't Buy Where You Can't Work" campaign. Hamid came back the next day, but she had given orders to the elevator boy not to let anyone in. Then he began writing letters for appointments until she allowed him to visit her again. From that moment on they were inseparable. Both were ambitious, passionate activists and neither was timid or conservative in voice or manner.[28]

Hamid was known for being a fiery orator. Harlem experienced more than 50 percent unemployment during the Great Depression, making it fertile ground for Hamid's message that Blacks needed to organize economically.

It struck a chord with the residents, and he recruited a significant number of followers. But when Hamid appealed to Blacks to "drive the Jews out of Harlem," he was vilified and accused of being a "Black Hitler," and his message was drowned in controversy.

Like Stephanie, he was also a flamboyant dresser who wore elaborate gold-lined capes, a purple turban, and expensive leather boots and a dagger in his belt. Like Stephanie, he had reinvented himself. Born Eugene Brown in Philadelphia, he converted to Islam while living in Chicago. He eventually styled himself "His Holiness Bishop Amiru Al-Mu-Minin Sufi A. Hamid," claiming that he had been born in Egypt beneath the shadow of a pyramid. In August, two months after they met, they were married, but instead of undergoing the traditional marriage ceremony, the couple signed a contract uniting them for ninety-nine years; it contained a clause allowing for a trial year, "during which time the feasibility of the plan could be tested." The *Amsterdam News* labeled them "two of Harlem's most exotic figures."

In less than two years, the marriage was on the rocks. Hamid disagreed with Stephanie's decision to call up district attorney Thomas Dewey in connection with the death of a Harlem woman. After a year, Hamid started to stay out all night, and Stephanie found out that he kept two apartments with two different women, and that he had a gambling addiction.[29] By December 1937, she had left him and her apartment, moving to another apartment at 580 St. Nicholas Avenue. Stephanie blamed their problems on a popular spiritualist named Madame Fu Futtam, who was described by one reporter as having "more curves than a winding mountain grace." The owner of a mystical store in Harlem, Madame Futtam was also the author of a *Dream Book,* which was widely read. Futtam approached Stephanie, requesting five thousand dollars to start a fertilizer business. When she turned her down, Futtam offered to "fix" Hamid for $250.

At some point, Hamid and Stephanie reconciled, but she became suspicious when an angry Madam Futtam called the house demanding to speak to Hamid. Stephanie decided to do a little digging, discovering that Futtam (whose real name was Dorothy Matthews) had been in business with Hamid five years previously. Madame Futtam claimed that she and Hamid had a "spiritual relationship." Despite her reservations, Stephanie tried to make the relationship work, but Hamid became abusive. One night she called Hamid at Futtam's apartment, and Hamid threatened to "kick her within an inch of her life and throw her out the window." Stephanie claimed that she didn't tell anyone about the abuse because she didn't want people to know.

In January 1938, Stephanie pulled out a gun and fired three shots at her cheating husband as he was on his way to an appointment with his lawyer. Hamid was nicked in the chin with one shot; a second tore through the left sleeve of his overcoat, inflicting a slight flesh wound, while a third went wild. Hamid grappled with Stephanie before she could fire a fourth shot.[30] The next day, she was arrested and held on six thousand dollars bail.[31] She was charged with first-degree assault and being in possession of an unlicensed pistol. Reporters couldn't wait to visit Stephanie at the 123rd Street police station, where she posed for photographers. As she walked into felony court to plead not guilty, she told bystanders and reporters: "I only wanted to scare him. If I had killed him, I would have died."[32]

A few days before her trial, she told reporters that Hamid had shot at her, and she was just attempting to defend herself. When she encountered Hamid at an office building on 125th Street, he tried to hit her. They struggled, and he went into his coat pocket and drew a gun. Stephanie insisted that she had grabbed the gun and three shots were fired. She maintained that Hamid always carried a gun because of his "mysterious business ventures."[33] Eager to get his side of the story out, Sufi gave several interviews in which he claimed that he wasn't surprised. According to him, Stephanie "had threatened his life," after he informed her that he "wanted no more to do with her."

The trial started on March 15, 1938. Hamid arrived wearing a dark blue English drape, a Malacca overcoat, and a black derby and carrying a mahogany and ivory cane. At one point during his testimony, he reenacted the struggle for the gun with Assistant District Attorney Thayer. Stephanie's attorney was fined one hundred dollars by Judge Wallace for repeated attempts to prejudice the jury by referring to Hamid as "the Black Hitler of Harlem." The elevator operator in the building testified that he saw Hamid holding the gun and that Stephanie had told him that Hamid was shooting at her. But a surprise witness for the prosecution, Edison McVey, testified that Stephanie had threatened Hamid the day before the shooting, declaring, "I am going to kill Sufi." The final witness for the prosecution, a police detective, testified there were no powder burns on Hamid's clothing, which meant that he couldn't have been the shooter, and that the gun was shot not at close range but at least eighteen inches away.

Stephanie didn't have a single witness to testify on her behalf. The court ruled out all evidence referring to her as a former Numbers Queen and nemesis of the late Dutch Schultz. On March 21, 1938, after three hours of deliberation, the jury composed of seven men and five women, all white, delivered a guilty verdict. Stephanie cried softly upon hearing the verdict. When she spied Captain McVey, as she was being carried out, she hissed through clenched teeth, "You louse."[34]

At her sentencing, her attorney pleaded for mercy, but the judge told the courtroom: "This woman has been living by her wits all of her life. She has a bad temper and must learn that she can't go around shooting at other people." The judge sentenced her from two to ten years in prison, the minimum and the maximum sentence. Stephanie, with a flair for the dramatic, kissed her hand and waved good-bye as she was led out of the courtroom.[35] Hamid was not in court when the sentence was pronounced. He went on to marry Futtam three weeks after Stephanie began serving her sentence. Four months later, in August 1938, Hamid was killed in a plane crash.

After she was released from prison, Stephanie faded from history as mysteriously as she had entered it. Her biographer, Shirley Stewart, speculates that she went to work for Ellsworth "Bumpy" Johnson, at one of his legitimate businesses. Johnson had worked for Stephanie, and then when he got out of prison in 1932, he was at her side as she fought against Dutch Schultz's encroachment on the policy game. After Bumpy's fatal heart attack in 1968, Stephanie was left without a benefactor. Stewart believes that she may have ended her days, not in a mansion on Long Island, but in a psychiatric hospital. She died in 1969, shortly before her seventy-third birthday.

NOTES

HENRIETTA ROBINSON

1. David Wilson, *Henrietta Robinson* (New York: Auburn, Miller, Orton & Mulligan, 1855), 12.

2. John D. Lawson, *American State Trials: XI* (St. Louis, Thomas Law Books, 1914–36), 560–61.

3. David Wilson, *Henrietta Robinson* (New York: Auburn, Miller, Orton & Mulligan, 1855), 148–51.

4. "Impeachment of John C. Mather," *New York Daily Times*, April 16, 1853, 5.

5. John D. Lawson, *American State Trials: XI* (St. Louis: Thomas Law Books, 1914–36), 543.

6. "Home Matters," *Troy Daily Times*, February 17, 1854.

7. John D. Lawson, *American State Trials: XI* (St. Louis: Thomas Law Books, 1914–36), 543–44.

8. John D. Lawson, *American State Trials: XI* (St. Louis: Thomas Law Books, 1914–36), 567.

9. Ibid., 560–61.

10. "Trial of Henrietta Robinson for the Murder of Timothy Lannagan," *New York Daily Times*, May 26, 1854, 3.

11. David Wilson, *Henrietta Robinson* (New York: Auburn, Miller, Orton & Mulligan, 1855), 109.

12. John D. Lawson, *American State Trials: XI* (St. Louis: Thomas Law Books, 1914–36), 547.

13. David Wilson, *Henrietta Robinson* (New York: Auburn, Miller, Orton & Mulligan, 1855), 103–06.

14. John D. Lawson, *American State Trials: XI* (St. Louis: Thomas Law Books, 1914–36), 545–46.

15. David Wilson, *Henrietta Robinson* (New York: Auburn, Miller, Orton & Mulligan, 1855), 108.

16. Ibid., 58–9.

17. John D. Lawson, *American State Trials: XI* (St. Louis: Thomas Law Books, 1914–36), 565–66.

18. "Is Mrs. Robinson Miss Wood?" *Troy Daily Whig*, June 8, 1854.

19. Mary Robinson (1757–1800) was actually the mistress of George IV when he was Prince of Wales. She was nicknamed "Perdita" for her role as Perdita in Shakespeare's *The Winter's Tale*. She was the first public mistress of the prince.

20. David Wilson, *Henrietta Robinson* (New York: Auburn, Miller, Orton & Mulligan, 1855), 10–37.

21. "The 'Veiled Murderess,' Her Life and History," *New York Daily Times*, July 31, 1855, 1.

22. Wilson, *Henrietta Robinson*, 67–68.

23. "Attempted Suicide by Mrs. Robinson," *Troy Daily Budget*, July 25, 1853.

24. "Another Poisoning Case: Attempted Suicide by Mrs. Robinson," *Troy Daily Whig*, July 25, 1853.

25. "Mrs. Robinson, the Alleged Murderess," *Troy Daily Times*, October 11, 1853.

26. David Wilson, *Henrietta Robinson* (New York: Auburn, Miller, Orton & Mulligan, 1855), 65.

27. "Trial of Mrs. Robinson at Troy," *Buffalo Daily Republic* (Buffalo, NY), May 25, 1854, 2.

28. David Wilson, *Henrietta Robinson* (New York: Auburn, Miller, Orton & Mulligan, 1855), 77–81.

29. John D. Lawson, *American State Trials: XI* (St. Louis: Thomas Law Books, 1914–36), 544.

30. David Wilson, *Henrietta Robinson* (New York: Auburn, Miller, Orton & Mulligan, 1855), 102–03.

31. John D. Lawson, *American State Trials: XI* (St. Louis: Thomas Law Books, 1914–36), 547–48.

32. John D. Lawson, *American State Trials: XI* (St. Louis: Thomas Law Books, 1914–36), 550–52.

33. David Wilson, *Henrietta Robinson* (New York: Auburn, Miller, Orton & Mulligan, 1855), 122–27.

34. John D. Lawson, *American State Trials: XI* (St. Louis: Thomas Law Books, 1914–36), 558–60.

35. David Wilson, *Henrietta Robinson* (New York: Auburn, Miller, Orton & Mulligan, 1855), 142.

36. John D. Lawson, *American State Trials: XI* (St. Louis: Thomas Law Books, 1914–36), 563.

37. "The Veiled Murderess," *Harrisburg Telegraph* (Harrisburg, PA), December 3, 1872, 1.

38. *Brooklyn Daily Eagle*, May 29, 1854, 2.

39. "Henrietta Robinson: The Poisoner at Troy," *New York Daily Times*, June 9, 1854.

40. "The 'Veiled Murderess,' Her Life and History—Who is Mrs. Robinson?" *Troy Times*, July 30, 1855.

41. "The Mysterious Murderess," *New York Daily Times*, June 21, 1855, 2.

42. "The 'Veiled Murderess,' Her Life and History," *New York Daily Times*, July 31, 1855, 1.

43. "Mrs. Robinson," *American Phrenological Journal (1838–1869)*, Sept. 1855, 22 (3), 62.

44. "Veiled Murderess Dies with 50 Years' Secret" *New York Times*, May 15, 1905, 7.

EMMA CUNNINGHAM

1. "Mrs. Emma Augusta Cunningham," *New York Daily Herald*, February 3, 1857, 8.

2. "The Murder of Dr. Burdell: The Testimony Sketch of Dr. Burdell's Life," *New York Daily Tribune*, February 2, 1857, 2.

3. "Horrible and Mysterious Murder in Bond Street," *The New York Herald*, February 1, 1857, 1.

4. "The Bond Street Butchery, Excitement Unabated," *New York Daily Tribune*, February 5, 1857, 6.

5. "The Bond Street Murder: Some Important Developments," *New York Daily Times*, February 6, 1857, 1.

6. "Horrible and Mysterious Murder in Bond Street," *New York Herald*, February 1, 1857, 1.

7. Henry L. Clinton, *Celebrated Trials*, New York: Harper & Brothers, 1897, 32.

8. "The Bond Street Murder," *New York Daily Times*, February 3, 1857, 2.

9. Ibid, 2.

10. "The Bond Street Tragedy; Additional Particulars of the Murder of Dr. Burdell," *New York Herald*, February 7, 1857, 1.

11. "Mysterious Midnight Murder," *New York Daily Tribune*, February 2, 1857, 5.

12. "Horrible and Mysterious Murder in Bond Street," *New York Herald*, February 1, 1857, 1.

13. "Mysterious Midnight Murder; An Eminent Citizen Assassinated," *New York Herald*, February 1, 1857, 1.

14. "The Bond Street Tragedy," *The New York Herald*, February 2, 1857, 1.

15. The Bond Street Tragedy: Additional Particulars of the Murder of Dr. Burdell, *New York Herald*, February 3, 1857, 1.

16. Horrible and Mysterious Murder in Bond Street: Assassination of Dr. Burdell in his own office, *New York Herald*, February 1, 1857, 1.

17. "The Bond Street Murder," *New York Daily Times*, February 3, 1857, 2.

18. "The Burdell Tragedy: Condensation of Testimony Up to Saturday," *Frank Leslie's Illustrated Newspaper*, 202.

19. "The Bond Street Murder—The Defense," *New York Herald*, May 8, 1857, 6.

20. "The Bond Street Tragedy; Additional Particulars of the Murder of Dr. Burdell," *New York Herald*, February 7, 1857, 1.

21. "Horrible and Mysterious Murder in Bond Street: Assassination of Dr. Burdell in His Own Office," *The New York Herald*, February 1, 1857, 1.

22. "The Evidence in the Burdell Case," *Harper's Weekly*, February 21, 1857, 114.

23. "The Bond Street Tragedy," *Frank Leslie's Illustrated Newspaper*, February 14, 1857, 14.

24. "Mysterious Murder: An Eminent Citizen Assassinated," *New York Daily Tribune*, February 2, 1857, 5.

25. "The Bond Street Murders: Personal Notes of Some of the Witnesses," *New York Daily Times*, February 6, 1857, 2.

26. "The Bond Street Murder: The Breach of Promise Suit was to be Recommended Three Weeks after the Alleged Marriage," *New York Daily Times*, Feb. 9, 1857, 1.

27. "The Bond Street Murders," *Brooklyn Daily Eagle*, February 4, 1857, 2.

28. "The Bond Street Murder: The Breach of Promise Suit was to be recommenced Three Weeks after the Alleged Marriage," *New York Daily Times*, Feb. 9, 1857, 1.

29. "The Bond Street Tragedy: Twelfth Day of the Investigation," *New York Herald*, February 12, 1857, 1.

30. "The Bond Street Tragedy," *New York Herald*, February 2, 1857, 1.

31. "Biography of Dr. Harvey Burdell," *American Phrenological Journal*, March 1857, 51.

32. "The Funeral of Dr. Burdell," *New York Daily Times*, February 5, 1857, 4.

33. "The Bond Street Tragedy: Funeral of the Victim," *New York Herald*, February 5, 1857, 8.

34. "The Bond Street Murder Case," *The Brooklyn Daily Eagle*, February 16, 1857, 2.

35. "The Burdell Murder – Verdict of the Coroner's Jury," *Boston Herald*, February 16, 4.

36. The Bond Street Tragedy: Interesting Interviews with Mrs. Cunningham, *New York Herald*, February 17, 1857, 1.

37. Ibid, 1.

38. "The Auction at 31 Bond Street: An Immense Crowd," *The New York Herald*, March 31, 1857, 1.

39. "The Widow Burdell Before the Surrogate: Proceedings on the Application of Administration," *New York Daily Times*, March 13, 1857, 1.

40. "The Murder of Doctor Burdell: Trial of Mrs. Cunningham and J. J. Eckel," *New York Daily Tribune*, May 6, 1867, 6.

41. "The Burdell Murder: Scenes in Court. Speeches of Counsel." *New York Daily Times*, May 11, 1857, 1.

42. "The Bond Street Murder – Acquittal of Mrs. Cunningham – Discharge of Eckel," *New York Herald*, May 10, 1857, 4.

43. "The End of the 'Burdell Trial'." *Frank Leslie's Illustrated Newspaper*, May 23, 1857, 389.

44. "31 Bond street Again: Same of Fraud Exposed . . . Cunningham would be a Mother . . . She is Caught in Her Own Trap . . . Adventures of a Borrowed Baby," *New York Daily Tribune*, August 5, 1857, 6.

45. "The Burdell Estate; She Gets None of the Property. It is Against Mrs. Cunningham," *New York Daily Times*, August 25, 1857, 1.

46. *Brooklyn Daily Eagle*, April 4, 1863, 3, col. 1.

47. "Henry Lauren Clinton 1820-1899," http://courts.state.ny.us/history/legal-history-new-york/luminaries-legal-figures/clinton-henry.html

48. "Obsequies of John J. Eckel; Clergymen Refusing to Officiate," *New York Herald*, December 8, 1896, 30.

49. "Mrs. Cunningham Again: A Part of Her Life Subsequent to the Burdell Murder—Married to a Man whom She Had Jilted Years Before," *San Francisco Chronicle*, February 9, 1876, 1.

50. Benjamin Feldman and Darleen Gumtow, *Evil Emma, Down Mexico Way*, New York: New York Wanderer Press in association with The Green-Wood Historic Fund, 2018, 61.

51. "A Clouded Life; Interview with Mrs. Cunningham-Burdell," *San Francisco Chronicle*, February 11, 1876, 3.

52. "An Old Crime Recalled: Mrs. Cunningham and the Tragedy in Which She Figured," *New York Times*, September 17, 1887, 1.

FREDERICKA "MARM" MANDELBAUM

1. "Old Mother Mandelbaum; A Character Dickens Would Have Delighted to Portray," *Boston Globe*, November 11, 1883, 16.

2. Marion Kaplan, *Jewish Daily Life in Germany 1618–1945* (New York: Oxford University Press, 2005), 130–32.

3. https://www.genealogy.com/forum/surnames/topics/lett/625/

4. Ronald Vern Jackson, ed. *Germans to America. Volume 1 January 1850–May 1851* (New York: Accelerated Indexing Systems International, Inc., 1988) 252.

5. Robert Greenleigh Albion, *The Rise of the New York Port, 1815–1860* (Boston: Northeastern University Press, 1984, 1967, 1939), 343–44.

6. Robert Ernst, *Immigrant Life in New York City, 1825–1863* (New York: Columbia University, 1949), 61–63.

7. Stanley Nadel, *Little Germany: Ethnicity, Religion, and Class in New York City, 1845–80* (Urbana: University of Illinois Press, 1990), 29, 37–39.

8. "A Queen Among Thieves," *New York Times*, July 24, 1884, 5.

9. "End of a Criminal Career; Old Abe Greenthal Dies of Old Age," *New York Times*, November 20, 1889, 8.

10. "Pawnbrokers; How Boys are Induced to Steal," *Brooklyn Daily Eagle*, February 4, 1874, 4.

11. "A Queen Among Thieves; Mother Mandelbaum's Vast Business," *New York Times*, July 24, 1884, 5.

12. "'Mother' Mandelbaum Dead," *New York Tribune*, February 27, 1894, 4.

13. James Lardner and Thomas Repetto. *NYPD: A City and Its Police* (New York: Henry Holt & Company, 2001), 15, 30.

14. Lawrence M. Friedman, *Crime and Punishment in American History* (New York; Basic Books, 1993), 110.

15. Oliver L. Barbour, *A Treatise on the Criminal Law of the State of New York; and Upon the Jurisdiction, Duty, and Authority of Justices of the Peace*, 2nd ed. (Albany: Gould, Banks 1852), 156.

16. John Steele Gordon, *An Empire of Wealth: The Epic of American History*, 1607–2001 (New York: Harper Collins Publishers, 2004), 208.

17. George W. Walling, Recollections of a New York Chief of Police (New York: Caxton Book Concern, 1887), 283.

18. Luc Sante, *Low Life: Lures and Snares of Old New York* (New York: Farrar, Straus, and Giroux, 2003), 324.

19. "Mr. Olney's Boomerang, Inspector Byrnes on The District Attorney's Office," *New York Times*, August 3, 1884.

20. Richard Rovere, *Howe & Hummel: Their True and Scandalous History* (New York: Farrar, Strauss and Giroux, 1974), 6.

21. Sophie Lyons, *Why Crimes Does Not Pay* (New York: J.S. Ogilvie Publishing Co., 1913), 143.

22. "A Queen Among Thieves," *New York Times*, July 24, 1884, 5.

23. Ibid.

24. Sophie Lyons, *Why Crimes Does Not Pay*, 144.

25. "A Queen Among Thieves," *New York Times*, July 24, 1884, 5.

26. "Queen of the 'Crooks' Mother Mandelbaum, the Famous Fence is Dead," *World* (New York), February 27, 1894, 14.

27. "A Queen Among Thieves," *The New York Times*, July 24, 1884, 5.

28. Ben Macintyre. *The Napoleon of Crime: The Life and Times of Adam Worth, Master Thief* (New York: Dell, 1997), 30.

29. "Receivers of Stolen Goods," *New York Times*, July 18, 1873, 8.

30. "The Great Bank Robbery: Fortunes of the Men Who Took Part in the Crime," *New York Times*, October 6, 1879, 8.

31. "Old Mother Mandelbaum," *Boston Globe*, November 11, 1883, 16.

32. Ben Macintyre. *The Napoleon of Crime: The Life and Times of Adam Worth, Master Thief* (New York: Dell, 1997), 33–35.

33. "Black Lena; The Notorious Shoplifter's Conviction Affirmed," *Brooklyn Daily Eagle*, December 11, 1878, 4.

34. "A Queen Among Thieves," *New York Times*, July 24, 1884, 5.

35. "A Robbed Merchant's Suite," *New York Times*, January 24, 1884, 8.

36. "Queer Mrs. Mandelbaum: The Trial of a Woman Whose Name Is A Proverb," *Sun* (New York), January 24, 1884, 4.

37. "Marm Mandelbaum's Bonanza," *Boston Daily Globe*, January 25, 1884, 4.

38. "Mary Hoey Pardoned," *New York Times*, January 6, 1885, 3.

39. "A Queen Among Thieves," *New York Times*, July 24, 1884, 5.

40. "Mother Mandelbaum Trapped; Arrested by Private Detectives and Held in Heavy Bail," *New York Times*, July 23, 1884, 5.

41. "Got Mother Mandelbaum," *Sun* (New York), July 24, 1884, 1.

42. "A Big Haul," *Chicago Daily Tribune*, July 25, 1884, 3.

43. "Bulldozing the Court; Mrs. Mandelbaum's Lawyer Rebuked by Judge Murray," *New York Times*, July 31, 1884, 5.

44. "Her Son Julius Bailed; Mrs. Mandelbaum Reused as Surety by the Justice," *New York Times*, July 26, 1884, 5.

45. "Bulldozing the Court," *New York Times*, July 31, 1884, 5.

46. "Mr. Olney's Boomerang," *New York Times*, August 3, 1884, 12.

47. "Inspector Byrnes and the District Attorney," *Brooklyn Daily Eagle*, August 5, 1884, 2.

48. "In and About The City; Is Detective Frank on Trial?" *New York Times*, September 16, 1884, 8.

49. "The Case of Mrs. Mandelbaum," *New York Times*, December 3, 1884, 8.

50. "'Mother' Mandelbaum's Departure; What Mr. Pinkerton Says About It," *New York Tribune*, December 6, 1884, 7.

51. "Mrs. Mandelbaum Missing; The Notorious Receiver Flies from The City," *New York Times*, December 6, 1884, 1.

52. "Mother Mandelbaum; A Belief That Her Diamonds Are Stolen Property," *New York Times*, December 10, 1884, 1.

53. "Mrs. Mandelbaum in Jail; The Fugitives Arrested in Canada," *New York Tribune*, December 9, 1884, 1.

54. "Mother Mandelbaum's Den; Canadians Buying New York Goods Remarkably Cheap," *National Police Gazette*, September 4, 1886, 7.

55. "Mother Mandelbaum's Mortgage," *New York Times*, February 19, 1885, 3.

56. "Mrs. Mandelbaum's Visit; Her Favorite Daughter's Death Brings Her Here," *New York Times*, November 12, 1885, 2.

57. "Julius Mandelbaum Surrenders," *New York Times*, June 23, 1888.

SOPHIE LYONS

1. Herbert Asbury, *The Gangs of New York: An Informal History of the Underworld* (New York: Vintage: Reprint Edition, 2008), 216.

2. "Jacob Alken," 1860 United States Federal Census: Census Place: New York Ward 8 District 4, New York, New York; Roll: M653_795; Page: 562; Image: 43; Family History Library Film: 803795. Ancestry.com.

3. "Famous Sophie Lyons, Princess of Crime," *National Police Gazette*, January 9, 1897, 69.

4. Sophie Lyons, *Why Crime Does Not Pay* (New York: J. S. Ogilvie Publishing Co., 1913), 12.

5. Ibid., 11.

6. Ibid., 11.

7. Sophie Lyons, *Why Crime Does Not Pay* (New York: J. S. Ogilvie Publishing Co., 1913), 13.

8. Ibid.

9. "Policeman's Salaries—The Mayor's Veto," *New York Times*, October 28, 1853.

10. Sophie Lyons, *Why Crime Does Not Pay* (New York: J. S. Ogilvie Publishing Co., 1913), 11.

11. David W. Maurer, *Whiz Mob: A Correlation of the Technical Argot of Pickpockets with Their Behavior Pattern* (New Haven: College & University Press, 1964), 71.

12. Ibid., 60, 175.

13. Sophie Lyons, *Why Crime Does Not Pay* (New York: J. S. Ogilvie Publishing Co., 1913), 13.

14. Sophie Lyons, *Why Crime Does Not Pay* (New York: J. S. Ogilvie Publishing Co., 1913), 11, 12.

15. Society for the Reformation of Juvenile Delinquents, "By-Laws of the Board of Managers of the Society of Juvenile Delinquents," 1861, 18–19.

16. "State of New York, Department of Correctional Services, House of Refuge, Inmate Case Histories and Record of Admissions, Discharges and Other," (New York: New York State Archives, 1859), case no. 7820.

17. "Court of General Sessions," *New York Times*, September 21, 1861.

18. "Famous Sophie Lyons, Princess of Crime," *National Police Gazette*, January 9, 1897, 69, 1011.

19. "Buying Out of Sing Sing," *Sun* (New York), July 11, 1873, 1.

20. W. F. Howe, "Sophie Lyons, Queen of Crime, Chapter II," *National Police Gazette*, January 16, 1897, 69, 1012.

21. "Buying Out of Sing Sing," *Sun* (New York), July 11, 1873, 1.

22. W. F. Howe, "Sophie Lyons, Queen of Crime, Chapter II," *National Police Gazette*, January 16, 1897, 69, 1012.

23. "Buying Out of Sing Sing," *Sun* (New York), July 11, 1873, 1.

24. Sophie Lyons, *Why Crime Does Not Pay* (New York: J. S. Ogilvie Publishing Co., 1913), 15.

25. Ibid.

26. Ibid.

27. "Buying Out of Sing Sing," *Sun* (New York), July 11, 1873, 1.

28. Ibid.

29. "Ned and Sophy Lyons," *Brooklyn Daily Eagle*, December 29, 1876.

30. "Important to Escaped Convicts," *New York Daily Herald*, December 28, 1876.

31. W. F. Howe, "Sophie Lyons, Queen of Crime," *National Police Gazette*, January 16, 1897, 69, 1012.

32. Thomas Byrnes, Professional Criminals of America, 1886, 141.

33. W. F. Howe, "Sophie Lyons, Queen of Crime," *National Police Gazette*, January 16, 1897, 69, 1012.

34. "Suspected Sophie," *Boston Globe*, October 27, 1880.

35. Thomas Byrne, *1886 Professional Criminals of America* (New York: Chelsea House Publishers, 1969), 206.

36. "The Sophie Lyons Case," *Detroit Free Press*, February 4, 1883, 4.

37. "Guilty: So Say the Jurors in the Lyons Case," *Detroit Free Press*, February 3, 1883, 7.

38. "Grinds Organ for Pennies," *Detroit Free Press*, November 17, 1908, 1.

39. "Accusing His Mother," *Sun* (New York), February 1, 1880.

40. Ibid.

41. "Said to Be a Son of Ned and Sophie Lyons," *Sun* (New York), August 31, 1884.

42. "George Lyons," https://www.findagrave.com/memorial/9152664/george-lyons.

43. W. F. Howe, "Sophie Lyons, Queen of Crime," *National Police Gazette*, January 16, 1897, 69, 1012.

44. "Once Queen of Crooks, Dies a Philanthropist," *New York Times*, May 18, 1924, 4.
45. "Says Pope Blessed Her," *Boston Post*, June 6, 1901.
46. "No Expense," *Detroit Free Press*, July 18, 1901.
47. "Wins Her Fight for Negro Home," *Detroit Free Press*, June 17, 1909, 1.
48. "Sophie Lyons is Glad She's No One Else," *Detroit Free Press*, August 16, 1908, 7.
49. "I Don't Care if Billie Has An Affinity—Sophie Lyons Burke," *Detroit Free Press*, August 6, 1911, 1.
50. "Queen of Crooks Reforms," *Daily Republican* (Rushville, IN), May 10, 1913.
51. "Sophie Lyons Offers Gift: Retired Thief Has Site for Criminals Home in Detroit," *New York Times*, February 2, 1916, 1.
52. "Grinds Organ for Pennies: Daughter of Sophie Lyons, In Desperate Straits, Begs For Living," *Detroit Free Press*, November 17, 1908, 1.
53. "'Perfumed Vagrant,' says Sophie Lyons of Child," *Detroit Free Press*, November 20, 1908, 6.
54. "Sophie Lyons Identifies Bandits Who Slugged Her," *Lansing State Journal*, April 4, 1924.
55. "Rob Ex-Confidence Woman: Burglars Sack Sophie L. Burke's Detroit Home—Get $20,000," *New York Times*, July 6, 1922, 8.

ROXALANA DRUSE

1. "Murdered by His Family, Wife, Daughter and Nephew Take Part in Killing Druse," *Sun* (New York), January 17, 1885, 1.
2. "A Wife's Terrible Crime, Killing Her Husband and Then Burning the Body," *New York Times*, January 17, 1885, 1.
3. "Killed by His Wife; A Nephew Confesses His Part in the Awful Crime," *Richwood Gazette* (Richwood, OH), January 22, 1885.
4. "The Druse Murder: Testimony of the Wife of the Dead Farmer," *The Post-Star* (Glens Falls, NY), January 21, 1885, 1.
5. "The Murder of William Druse," *New York Times*, January 20, 1885, 5.
6. "The Druse Murder," *Post-Star* (Glens Falls, NY), January 21, 1885, 1.
7. "Murdered by His Wife and Family," *Oshkosh Daily Northwestern* (Oshkosh, WI), January 30, 1885.
8. "The Murder of William Druse," *New York Times*, March 19, 1885.

9. "Ghastly Find; Supposed to be the Head of a Murdered Man," *Buffalo Commercial* (Buffalo, NY), March 19, 1885, 1.

10. "The Druse Murder; Inquest Concluded—The Accused in Jail," *Herkimer Democrat* (Herkimer, NY), February 4, 1885, 2.

11. W. H. Tippet, *Herkimer County Murders: This Book Contains an Accurate Account of the Capital Crimes Committed in Herkimer County from the Year 1783 Up to the Present Time* (Herkimer, NY), 1885.

12. "Criminal," *Herkimer Democrat* (Herkimer, NY), April 22, 1885, 3.

13. "Foreclosure Sale," *Herkimer Democrat* (Herkimer, NY), May 30, 1885, 4.

14. "Druse Trials; Frank Gates the First Witness," *Herkimer Democrat* (Herkimer, NY), September 30, 1885, 1.

15. "News of the Week," *Plattsburgh Sentinel*, October 16, 1885.

16. "The Druse Trial; Mrs. Druse Convicted of Murder in the First Degree at Herkimer," *Plattsburgh Sentinel*, October 9, 1885.

17. Ibid.

18. "Mrs. Druse Sentenced; The Woman Who Killed Her Husband and Boiled His Body," *Democrat and Chronicle* (Rochester, NY), November 9, 1886, 1.

19. "Her Sex Her Only Hope; Governor Hill Postpones the Execution of Mrs. Druse," *Detroit Free Press*, December 23, 1886, 2.

20. "Horrible Crime of Mrs. Druse; Condemned to Death, She is Respited to Allow Time for Legislative Action, *Chicago Daily Tribune*, December 23, 1886, 1.

21. "Mrs. Druse Facing Death; Fears That She Will Break Down At Last," *New York Times*, February 27, 1887.

22. Ibid.

23. "Squared. The Vengeful Account of the Law with Roxalana Druse, the Husband Butcher, *National Police Gazette*, March 12, 1887, 6.

24. "Roxalana Druse Hanged; The Herkimer Butchery Avenged By the Law," *New York Times,* March 1, 1887, 2.

25. "The Law is Satisfied; Mrs. Roxalana Druse Hanged for the Murder of Her Husband," *Detroit Free Press*, March 1, 1887, 2.

26. "Roxalana Druse Hanged," *New York Times*, March 1, 1887, 2.

27. "Violent Grief of Mary Druse," *The Fort Covington Sun* (Franklin County), July 7, 1887, 1.

28. "Pardoned by the Governor," *New York Times*, June 26, 1895, 5.

29. "Mary Druse, Overcome with Joy," *Democrat and Chronicle* (Rochester, NY), June 27, 1895, 1.

30. "The Rights of Criminals: Modern Legislation Has Tended to Their Enlargement," *New York Times*, Aug. 11, 1895, 20.

31. James M. Greiner, *Last Woman Hanged: Roxalana Druse* (Keene, NH: Pumpelly Press), 2010.

LIZZIE HALLIDAY

1. "Lizzie Halliday Soon to Be Tried," *New York Times*, June 10, 1894, 8.

2. Blumer G. Alder, "The Halliday Case," *Brooklyn Medical Journal* 9, 165.

3. Ibid., 169.

4. "Lizzie Borgia: Mrs. Halliday, The Triple Murderess, Confesses to Nellie Bly," *St. Louis Post-Dispatch*, November 5, 1893, 6.

5. "A Woman Without a Heart," *The World* (New York), November 5, 1893, 1.

6. "Mrs. Halliday's Case Called: Three Jurors Secured to Try the Alleged Murderess, *New York Times*, June 19, 1894.

7. "A Woman Without a Heart," *The World* (New York), November 5, 1893, 1.

8. "Lizzie Borgia," *St. Louis Post-Dispatch*, November 5, 1893, 1.

9. "A Woman Without a Heart," *The World* (New York), November 5, 1893, 26.

10. Adler G. Blumer, "The Halliday Case," *Brooklyn Medical Journal* 9, 167.

11. "A Woman Without a Heart," *The World* (New York), November 5, 1893, 26.

12. "Weird Life of Crime: Mrs. Halliday's Many Marriages and Murders," *Morning Star* (Glens Falls, NY), June 19, 1894.

13. "Lizzie Borgia," *St. Louis Post-Dispatch*, November 5, 1893, 1.

14. "A Woman Without a Heart," *The World* (New York), November 5, 1893, 26.

15. "Weird Life of Crime; Mrs. Halliday's Many Marriages and Murders," *The Morning Star* (Glens Falls, NY), June 19, 1894.

16. Eastern State Penitentiary; America's Most Historic Prison, website. www.easternstate.org

17. "Lizzie Borgia; Mrs. Halliday, the Triple Murderess," *St. Louis Post-Dispatch*, November 5, 1893, 6.

18. "A Female Fiend; Lizzie Halliday, the Triple Murderess in the Toils," *St. Louis Post-Dispatch*, September 10, 1893, 6.

19. "Lizzie Halliday's Past: Light on Alleged Crimes" *New York-Tribune*, September 9, 1893, 1.

20. "A Woman Without A Heart," *The World* (New York), November 5, 1893, 26.

21. "Lizzie Halliday's Past,";. Light on Alleged Crimes," *New York Tribune*, September 9, 1893, 1.

22. "Horrible Crimes; Tomorrow Will Begin the Trial of Mrs. Lizzie Halliday," *St. Louis Post-Dispatch*, June 17, 1894, 5.

23. "A Murderous Maniac: The Many Crimes Charged Against Lizzie Halliday," *Frederick News* (Maryland), September 11, 1893.

24. "Nellie Bly Visits Mrs. Halliday; Strange Story of the Triple Murder as Told by the Prisoner in the Monticello Jail," *The World* (New York), October 22, 1893, 17.

25. "Mrs. Halliday Seemed Sane: So Testify Several Witnesses in the Murder Trial," *New York Times*, June 19, 1894, 9.

26. Ibid.

27. "Murdered by a Woman: Two Women and a Man Killed by Mrs. Halliday," *National Police Gazette*, September 23, 1893, 6.

28. "A Horrible Crime: The Bodies of Two Women Found Under a Barn Near Burlingham," *Middletown Times-Press*, September 5, 1893, 3.

29. "Is She A Murderess? Not a Clew to the Ghastly Mysteries on the Halliday Farm," *The World* (New York), September 6, 1893, 1.

30. "A Horrible Crime: The Bodies of Two Women Found Under a Barn Near Burlingham," *Middletown Times-Press*, September 5, 1893, 3.

31. "Hired by Mrs. Halliday: Some Light on the Murders," *New York Tribune*, September 7, 1893, 1.

32. "A Horrible Crime," 3.

33. "Old Paul Killed, Too; His Body Found Under the Floor of the Halliday House," *Evening World* (New York), September 7, 1893, 1.

34. "Paul Halliday's Body Found: Buried Beneath the Kitchen Floor of His House," *New York Times*, September 8, 1893, 8.

35. "Hired by Mrs. Halliday: Some Light on the Murders," *New York Tribune*, September 7, 1893, 1.

36. "Mrs. Halliday Is in Monticello Jail," *Chicago Daily Tribune*, September 9, 1893, 6.

37. "More Mystery; The Halliday Woman in Monticello Jail Induced to Eat and Talk," *Middletown Times-Press*, September 11, 1893, 3.

38. "A Plausible Theory; Did Mrs. Halliday Have a Lover?" *Middletown Times-Press*, September 15, 1893.

39. "Cuts Her Throat with Broken Glass," *Chicago Daily Tribune*, December 12, 1893, 3.

40. "The Horror Thickens," *Middletown Times-Press*, September 7, 1893, 3.

41. "Mrs. Halliday Tries to Burn Jail," *New York Times*, November 24, 1893, 1.

42. "Nellie Bly Visits Mrs. Halliday; Strange Story of the Triple Murder as Told by the Prisoner in the Monticello Jail," *The World* (New York), 17.

43. A Woman Without A Heart," *The World* (New York), November 5, 1893, 1.

44. "Murderess Halliday" *Star-Gazette* (Elmira), December 2, 1893, 1.

45. "More About Mrs. Halliday," *Middletown Times-Press*, December 4, 1893.

46. "Horrible Crimes; Tomorrow Will Begin the Trial of Mrs. Lizzie Halliday," *St. Louis Post-Dispatch*, June 17, 1894, 5.

47. Blumer, "The Halliday Case," 169.

48. "Mrs. Halliday's Trial Near At Hand," *New York Times*, June 4, 1894, 9.

49. "To Stop The Insanity Dodge," *Chicago Daily Tribune*, April 21, 1898, 6.

50. *Transactions of the Medical Society of the State of New York*, 1895, 241.

51. "Mrs. Halliday's Assistant," *Sun* (New York), September 17, 1893, 21.

52. "Lizzie Halliday Soon To Be Tried," *New York Times*, June 10, 1894, 8.

53. Ibid., *New York Times*, June 10, 1894, 8.

54. "Mrs. Halliday Seemed Sane; So Testify Several Witnesses in the Murder Trial," *New York Times*, June 19, 1894, 9.

55. "The Halliday Murder Case: Bodies of the Female Victims Fully Identified," *New York Times*, September 7, 1893, 8.

56. "Mrs. Halliday Seemed Sane," *New York Times*, June 19, 1894, 9.

57. "A Weird Murderess," *Evening World* (New York), June 20, 1894, 1.

58. "Was Like a Tigress," *Evening World* (New York), June 21, 1894, 1.

59. "Mrs. Halliday Found Guilty; Jury Decides She Did Murder in the First Degree," *New York Times*, June 22, 1894, 5.

60. "Poisoned by Mrs. Halliday's Bite. The County Sheriff in Danger of Losing His Arm," *New York Tribune*, August 25, 1894.

61. "Lizzie Halliday Examined," *Middletown Daily Argus*, July 14, 1894, 4.

62. "Two Murderous Lunatics; They Assault an Asylum Attendant and Beat Her Nearly to Death," *Washington Post*, September 2, 1895, 7.

63. "Ex-Gypsy Queen Shoots Another Woman to Death; Lizzie Halliday Kills Nellie Wickes, Attendant at Matteawan Asylum," *Evening World* (New York), September 27, 1906, 10.

64. "Multimurderess Dies in Asylum; Lizzie Halliday Known to Have Killed at Least Eight," *Washington Post*, June 30, 1918, 8.

MARY ALICE LIVINGSTON

1. "Mrs. Fleming's Ordeal On; The Legal Battle For Her Life Begun in Earnest," *Sun* (New York), May 27, 1896, 1.

2. "Bliss Poisoning Case: Mrs. Fleming Takes Her Imprisonment Calmly," *Sun (New York)*, September 5, 1895, 2.

3. "From A Child's Lips; Florence King's Evidence Against Mrs. Fleming," *The World* (New York), June 9, 1896, 1.

4. "Bliss Poisoning Case: Only Circumstantial Evidence for Coroner's Jury Tomorrow," *New York Times*, September 9, 1895, 8.

5. "Bliss Accused Her," *The World* (New York), June 10, 1896, 16.

6. *New York Herald*, September 1, 1895, 1.

7. "Mrs. Fleming Arrested," *New York Times*, September 4, 1895, 1.

8. "Did She Kill Her Mother?" *Evening World*, September 4, 1895, 2.

9. "Mrs. Fleming Arrested," *New York Times*, September 4, 1895, 1.

10. "Poisoning Trial Opens," *Sun* (New York), May 12, 1896, 1.

11. "The Bliss Poisoning Case," *New York Tribune*, September 5, 1895, 1

12. "The Bliss Poisoning Case," *New York Tribune*, September 5, 1895, 1

13. "Poisoning Trial Opens," *Sun* (New York), May 12, 1896, 1.

14. "For Breach of Promise, Miss Livingston Wants $75,000 from Mr. Fleming," *New York Times*, January 10, 1883, 3.

15. Ibid.

16. "Did She Kill Her Mother?" *Evening World*, September 4, 1895, 2.

17. "A Suit for Breach of Promise," *New York Times*, June 14, 1882, 3.

18. "For Breach of Promise, Miss Livingston Wants $75,000 from Mr. Fleming," *New York Times*, January 8, 1883, 3.

19. Ibid.

20. "The Bliss Poisoning Case," *New York Tribune*, September 5, 1895, 1.

21. "A Verdict for Miss Livingston," *New York Times*, January 12, 1883, 8.

22. "Relying on a Diary; It is Brought into Court by Miss Livingston," *New York Times*, October 12, 1886, 3.

23. Ibid.

24. "Left All to His Wife," *New York Times*, April 21, 1887, 2.

25. "Lawyer Willis's Story; He Considers Himself the Victim of a Wicked Plot," *New York Times*, October 15, 1886, 8.

26. "Will Wed Mrs. Fleming," *The World* (New York), May 25, 1896, 1.

27. "Mrs. Fleming Not Free," *New York Times*, September 11, 1895.

28. Ibid.

29. Ibid.

30. "Mrs. Fleming Denies Guilt," *Evening World* (New York), September 12, 1895, 2.

31. "No Inheritance by Murder," *Sun* (New York), October 17, 1895, 5.

32. "$82,000 Mrs. Fleming Can't Get," *Sun* (New York), February 14, 1896, 7.

33. Ibid., 2.

34. "Mrs. Fleming a Mother Again," *Sun* (New York), December 9, 1895, 1.

35. "Career of the Recorder Elect," *New York Times*, November 7, 1894.

36. "Strong! Tammany Overwhelmed by a Plurality of 50,000," *New York Times*, November 7, 1894.

37. "Recorder Goff's Errors; So Says the Court of Appeals," *New York Times*, April 22, 1896, 9.

38. "Charles W. Brooke Dead," *New York Times*, February 8, 1897, 1

39. "John F. McIntyre, Jurist, Dies at 72," *New York Times*, January 10, 1927, 1.

40. "Poisoning Trial Begins," *Sun* (New York), May 12, 1896, 1.

41. "Fleming Trial Goes Slow: Talesmen Don't Want to Try a Woman for Murder," *Sun* (New York), May 13, 1896, 2.

42. "The Poisoning Trial; Mrs. Fleming's Legitimacy, It is Said, Will Be Called in Question," *Sun* (New York), May 10, 1896, 7.

43. "Her Life at Stake; Yet Mrs. Fleming Sees Nothing but Humor in Her Trial," *The World* (New York), May 12, 1896, 4.

44. "Will Wed Mrs. Fleming," *The World* (New York), May 25, 1896, 1.

45. "Mrs. Fleming Out of Court," *The World* (New York), May 15, 1896, 8.

46. "Fleming Trial Stories; State Sends Witness Florrie King out of the City," *Sun* (New York), May 24, 1896, 5.

47. "Her Life at Stake," *The World*, May 12, 1896, 4.

48. "Mrs. Fleming's Ordeal On," *Sun* (New York), May 27, 1896, 2.

49. Ibid.

50. "Plenty of Poison Found," *Sun* (New York), October 3, 1895, 3.

51. "Mrs. Fleming's Board Bills," *New York Tribune*, June 2, 1896, 3.

52. "Brooke's Bombshell; Says A Conspiracy was Formed To Convict Mrs. Fleming," *The World* (New York), June 6, 1896, 3.

53. "From a Child's Lips; Florence King's Evidence Against Mrs. Fleming," *The World* (New York), June 9, 1896, 1.

54. "Bliss Accused Her. Indirectly Charged Mrs. Fleming with Her Mother's Death," *The World* (New York), June 10, 1896, 16.

55. "Shielded by Wilckes," *The World* (New York), June 12, 1896, 14.

56. "Now for the Defense; Mrs. Fleming's Side of the Case Will Begin Today," *The World* (New York), June 16, 1896, 16.

57. "Her Love The Motive," *The World* (New York), June 13, 1896, 4.

58. "*World's* Woman Jury Speaks For Itself," *The World* (New York), June 7, 1896.

59. "Mrs. Fleming Thanks 'The World's' Jury, *The World* (New York), June 21, 1896, 21.

60. "May Allege Suicide; Lawyer Brooke Gives A Hint As To Mrs. Fleming's Defense," *The World* (New York), June 3, 1896, 3.

61. "Defense Begins; Strong Declarations Today at the Fleming Trial," *Standard Union* (Brooklyn), June 16, 1896, 4.

62. "Has Got To Die; Dr. Scheele's Statement Regarding Mrs. Fleming," *Standard Union* (Brooklyn), June 17, 1896.

63. "Mrs. Fleming Free; Found Not Guilty By the Jury At 12:50 A.M." *The World* (New York), June 24, 1896, 1.

64. "Fascinated by Freedom," *The World* (New York), June 25, 1896, 3.

65. "Mrs. Fleming to Long Branch," July 2, 1896, *The World* (New York), July 2, 1896, 3.

66. "*World's* Woman Jurors Give Their Impressions," *The World* (New York), June 21, 1896.

MARY FARMER

1. "Woman Sentenced to Electrocution," *Evening Tribune* (San Diego, CA), June 20, 1908, 1.

2. "Brutally Murdered, Body Concealed," *Watertown Daily Times*, April 28, 1908, 1, 3.

3. The Farmer Trial, *Watertown Re-union*, June 17, 1908, 1.

4. "Cruel Murder," *Watertown Re-Union*, April 29, 1908.

5. "Farmers are Held for Grand Jury," *Watertown Re-Union*, May 9, 1908, 1.

6. "A Woman Murdered," *Ogdensburg Daily Journal*, April 29, 1908, 1.

7. "Brutally Murdered, Body Concealed," *Watertown Daily Times*, April 28, 1908, 3.

8. "A Woman Murdered," *Ogdensburg Journal*, April 29, 1908, 1.

9. "Cruel Murder," *Watertown Re-Union*, April 29, 1908, 1.

10. "Man and Wife Under Arrest in Connection with Brutal Murder," *The Ogdensburg News*, April 29, 1908, 1.

11. "In Woman's Prison. There Mary Farmer Will Remain for Present at Least," *Auburn Democrat-Argus*, June 23, 1908, 8.

12. "Confesses Brennan Murder," *New York Times*, April 29, 1908, 1.

13. "Mrs. Farmer Held for the Grand Jury," *Watertown Daily Times*, May 7, 1908, 5.

14. "Farmer and Wife Plead Not Guilty," *Watertown Re-Union*, May 6, 1908, 7.

15. "Both Are Indicted," *Watertown Re-Union*, May 16, 1908, 1.

16. "Trying to Show Motive," *Syracuse Herald*, June 13, 1908, 11.

17. "The Farmer Trial: The Actions of Dead Woman Traced with Care," *Watertown Re-Union*, June 17, 1908, 1.

18. "The Farmer Trial: The Actions of Dead Woman Traced with Care," *Watertown Re-Union* June 17, 1908, 1.

19. "The Farmer Trial," *The Watertown Re-Union*, June 17, 1908, 6.

20. "Held for Murder," *Watertown Herald*, May 9, 1908, 1.

21. "Farmer Trial—Defense Witnesses Testify," *Watertown Re-Union*, June 20, 1908, 1.

22. "Mrs. Farmer Taken to Auburn," *New York Tribune*, June 21, 1908, 5.

23. "Jas. D. Farmer on Trial for Murder," *Watertown Daily Times*, October 19, 1908, 8.

24. "First Witnesses in Farmer Case," *Watertown Daily Times*, October 21, 1908, 3, 6.

25. "Is Indifferent to her Fate," *Oswego Palladium*, February 15, 1900, 1.

26. "Test Death Chair for Mrs. Farmer," *New York Times*, March 28, 1909, 11.

27. "Mrs. Farmer Calm, Facing Death Today," *New York Times*, March 29, 1909, 1.

28. "Mrs. Farmer Calm, Facing Death Today," *New York Times*, March 29, 1909, 2.

29. "The Case of Mrs. Farmer: A Woman Lawyer's Reasons Why She Should Not Be Executed," *New York Times*, March 29, 1909, 2.

30. "Jury Finds Farmer 'Is Not Guilty,'" *Watertown Daily Times*, March 5, 1910, 8.

31. "The Late James Farmer," *Journal and Republican*, June 14, 1934, 8.

CELIA COONEY

1. "Bobbed Haired Bandit's Own Story," Part III, *New York American*, April 30, 1924.

2. "What the World Didn't Know," *Modern Romances*, March 1940, 87.

3. "Bobbed Haired Bandit's Own Story," Part III, *New York American*, April 30, 1924.

4. Ibid.

5. "Bobbed Haired Bandit's Own Story," IV, *New York American*, May 1, 1924.

6. "Robbed to Get Home for Baby Girl, Bandit Says," *New York Herald Tribune*, April 23, 1924, 9.

7. "Woman with Gun Holds up Six Men as Pal Robs Store," *Brooklyn Eagle*, January 6, 1924, 1.

8. "Bobbed Hair Bandit's Mate Located by Police," *Brooklyn Daily Times*, April 17, 1924, 13.

9. "Bobbed Hair Bandit's Own Story," Part V, *New York American*, 10.

10. "Armed Girl Bandit Holds Up 2 Stores, Slight and Bobbed Haired, She Gets $450 Loot, Aided By Tall Companion," *New York Times*, January 13, 1924, 1.

11. "Bobbed Hair Bandit's Own Story," Part VI, *New York American*, 6.

12. "Bobbed Haired Girl Captured as Store Bandit," *New York Herald*, January 15, 1924, 1.

13. "Who's Who in Girl Banditry Baffles Police," *New York Herald Tribune*, January 17, 1924, 24.

14. "'Cops Got Wrong One,' Girl Bandit Asserts in Note," *New York Herald Tribune*, January 16, 1924, 1.

15. Helen Quigley was finally released from custody after a month and a half in jail.

16. "Flapper Bandit Comes Back to Rob Same Shop," *New York Herald Tribune*, February 7, 1924, 11.

17. "Gun Girl Robs Store as 250 Police Hunt Her," *New York Herald Tribune*, March 6, 1924.

18. "Good Looks and Bobbed Hair Unlucky Charms in Brooklyn," *New York Herald Tribune*, March 8, 1924.

19. "The Bob-Haired Raider," *New York Herald Tribune*, March 7, 1924, 12.

20. "Bob-Haired Bandit Attempts A Murder," *New York Times*, April 2, 1924.

21. "Cooney Girl Sought As Bobbed Bandit Caught in Florida," *New York Times*, April 21, 1924, 1.

22. "Victim Threatens to Kill Girl Bandit—Next Time," *Brooklyn Standard Union*, April 3, 1924, 1.

23. "Bobbed Hair Bandit's Own Story," Part I, *New York American*, April 28, 1924, 2.

24. "Girl Bandit Proudly Describes 10 Crimes," *New York Times*, April 23, 1924, 1.

25. "Police Get A Clue To Bob-Hair Bandit; Circular Sent All Over Country," *New York Times*, April 16, 1924, 24.

26. "Girl 'Bandit' Still Smiles," *Los Angeles Times*, April 22, 1924, 1.

27. "Stork Leads to Bobbed Bandit's Arrest in South," *Chicago Daily Tribune*, April 22, 1924, 6.

28. "Bobbed Hair Bandit Home Today, Her Baby Dead," *New York Herald Tribune*, April 22, 1924, 1.

29. "Bobbed Bandit Steals Eye of Public From President," *Atlanta Constitution*, April 23, 1924, 22.

30. "Bobbed-Hair Bandit Loses First Fight," *Boston Daily Globe*, April 23, 1924, 2.

31. "Potent Mother Love Softens Heart of Bob-Haired Bandit," *Atlanta Constitution*, April 22, 1924, 2.

32. "Bobbed Bandit Pleads Guilty; Teases Victims," *New York Herald Tribune*, April 24, 1924, 1.

33. "13 Victims Identify Bobbed Hair Bandit," *Boston Daily Globe*, April 24, 1924, 13.

34. "Bobbed Bandit Pleads Guilty; Teases Victims," *New York Herald Tribune*, April 24, 1924, 1.

35. "Bobbed Girl Pleads Guilty of Robbery With Her Husband," *New York Times*, April 24, 1924, 1.

36. "Robbed to Get Home for Baby Girl, Bandit Says," *New York Herald Tribune*, April 23, 1924, 9.

37. "Bob-Haired Bandit Decides to Fight," *New York Times*, April 27, 1924, 17.

38. "Cooney Opens Fight to Save Bandit Wife," *New York Herald Tribune*, April 28, 1924, 1.

39. "Alienists Named to Examine Girl Bandit and Mate," *Brooklyn Daily Eagle*, April 28, 1924, 1.

40. "Alienists to Test Cooney for Sanity," *New York Times*, April 27, 1924, 1.

41. "Bob-Haired Bandit and Husband Consult Judge," *New York Herald Tribune*, April 30, 1924, 12.

42. "Bob-Haired Bandit Decides to Stick to Guilty Plea," *Brooklyn Daily Eagle*, April 30, 1924, 1.

43. "Bobbed-Hair Bandit and Hubby Sane, Say 4 Alienists," *Atlanta Constitution*, May 6, 1924, 1.

44. "Matron's Report On Celia's Life Bares Girl Bandit's History From Coal Pile Bed," *Brooklyn Daily Eagle,* May 6, 1924, 3.

45. "Bobbed Bandit Gets Ten Years in Prison; Warns Other Girls," *New York Times*, May 7, 1924, 1.

46. "Bobbed Hair Bandit Weeps At Sentence of 10 to 20 Years," *Washington Post*, May 7, 1924, 4.

47. "Gotham Indulges in Spree of Tears for Bandit Couple," *Atlanta Constitution*, May 9, 1924, 1.

48. "Hardboiled Gun Moll Defies Police as Well as Judge," *New York Daily News*, March 19, 1931.

49. "Girl Bandit's Husband Has Hand Amputated," *New York Herald Tribune*, September 1, 1924.

50. "'Bob-Haired Bandit' Wins Parole Plea" *New York Times*, October 17, 1931, 7.

51. "Cooney Will Get $12,000; State Award to Brooklyn Bandit for Loss of Hand in Prison," *New York Times*, December 25, 1931, 25.

52. "How We Forgot the Bobbed Haired Bandit," *Atlas Obscura*, January 26, 2017.

RUTH SNYDER

1. "Wife, Tied Up, Says Burglars Killed Mate," *New York Daily News*, March 21, 1927.

2. "Wife, Tied Up Says Burglars Killed Mate," *New York Daily News*, March 21, 1927.

3. "Girl Finds Mother Bound; Woman Tells of Quarrel at Card Party and of Strangers in House," *New York Times*, March 21, 1927.

4. "Art Editor's Wife Tells Death Plot; False, Says Suitor," *Washington Post*, March 22, 1927.

5. "Wife Betrays Paramour As Murderer of Snyder and He Then Confesses," *New York Times*, March 22, 1927.

6. "Gray's First Story Was A Full Denial; Had Not Been in New York for Weeks, He Told Detectives in Syracuse," *New York Times*, March 22, 1927.

7. "Wife Betrays Paramour as Murderer of Snyder and He Then Confesses," 1.

8. "Slayers of Snyder Face Speedy Trial," *New York Times*, March 23, 1927.

9. "Text of Confession Mrs. Snyder Made; Statement Given After Murder," *New York Times*, April 27, 1927.

10. "Home Life Unhappy," *New York Daily News*, March 22, 1927.

11. "Mrs. Snyder Sobs Innocence, Shifts All Blame to Gray," *New York Tribune*, April 30, 1927, 1.

12. "Gray's First Story Was A Full Denial," *New York Times*, March 22, 1927.

13. "Letters to Gray Found: Unclaimed in Easton, PA," *New York Times*, March 27, 1927, 22.

14 Ibid.

15. "Snyder Was Tricked into Big Insurance State Witness Says," *New York Times*, April 26, 1927

16. "Says Gray Was Hypnotized," *New York Times*, March 26, 1927.

17. "Mrs. Snyder Hypnotized Him, He Says in Cell," *New York Daily News*, April 1, 1927, 3.

18. Penelope Pelizzon and Nancy M. West, "Multiple Indemnity; Film Noir, James M. Cain, and Adaptations of a Tabloid Case," *Narrative*, Vol. 13, No. 3 (Columbus: Ohio State University Press, October 2005), 213.

19. Founded and owned by Joseph Medill Patterson in 1919 as the *Illustrated Daily News*, it was the first U.S. daily printed in tabloid format.

20. The *New York Evening Graphic*, owned by Bernarr Macfadden, was published from 1924 to 1932. It launched the careers of Walter Winchell and Ed Sullivan. Unfortunately, the issues of the *Evening Graphic* that covered the Snyder/Gray Trial have been lost. No archive has them.

21. "Lovers Enter Murder: Gray and Mrs. Snyder Start Court Fight Against Chair," *New York Daily News*, March 23, 1927, 3.

22. "'Can't Believe It,' Gray's Wife Cries at Confession," *New York Daily News*, March 22, 1927.

23. "Lovers Enter Murder: Gray and Mrs. Snyder Start Court Fight Against Chair," *New York Daily News*, March 23, 1927, 4.

24. "Why Gray Killed, Puzzle to Mother," *New York Times*, April 12, 1927.

25. "Gray Undergoes 2nd Sanity Test in Queens Jail," *New York Herald Tribune*, April 16, 1927, 2.

26. "Gray Swears Mrs. Snyder Broached Murder Plot; Her Story Wavers at End," *New York Times*, May 1, 1927, 1.

27. "Defense Divided in Snyder Murder," *New York Times*, March 30, 1927.

28. "Gray, Cast Off By Woman, to Plead Insanity," *New York Herald Tribune*, April 14, 1927, 2.

29. "The Lantern: The Low Down," *New York Herald Tribune*, April 20, 1927.

30. "Mrs. Snyder Hopeful, Gray Expects Chair," *New York Tribune*, May 8, 1927, 1.

31. "Mrs. Snyder Makes Appeal for Sympathy of Mothers," *Atlanta Constitution*, April 16, 1927, 3.

32. "Gray Undergoes 2nd Sanity Test in Queens Jail," *New York Herald Tribune*, April 16, 1927, 2.

33. "Court Sets April 18th for Snyder Trial," *New York Times*, April 6, 1927.

34. "Mrs. Snyder Breaks as Trial Day Nears," *New York Times*, April 17, 1927.

35. "Snyder Was Tricked Into Big Insurance," *New York Times*, April 26, 1927, 1.

36. "Death Penalty Plea Shakes Mrs. Snyder; Woman Shows Fear, then Anger as Prosecution, Opening Murder Trial, Centers Its Fire On Her, *New York Tribune*, April 26, 1927, 1.

37. "Snyder Jury Hears Widow's Confession," *New York Times*, April 27, 1927, 1.

38. "Widow on Stand Swears Gray Alone Killed Snyder As She Tried to Save Him," *New York Times*, April 30, 1927, 1.

39. "Crowd Fights to Hear Story of Mrs. Snyder," *New York Herald Tribune*, April 30, 1927, 7.

40. "'We Slew Snyder,' Says Gray, as Both Prisoners Collapse," *New York Tribune*, May 5, 1927, 1.

41. "Mrs. Snyder Hopeful, Gray Expects Chair," *New York Tribune*, May 8, 1927, 1.

42. Mrs. Snyder and Gray to Die; Jury in Hour Convicts both of Murder in First Degree," *New York Tribune*, May 10, 1927, 1.

43. Two Snyder Slayers Hear Doom Calmly: Judge, Opposed to Death Penalty, Sets Week of June 20 for Widow and Gray to Die in Chair," *New York Herald Tribune*, May 14, 1927, 1.

44. "Mrs. Snyder's 'Insanity' Held Only Hysteria," *New York Herald Tribune*, May 11, 1927, 1.

45. "Snyder Slayers Occupy Cells in Death House," *New York Herald Tribune*, May 17, 1927, 1.

46. Ibid.

47. "Alienists Visit Snyder Slayers in Death Cells," *New York Herald Tribune*, May 18, 1927, 3.

48. "Mrs. Snyder's Plea Revealed; Appeal Will Charge Abuse of Discretion by Trial Judge," *New York Herald Tribune*, August 29, 1927, 2.

49. "Gray's Wife Unemotional on Death House Visit," *New York Herald Tribune*, June 3, 1927, 7.

50. "Mrs. Snyder's Execution Stayed by Her Appeal," *New York Herald Tribune*, May 28, 1927, 2.

51. "Mrs. Snyder Fears Fat; Condemned Woman Asks for Ball so She Can Exercise," *Los Angeles Times*, May 23, 1927, 4.

52. "Ruth Snyder Hysterical, but Gray is Calm," *New York Tribune*, November 23, 1927, 6.

53. "Grandmothers Ask Chair for Ruth," *New York Daily News*, January 6, 1928, 12.

54. "If Vote Majority 2,299 for Ruth," *New York Daily News*, January 12, 1928, 5.

55. "Mother, in Tears, Begs Gov. Smith to Spare Mrs. Snyder," *New York Tribune*, December 9, 1927, 3.

56. "Alienists Doom Mrs. Snyder and Gray as Sane," *New York Tribune*, December 22, 1927.

57. "Ruth Snyder Dies First; Then Judd Gray Goes to Chair," *Los Angeles Times*, January 13, 1928, 1.

58. "Executed Pair at End of Trail, Mrs. Snyder and Gray Buried in Separate Cemeteries," *Los Angeles Times*, January 14, 1928, 3.

59. "Dual Execution Makes Trio Ill," *Pittsburgh Press*, January 14, 1928, 1.

60. "Appeal Ruling Against Child; Lawyer Says Lorraine Snyder is Destitute," *Pittsburgh Press*, November 11, 1928, 41.

61. "Girls, Orphaned Year Ago By Chair, Happy," *Toledo News-Bee*, January 12, 1929, 1.

STEPHANIE ST. CLAIR

1. Herbert Mitgang, *The Man Who Rode the Tiger: The Life and Times of Judge Samuel Seabury* (New York: J.B. Lippincott Co., 1963), 204.

2. Shirley Stewart, *The World of Stephanie St. Clair* (New York: Peter Lang Publishing, Inc., 2014), 2.

3. Ibid., 24–25.

4. Agnes Calliste, "Race, Gender and Canadian Immigration Policy: Blacks from the Caribbean, 1900-1932," *Journal of Canadian Studies* 28 (Winter 1993/94): 131–48.

5. Herb Boyd, ed. *The Harlem Reader* (New York: Random House, 2003), 45–52.

6. "Madame Gachette Gets Judgment for $1,000," *New York Amsterdam News*, February 14, 1923, 3.

7. Irma Watkins-Owens, *Blood Relations: Caribbean Immigrants and the Harlem Community, 1900–1930* (Bloomington: Indiana University Press, 1996), 137.

8. Rufus Schatzberg, *Black Organized Crime*, Chapter 7 (New York: Garland Publishing, 1993).

9. T. R. Poston, "Harlem Shadows: Harlem Moon," *Pittsburgh Courier*, December 27, 1930, 2.

10. "Mme St. Clair asks for $25,000 from the *New York Tattler* for Libel," *New York Age*, December 12, 1921 5.

11. "An Address that Drew the City's Black Elite," Christopher Gray, *New York Times*, July 24, 1994, R7.

12. Katherine Butler Jones, "409 Edgecombe, Baseball and Madame St. Clair," *The Harlem Reader: A Celebration of New York's Most Famous Neighborhood from the Renaissance Years to the Twenty-First Century* (New York: Three Rivers Press, 2003), 136.

13. "Graft on Gambling Laid to the Police by 'Policy Queen,'" *New York Times*, December 9, 1930, 1.

14. "Grandmother, Age 65, Goes Free on 'Policy' Charge 5,000 Slips," *New York Amsterdam News*, January 16, 1929, 1.

15. "Graft on Gambling Laid to the Police by 'Policy Queen,'" *New York Times*, December 9, 1930, 1.

16. "Complains to Mayor about Harlem Police," *New York Amsterdam News*, August 21, 1929, 12.

17. *New York Amsterdam News*, September 4, 1929.

18. Display Ad 26—No Title, *New York Amsterdam News*, September 18, 1929, 6.

19. "Mme St. Clair held in $5,000 Bail for Special Sessions," *New York Amsterdam News*, January 22, 1930, 1.

20. "Display Ad 4—No Title: Mme Stephanie St. Clair, *New York Amsterdam News*, January 1, 1930, 2.

21. "Mme St. Clair Convicted: Confessed 'Banker' of 'Numbers' Given Sentence to Island," *New York Amsterdam News*, March 19, 1930 1

22. "Mme St. Claire Bares 'Policy' Protection," *New York Amsterdam News*, December 10, 1930, 1.

23. "Harlem Cops Drawn Into 'Numbers Investigation,'" *New York Amsterdam News*, December 24, 1930, 1.

24. "Things I Couldn't Tell Till Now," *Collier's*, July 29, 1939, 37.

25. "Harlem Policy Queen Declares War on Rival," *The Pittsburgh Courier*, January 5, 1935, 6.

26. "Only Stephanie Defied Schultz: Says Ex-Wife of Black Hitler Did Not Fear Racket Boss," *New York Amsterdam News*, August 27, 1938, 1.

27. "14 in Office Seized as Schultz Aides, Police Raiders Say More Than 5,000,000 Policy Slips Were Found in Uptown Flat," *New York Times*, March 16, 1933, 8.

28. "Sufi Wooed St. Clair in 'Darkened Room,'" *New York Amsterdam News*, January 29, 1938, 3.

29. "Sufi Wooed St. Clair in 'Darkened Room,'" *New York Amsterdam News*, January 29, 1938, 3.

30. "Mme. St. Clair's Shot Nicks Hamid in Chin," *Baltimore Afro-American*, January 29, 1938, 12.

31. $6,000 Bail for Mme St. Clair: Mme St. Clair Just Wanted Conciliation," *New York Amsterdam News*, January 22, 1938, 1.

32. "Didn't Want to Kill Him," *New York Amsterdam News*, January 22, 1938, 1.

33. "Self-Defense Will Be Plea," *New York Amsterdam News*, February 19, 1938, 1.

34. "Former Numbers Queen is Jailed," *New York Age*, March 19, 1938, 1.

35. "Mme St. Clair Gets Ten Years," *New York Amsterdam News*, March 26, 1938, 1.

SELECTED
BIBLIOGRAPHY

HENRIETTA ROBINSON

Adler, Jeanne Winston. *The Affair of the Veiled Murderess: An Antebellum Scandal and Mystery.* Excelsior Editions, State University of New York Press, 2011.

Palmer, Dr. Hollis A. *Curse of the Veiled Murderess.* New York. Deep Roots Publishing, 2004.

Schechter, Harold. *Psycho USA: Famous American Killers You Never Heard of.* New York: Ballantine Books, 2012.

Wilhelm, Robert. *The Bloody Century: True Tales of Murder in 19th Century America.* Night Stick Press, 2014.

Wilson, David. *Henrietta Robinson.* New York: Miller, Orton & Mulligan, 1855.

EMMA CUNNINGHAM

Clinton, Henry L. *Celebrated Trials.* New York: Harper & Brothers, 1897.

Feldman, Benjamin. *Butchery on Bond Street—Sexual Politics and The Burdell-Cunningham Case in Ante-Bellum New York.* New York: New York Wanderer Press in association with The Green-Wood Cemetery Historic Fund, 2007.

Feldman, Benjamin with Darleen Gumtow. *Evil Emma, Down Mexico Way: The Gruesome Sequel to Butchery on Bond Street.* New York: New Yorker

Wanderer Press in association with The Green-Wood Cemetery Historic Fund, 2018.

Finney, Jack. *Forgotten News: The Crime of the Century and Other Lost Stories.* New York: Doubleday, 1983.

Jenkins, Brian. *The Trial of Emma Cunningham: Murder and Scandal in the Victorian Era.* North Carolina: McFarland, 2019.

Sachsman, David B. and David W. Bulla. *Sensationalism: Murder, Mayhem, Mudslinging, Scandals, and Disasters in 19th-century Reporting.* New Brunswick: Transaction Publishers, 2013.

FREDERICKA "MARM" MANDELBAUM

Anbinder, Tyler. *Five Points: The Nineteenth-Century New York City Neighborhood.* New York: Free Press, 2001.

Asbury, Herbert. *The Gangs of New York.* New York: Alfred A. Knopf, 1927.

Conway, J. North. *Queen of Thieves: The True Story of "Marm" Mandelbaum and Her Gangs of New York.* New York: Skyhorse Publishing, 2014.

Ernst, Robert. *Immigrant Life in New York City, 1825–1863.* New York: Columbia University, 1949.

Holub, Rona. "Fredericka 'Marm' Mandelbaum 'Queen of the Fences:' The Rise and Fall of a Female Immigrant Criminal Entrepreneur in the Nineteenth-Century." New York: Columbia University doctoral dissertation, 2007.

Jackson, Robert Vern, ed. *Germans to America.* Volume 1 January 1850–1851. New York: Accelerated Indexing Systems International, Inc., 1988.

Lardner, James and Thomas Reppetto. *NYPD: A City and Its Police.* New York: Henry Holt & Co., 2000.

Macintyre, Ben. *The Napoleon of Crime: The Life and Times of Adam Worth, Master Thief.* New York: Farrar, Straus & Giroux, 1997.

Morton, James. *The Mammoth Book of Gangs* (Mammoth Books). New York: Running Press, 2012.

Murphy, Cait. *Scoundrels in Law: The Trials of Howe & Hummel, Lawyers to the Gangsters, Cops, Starlets, and Rakes Who Made the Gilded Age.* Washington, DC: Smithsonian Books, 2010.

Nadel, Stanley. *Little Germany: Ethnicity, Religion, and Class in New York City, 1845–80.* Urbana: University of Illinois Press, 1990.

Rovere, Richard. *Howe & Hummel: Their True and Scandalous History.* New York: Farrar, Strauss and Giroux, 1974.

Sante, Luc. *Low Life: Lures and Snares of Old New York.* New York: Farrar, Straus & Giroux, 1991.

Van Elkan Lyons, Sophie. *Why Crime Does Not Pay.* New York: J. S. Ogilvie, 1913.

Walling, George W. *Recollections of a New York Chief of Police.* New York: Caxton Book Concern, 1887.

SOPHIE LYONS

Anbinder, Tyler. *Five Points: The Nineteenth-Century New York City Neighborhood.* New York: Free Press, 2001.

Asbury, Herbert. *The Gangs of New York.* New York: Alfred A. Knopf, 1927.

Byrnes, Thomas. *1886 Professional Criminals of America.* New York: Chelsea House Publishers, 1969.

Davidson, Shayne. *Queen of the Burglars: The Scandalous Life of Sophie Lyons.* Jefferson, NC: Exposit Books, 2020.

Lardner, James and Thomas Reppetto. *NYPD: A City and Its Police.* New York: Henry Holt & Co., 2000.

Macintyre, Ben. *The Napoleon of Crime: The Life and Times of Adam Worth, Master Thief.* New York: Farrar, Straus & Giroux, 1997.

Sante, Luc. *Low Life: Lures and Snares of Old New York.* New York: Farrar, Straus & Giroux, 1991.

Van Elkan Lyons, Sophie. *Why Crime Does Not Pay.* New York: J. S. Ogilvie, 1913.

Walling, George W. *Recollections of a New York Chief of Police.* New York: Caxton Book Concern, 1887.

ROXALANA DRUSE

Greiner, James M. *Last Woman Hanged: Roxalana Druse.* Keene, NH: Surrey Cottage Books, 2010.

Hopson, Caryl. *Murder & Mayhem in Herkimer County.* Charleston, SC: The History Press, 2019.

Tippetts, William Henry. *Herkimer County Murders: This book contains an accurate account of the capital crimes committed in the County of Herkimer, from the year 1783 up to the . . . Druse butchery, and the Middleville tragedy.* Herkimer, NY: H. P. Witherstine & Co., Steam Book and Job Printers, 1885.

Mrs. Druse's case and Maggie Houghtaling; Innocent woman hanged; Mrs. Druse. A sad mistake: An innocent woman hanged. The truth revealed at last. A startling confession. Dying innocent to save those she loved. Philadelphia: Old Franklin Publishing House, 1887.

Hill, David Bennett. *Public Papers of David B. Hill, governor.* 1885– [1891]. Albany: The Argus Company Printers, 1886.

Walsh, Robert. *Murders, Mysteries and Misdemeanors in New York.* Charleston, SC: America Through Time. 2019.

LIZZIE HALLIDAY

Amelinck, Andrew K. *Hudson Valley Murder & Mayhem.* Charleston, SC: The History Press, 2017.

Conway, John. *Remembering the Sullivan County Catskills (American Chronicles).* Charleston, SC: The History Press, 2008.

Keene, Michael T. *Question of Sanity: The True Story of Female Serial Killers in 19th Century New York.* Pittsford, NY: Ad-Hoc Productions, 2017.

March, C. J. *Murderer's Gulch: Carnage in the Catskills* (Dead True Crime). Coppell, TX: Slingshot Books, 2019.

Owen, Kevin. *Killing Time in the Catskills: The Twisted Tale of the Catskill Ripper Elizabeth "Lizzie" McNally Halliday.* New York: Moonlight Press, 2019.

Schechter, Harold. *Psycho USA: Famous American Killers You Never Heard of.* New York: Ballantine Books, 2012.
Telfer, Tori. *Lady Killers: Deadly Women Throughout History.* New York: Harper Perennial, 2017.

MARY ALICE LIVINGSTON

Livingston, James D. *Arsenic and Clam Chowder: Murder in Gilded Age New York.* New York: Excelsior Editions, State University of New York Press, 2010.

MARY FARMER

Farnsworth, Cheri L. *Murder & Mayhem in Jefferson County.* Charleston, SC: The History Press, 2011.
Grossman, Mark. *The Trunk Dripped Blood: Five Sensational Murder Cases of the Early 20th Century.* Jefferson, NC: McFarland Publishers, 2018.
"People v. Farmer (Court of Appeals of New York, Oct. 19, 1909.)" *Northeastern Reporter.* St. Paul: West Publishing Co., 1910.

CELIA COONEY

Duncombe, Stephen and Andrew Mattson. The Bobbed Haired Bandit: *A True Story of Crime and Celebrity in 1920s New York.* New York: New York University Press, 2005.

RUTH SNYDER

Bryson, Bill. *One Summer: America, 1927.* New York: Doubleday, 2013.
Jones, Anne. *Women Who Kill.* New York: The Feminist Press at CUNY, 2009.

MacKellar, Landis. *The "Double Indemnity" Murder: Ruth Snyder, Judd Gray, & New York's Crime of the Century.* Syracuse, NY: Syracuse University Press, 2006.

Margolin, Leslie. *Murderess! The Chilling True Story of the Most Infamous Woman Ever Electrocuted.* New York: Kensington Books, 1999.

Pelizzon, Penelope and Nancy M. West, "Multiple Indemnity: Film Noir, James M. Cain, and Adaptations of a Tabloid Case," *Narrative,* Vol. 13, No. 3 (Ohio State University, October 2005), 213.

Ramey, Jessie: "The Bloody Blonde and the Marble Woman: Gender and Power in the Case of Ruth Snyder," *Journal of Social History,* Vol. 37, No. 3 (Spring, 2004), 625–50.

STEPHANIE ST. CLAIR

Boyd, Herb, ed. *The Harlem Reader: A Celebration of New York's Most Famous Neighborhood, from the Renaissance Years to the 21st Century.* New York: Random House, 2003.

Agnes Calliste, "Race, Gender and Canadian Immigration Policy: Blacks from the Caribbean, 1900–1932," *Journal of Canadian Studies,* 28 (Winter 1993/94) 131–48.

Chepesiuk, Ron J. *Queenpins: Notorious Women Gangsters of the Modern Era.* Rockhill, SC: Strategic Media Books, 2011.

Chepesiuk, Ron J. *Gangsters of Harlem: The Gritty Underworld of New York City's Most Famous Neighborhood.* Fort Lee, NJ: Barricade Books, 2010.

Harris, LaShawn. "Playing the Numbers Game: Madame Stephanie St. Clair & African-American Policy Culture in Harlem," *Black Women, Gender and Families* 2: 2 (2008), 53–76.

Johnson, Mayme and Karen E. Quinones Miller. *Harlem Godfather: The Rap on My Husband, Ellsworth "Bumpy" Johnson.* Philadelphia: Oshun Publishing Company, 2008.

Mitgang, Herbert, *The Man Who Rode the Tiger: The Life and Times of Judge Samuel Seabury.* New York: J. B. Lippincott Co., 1963.

Stewart, Shirley. *The World of Stephanie St. Clair: An Entrepreneur, Race Woman, and Outlaw in Early Twentieth Century Harlem.* New York: Peter Lang Publishing Inc., 2014.

Watkins-Owens, Irma. *Blood Relations: Caribbean Immigrants and the Harlem Community, 1900–1930 (Blacks in the Diaspora).* Bloomington: Indiana University Press, 1996.

White, Shane, Stephen Garton, and Stephan Robertson. *Playing the Numbers: Gambling in Harlem Between the Wars.* Cambridge, MA: Harvard University Press, 2010.

ABOUT THE AUTHOR

Elizabeth Kerri Mahon is a native New Yorker, actress, and history geek. Her book, *Scandalous Women*, was released in March 2011 to enthusiastic reviews. *Scandalous Women* was an RT Book Review Non-Fiction Pick for April 2011. She has spoken at the We Move Forward Conference on Isla Mujeres, Mexico and the Historical Novel Society North America Conference, and she participated in Chick History's yearlong project #HerStory. Elizabeth has been interviewed by *Marie Claire Malaysia, NPR, Extraordinary Women TV, The West Side Spirit, Vogue, Times of London,* NBC online, and the *Pittsburgh Historical Fiction Examiner.* She has been featured in the H2 show *How Sex Changed the World,* as well as the Travel Channel's *Monumental Mysteries* and the Investigation Discovery show *Tabloid.* A pop-culture diva, Elizabeth has written for *The Royal Representative, Heroes and Heartbreakers, Ever After Romance,* and *Criminal Element.*